FOUCAULT IN IRAN

MUSLIM INTERNATIONAL

Sohail Daulatzai and Junaid Rana
Series Editors

FOUCAULT IN IRAN

Islamic Revolution
after the Enlightenment

Behrooz Ghamari-Tabrizi

MUSLIM INTERNATIONAL

UNIVERSITY OF MINNESOTA PRESS
MINNEAPOLIS | LONDON

A different version of chapter 2 was published as "'When Life Will No Longer Barter Itself': In Defense of Foucault on the Iranian Revolution," in *A Foucault for the 21st Century: Governmentality, Biopolitics and Discipline in the New Millennium,* ed. Sam Binkley and Jorge Capetillo, 270–90 (New Castle: Cambridge Scholars Publishing, 2009). Published with the permission of Cambridge Scholars Publishing.

Published by the University of Minnesota Press
111 Third Avenue South, Suite 290
Minneapolis, MN 55401-2520
http://www.upress.umn.edu

Printed in the United States of America on acid-free paper

The University of Minnesota is an equal-opportunity educator and employer.

23 22 21 20 19 18 17 16   10 9 8 7 6 5 4 3 2 1

Library of Congress Cataloging-in-Publication Data
Names: Ghamari-Tabrizi, Behrooz, author.
Title: Foucault in Iran : Islamic Revolution after the Enlightenment / Behrooz Ghamari-Tabrizi.
Description: Minneapolis : University of Minnesota Press, [2016] | Series: Muslim international | Includes bibliographical references and index.
Identifiers: LCCN 2015036894 | ISBN 978-0-8166-9948-3 (hc) | ISBN 978-0-8166-9949-0 (pb)
Subjects: LCSH: Foucault, Michel, 1926–1984—Influence. | Iran—History—Revolution, 1979. | Iran—History—Revolution, 1979—Historiography.
Classification: LCC B2430.F724 G52 2016 | DDC 955.05/42—dc23
LC record available at http://lccn.loc.gov/2015036894

TO GOLROKH

The country that is more developed industrially only shows, to the less developed, the image of its own future.

—Karl Marx, *Das Kapital*

Modernity can and will no longer borrow the criteria by which it takes its orientation from the models supplied by another epoch; it has to create its normativity out of itself. Who else but Europe could draw from its own traditions the insight, the energy, the courage of vision to shape our mentality?

—Jürgen Habermas, *Philosophical Discourse of Modernity*

If philosophy of the future exists, it must be born outside Europe or equally born in consequence of meetings and impacts between Europe and non-Europe.

—Michel Foucault, *On Zen Buddhism*

CONTENTS

PREFACE

I REMEMBER VIVIDLY that cold, rainy Friday in October 1977 when, after a day of strenuous climbing in the Tehran mountains, my comrades and I descended on the Goethe Institute, where the second night of a ten-night poetry reading was underway. Thousands sat under the pouring rain, some with (and others, like me, without) umbrellas, in the enormous garden of the institute. I saw for the first time faces of those major literary figures whose works I had keenly read and with whose ideas I associated closely. Although it was hard to hear the words in that overcrowded garden, I, like everyone else there, knew what was said. The quiet crowd was the main speaker.

The Ten-Nights, as it became known in the lexicon of the Iranian Revolution, led to more gatherings, this time on university campuses, without the immunity that the grounds of the German Cultural Mission afforded the original meetings. What appeared to me as a seamless expansion of this protest movement turned into marches on the streets and eventually into the uprising of an entire nation that articulated what that quiet crowd could not utter freely only a few months earlier, *Down with the Shah, down with the U.S. imperialism.*

Very soon after I began the research on this book I realized that the main challenge for me writing about the revolutionary movement of 1978–79, and the philosophical contemplations of an astute observer like Michel Foucault, was to find a meaningful way to navigate the volatile terrains of memory, myth, ideology, and history. My own proximity to the events as a militant Marxist-Leninist student who organized rallies, wrote pamphlets, recruited other students to the *cause*, and fought daily battles on the streets of Tehran during the ghastly period of martial law, made writing about them that much more complex. I found myself in the precarious position of the one who lives *in* a particular historical moment as well as *through* its telling. As I began to research this book and examine archival material related to the same period, many of my memories, like the one at the Goethe Institute, had to be resituated in a wider context, which at times challenged the significance I had originally attributed to them. I realized how, either subconsciously or consciously, I had generated in my mind a particular arc of events that was situated in a field of competing, affectively charged and mobilizing, narratives.

During research it became increasingly equivocal whether I should regard my own participatory and eyewitness accounts as a form of privileged knowledge or, in contrast, a distortion of reality. I do understand the problem of correspondence and the representation of reality, and do not wish to claim that I had to weigh my own accounts against the *reality* of what had happened. Rather I needed to reevaluate the historical significance I attributed to the influence of my own revolutionary milieu. And perhaps the biggest challenge for me was to advance an understanding of the revolution within its own temporal unfolding, resisting the temptation to cast the shadow of the Islamic republic over the revolutionary movement that led to its foundation.

I have given the latter point the most earnest attention. This was necessary because both sides of the postrevolutionary power struggle, those who dominated the state and those who were purged and suppressed, came to view the revolutionary movement as an instance of a bifurcated Islamist versus secular politics. The postrevolutionary regime sanctified its rule as the indubitable outcome of the revolution. It transformed the religious rituals and the symbolic universe through which revolutionary demands were articulated into a formal, juridical, and doctrinal foundation of an Islamic state. The opposition to the establishment of the Islamic Republic also followed the same steps by calling the postrevolutionary theocratic reign of terror the *inevitable* consequence of the Islamic character of the revolutionary movement.

The revolutionary movement in Iran offered a world-historical possibility to move away from a binary Islamist/secular politics, to imagine a form of unscripted politics practices at the "threshold of a novelty." But that possibility collapsed in the wake of the way the postrevolutionary *realpolitik* colonized revolutionary ideals. I do not use this as a euphemism to cover the *real* costs of this colonization. A vicious campaign of assassination, mass executions, and massive incarceration, along with a bloody eight-year war and the unprecedented flight of the "unwanted," evokes the unfathomable emotional mark, the sheer human stakes that the (post)revolutionary process in Iran has produced. I mention this instead to highlight the convolution that is involved in reconciling the memory of events with historical processes and conceptual assertions.

As I was writing this book, many colleagues and critics have asked me, "Why should we care about what Foucault says about the Iranian Revolution?" "Is he not just another abstruse French intellectual with the colonial habit of poking his nose into another peoples' affairs?" I think these are legitimate questions. I have conceived this book, not as an exegesis of Foucault's intellectual oeuvre. Rather, I found his essays on the Iranian Revolution a perfect window through which one could look at the revolutionary events in Iran outside the discursive frames that make revolutions legible. The fact that the revolution in Iran transformed his theory of power and subjectivity also has less to do with Foucault, in my mind, than with the generative *conceptual* significance of the Iranian Revolution.

At the very core of Eurocentrism is the attribution of *theoretical* significance to European historical experiences—class formation, race and gender relations, state and politics, life-course and aging, power and subjectivity, and so on. The *universal* is the generalizable European *concrete*. Both in his essays and in his later transformations, Foucault offers important clues on how to comprehend the Iranian Revolution not as an instance of Eurocentric theories of power, politics, and history. While writing the book, I realized that Foucault failed to acknowledge the theoretical significance of the Iranian experience. Although he advances a theory of subjectivity in his late writings, he never articulated that theory in relation to its origins in the *political spirituality* of the revolutionary subjects in the streets of Tehran.

Introduction

FOUCAULT'S INDICTMENT

IS IT POSSIBLE FOR A PEOPLE to envision and desire futures uncharted by already existing schemata of historical change and patterns of social change? Is it possible to think of dignity, humility, justice, and liberty outside Enlightenment cognitive maps and principles? These are the types of questions that motivate the writing of this book.

I was in Berlin, finishing the first draft of this book, when the massive uprisings of 2010–11 swept North Africa and the Middle East. Remarkably, for a number of weeks, reading and writing about Foucault's essays on the Iranian Revolution of 1979 corresponded with events that were unfolding more than three decades later. The same kind of inexplicability that puzzled Foucault about "a man in revolt" in Tehran, the same kind of transformative exuberance that he called *political spirituality*, and the same kind of ambiguity about the future direction of these uprisings that fascinated Foucault during the Iranian Revolution seemed to define those moments. There was another important similarity in what was happening in 2010–11 with the Iranian Revolution of 1978–79. Pundits and scholars tried to make sense of this sudden upsurge of protest, analyze its causes, and attribute meaning to the demands of the insurgent masses in order to make these historical events *legible* to a global audience.

Unlike the Iranian Revolution thirty years earlier, the Arab uprisings not only overtook the streets of major cities and squares but also dominated the global mediascape that operated paradoxically both as an instrument of the effective dissemination of its existence and, at the same time, as a means of its discursive reticence. Although by and large the masses on the streets identified their movement as a call for human dignity *(kerāma)* and an end to social injustice and corruption *(kefāya)*, only a few weeks after their emergence the news reports and scholarly analyses identified the moment as the "Arab Spring." In order to make a phenomenon legible, one has to operate within a recognizable assembly of points of references. By naming it the "Arab Spring," the uprisings entered a conceptual and discursive universe with a written past and a known future direction.

In Iran, Foucault tried to see the revolution as a phenomenon of history and, at the same time, as a phenomenon that defies it. He perceived those who marched on the streets of Tehran as subjects of history who had risen to make history the subject of their revolutionary acts. He encouraged his readers to see Iranians at the threshold of a novelty rather than subjects of the discursive authority of a world that is perpetuated in tired conceptions of "History." In Iran, Foucault tried to introduce the revolution without closing the window of possibilities, without subjecting the revolutionary movement to the logic of historical inevitabilities.

The "Arab Spring" was a discourse, in the making for five years, constructed to do exactly the opposite, close the window of possibilities and subject the uprisings to historical inevitabilities. After the massive rallies to condemn the assassination of the former Lebanese prime minister, Rafik Hariri, in February 2005, conservative as well as a number of liberal and Left columnists began to ponder the wisdom of George W. Bush's Middle East project. They considered the mass protests against the Syrian influence in Lebanon, the "Cedar Revolution," an "Arab Spring" that heralded the fruition of the Bush policy of exporting democracy to the land of the unfriendly tyrants. In a self-congratulatory op-ed, the staunch conservative columnist Charles Krauthammer compared the Beirut protests to the 1848 revolutions that "did presage the coming of the liberal idea throughout Europe." "The Arab Spring of 2005," he proclaimed, "will be noted as a similar turning point for the Arab world."[1] Krauthammer was not alone in identifying the emergence of an Arab Spring. A series of editorial columns in *Le Monde*, *The Independent*, *Der Spiegel*, and *Foreign Policy* debated whether the "Cedar Revolution" of 2005 invoked the "Spring Time of Nations" in Europe of 1848, Prague Spring of 1968, or Eastern Europe of 1989.

The Arab Spring of 2005 did not materialize the way the pundits predicted. But the uprisings of 2010–11 turned into a full bloom "Spring," albeit a short-lived one. The dominant explanations of the uprisings interpreted this Spring, whether it was a reference to Prague of 1968, or Europe of 1848, as a triumph of liberalism and the discovery of Enlightenment in the Arab world. In Alain Badiou's words, "Our rulers and our dominant media have suggested a simple interpretation of the riots in the Arab world: what is expressed in them is what might be called a *desire for the West*."[2] Not only did this view conflate competing interests of the uprising in single reductionist desire for the West, but more significantly, it subjected those who rose up to *make* history to the unfolding of its inherent logic.

Foucault highlighted in Iran the struggle of a nation asserting itself for both an *inclusion* (in making history) and an *exit* (from terminal history). He conceived the indeterminacy of the revolutionary movement in Iran as a possible source of creativity and inspiration rather than an expression of backwardness finally unleashed forward toward progress. The narrative of Arab Spring denied the 2010–11 uprisings the *singularity* with which they could be comprehended and advanced outside the recognized patterns of revolutionary transformation. The discourse of Arab Spring devoured the Egyptian liberals and revolutionaries and denied them the impetus to articulate the significance of their uprising notwithstanding the burdens of a universal history. They considered any deviation from the conventional narratives of revolution to be failure and inauthentic to their movement. The election of Mohamed Morsi of the Muslim Brotherhood invariably and quickly became the case in point. Even before the Morsi Administration showed its incompetence and autocratic tendencies, liberals and many actors on the Left regarded a Muslim Brother president as the epitome of *one step forward, two steps back*, thus their Orwellian jubilance over the July 2013 military coup to save democracy.

Liberal and Left parties hastily celebrated the Arab Spring as the end of the ideological significance of political Islam. They believed that these revolutions would restore the authority of secular politics that had been obscured by the Iranian Revolution since 1979. The secularists of the Left and the Right vowed that they would not allow Egypt to become a second Iran. Not thinking through the *singularity* of the Egyptian moment, they deemed irrelevant the conspicuous facts that the incompetent Morsi lacked anything in common with the charismatic Khomeini, that the Brotherhood institutionally lacked the same effective Shi'a clerical network, and that the Brotherhood's political philosophy shared no affinity with the Shiʻa liberation theology.

I do not wish to suggest an intellectual commitment to a linear progressive conception of History was the reason a military coup in Egypt halted the Arab uprisings of 2010–12. But the desire to turn Arabs into legible subjects of the March of History rather than making history the subject of their uprising made the self-proclaimed secular actors ambivalent about, if not unashamedly promoting, a military intervention to save the nation from the "unyielding Islamist reactionaries." On August 14, 2013, the military forces massacred 1,250 Brotherhood supporters in two protest camps in Cairo. After the massacre, the only audible voice was the sigh of relief of the former revolutionaries who thought that they had brought the nation from the brink of an electoral catastrophe back to the mainstream of history. *You can take the country back from a military junta, you can't redeem the nation from the yoke of the Messengers of God,* was the word on the streets.

The bifurcation of political actors into secular versus Islamist generated alliances on the ground that otherwise one would deem implausible. As we know by now, the fragility of a secular coalition between the military and the Egyptian Left and liberals became evident soon after the coup. But the basic premise on which that coalition was justified remains in place on the ground and in intellectual circles. The binary conception of secular versus religious politics assumes actual uniformities on both sides of the dichotomy that correspond neither to a coherent conceptual project nor to the shared experience of a *particular* politics.[3]

The same Whiggish narrative has recast the revolutionary movement in Iran of 1978–79 and has dominated its historiography. Many of these revisionist accounts are motivated by ideological commitments to a universal history that renders the entire history of the twentieth-century Middle East as a struggle between progressive, democratic, secular forces against reactionary, autocratic Islamists. This was exactly the kind of epistemic violence inherent in bifurcated historiographies in contradistinction to which Foucault wrote his essays on the Iranian Revolution. Those who celebrated the Arab Spring not as a moment of defiance but as a desire for inclusion in and conformity to History could have learned important lessons from Foucault's writings on the Iranian Revolution.[4]

The interest in Foucault's contemplations on Islam and Iran, for the most part, remained a Parisian-Persian affair during the time of the revolution in 1978–80. Although a number of essays published in the early 1990s engaged his Iranian musings,[5] it was not until the terrorist attacks of September 11, 2001, that renewed interest in his thoughts about the Iranian Revolution appeared. One might reasonably ask what Foucault had to do with acts of atrocity committed on American soil years after his death? But as I shall demonstrate here, a host of philosophers, sociologists, historians, and essayists of the Left and liberal persuasion exploited the terrorist assaults of 9/11, and other recent violent encounters in Europe involving Muslims, to launch a feverish attack on the proponents of what they dubbed "cultural relativism." Nihilism and the awakening of the antiquated regimes of power, these scholars warned, was the inevitable consequence of the loss of the Enlightenment as the Universal Referent.

In 2005 coauthors of a book on Foucault and the Iranian Revolution went even further to indict and convict Foucault as the main poststructuralist culprit of this insidious cultural relativism.[6] They raised fundamental challenges to Foucault's historiography in order to divulge the inherent link between his philosophical oeuvre and his revolutionary sympathies toward the alleged pseudofascist core of Islamism.

Foucault's essays on the Iranian Revolution are either dismissed as another botched Orientalist venture or disparaged as an "infantile leftism" of a romantic European philosopher.[7] But the centerpiece of the new debate is a problem that extends far beyond Foucault. Such a perspective warns against the calamity of Islamism and the failure of poststructuralist philosophers, led by Michel Foucault, to reckon with the catastrophic consequences of deviating from the project of the Enlightenment. Affected by the civilizational ardor of the post-9/11 moment, the authors of *Foucault and the Iranian Revolution* hold poststructuralists (and their unlikely allies Noam Chomsky and Howard Zinn!)[8] responsible for affording postmodern discursive legitimacy to premodern Islamists and their mission to obliterate modernity. They set up their position in the question framing their book: "Did not a post-structuralist, leftist discourse, which spent all of its energy opposing the secular liberal or authoritarian modern state and its institutions, leave the door wide open to an uncritical stance toward Islamism and other socially retrogressive movements?"[9]

Afary and Anderson trace the roots of the horrific terrorist acts of 9/11 back to the Iranian Revolution and its ensuing radical Islamist politics. They argue that the Jihadist politics of total annihilation is the ultimate extremity of being seduced by what Foucault called "political spirituality." They chastise the Left in Western countries for ignoring "the specific social and political context in which al-Qaeda arose, [namely], that of two decades of various forms of radical Islamist politics, beginning with the Iranian Revolution" (169). They situate their own critique of Foucault's reporting of the Iranian Revolution as a critical engagement with root causes of 9/11!

What distinguishes Afary and Anderson's account of Foucault from earlier critiques is that they see his writing as the manifestation of, rather than an aberration from, his philosophical skepticism and genealogical historiography. In this book, I shall argue that Foucault's sympathies had nothing to with a romantic fascination with a premodern world and the pastoral exercise of power. Rather, his enthusiasm was kindled by witnessing a moment of *making history* outside the purview of a Western teleological schema.

The second major argument Afary and Anderson propose is that Foucault's experience of the Iranian Revolution informed his later writings, especially the second and third volumes of *The History of Sexuality* and his renewed interest in the question of ethics. They suggest (and offer his essay "What Is Enlightenment?" as evidence) that the postrevolutionary reign of terror in Iran forced Foucault to recant and "alter his stance toward both the Enlightenment and humanism"[10] as immutable Universal Referents. But, in order to justify their case, these authors misconstrue Foucault's earlier works and look for the footprint of the Iranian Revolution in the wrong places in his later writing.

This assumption is one of the common misinterpretations of Foucault's later writings and his interest in questions of ethics, care of the self, and Enlightenment. Even Slavoj Žižek, who defends Foucault's engagement with the Iranian Revolution and argues that "he *correctly* detected the emancipatory potential in the events,"[11] repeats the same standard narrative that "one should read his turn to Kant a couple of years later as his response to this failed engagement."[12] I have dedicated the last chapter of this book to a detailed discussion on how Foucault's engagement with the Iranian Revolution transformed his later writings, particularly on the question of the hermeneutics of the subject.

The significance of how Foucault made sense of the Iranian Revolution and how his encounter with the revolutionary movement informed his later writings go beyond a scholarly interest in Foucault. Neither was he an expert on Shi'ism nor did he have a deep understanding of Iranian history. What made his essays on the Iranian Revolution exceptional was his willingness to observe the revolution without a commitment to the temporal map of a universal history. He observed the revolution as a moment at the threshold of a novelty, as something radically new outside the tired conceptions of linear revolutionary politics. Not only did the revolution, and the way its actors lived it, give Foucault a conduit to reflect on his own genealogical method, more importantly, it afforded him a conceptual awareness to project the indeterminacies of the revolutionary movement back to the Enlightenment.

Although I offer a close reading of Foucault's essays on the Iranian Revolution and the way it transformed his ideas, I do not consider this book to be an extended commentary on Foucault. Rather, through this engagement with Foucault's writings, I hope to introduce a new historiography in which trajectories, ideas, relationships, and other eventful contingencies are understood as elements in a condition of historical possibilities.

In the following introduction, I show how the 9/11 attacks honed a civilizational alliance in the West against Islamism. I argue that despite their fundamental political differences, Euro-American neoconservative militarists and the militant defenders of the Enlightenment on the liberal and Left continuum share a conceptual angst against an undifferentiated Islamism as *the* global threat to democracy and human rights.

In chapter 1 I introduce a dramaturgy of the events to highlight the significance of Shi'a-Islamic rituals and symbolic language in shaping and sustaining the revolutionary movement. My use of the word "dramaturgy" is not meant to imply any artificial staging, but rather refers to the dramatic character of events as they unfolded and simultaneously emplotted in time and space. I also emphasize how a binary representation of actions and ideologies of political parties and leaders with references to their secular or religious orientation distorts the realities of the revolutionary movement. In order to show what Foucault saw in 1978 and how he made sense of his observations, I end the chapter with his arrival in Tehran in September 1978.

In chapter 2 I introduce Foucault's writings on the Iranian Revolution. I show how his critique of modernity and genealogical history informed his conception of *political spirituality*. The chapter also highlights the distinction Foucault draws between the revolt and the outcome of the revolution and the significance he attributes to the transformative power of revolt on revolutionary subjects.

Chapter 3 examines Afary and Anderson's misreading of Foucault and their misrepresentation of the revolutionary events. I illustrate how they present Foucault as a romantic advocate of pastoral power, "seduced by the 'authentic' touch of violent spectacles and outbursts, in love with the ruthless exercise of power."[13] I also show that in order to support their interpretive liberties, they use passages from Foucault's writings out of context. I argue that analyses such as theirs are trapped in a teleology that cannot account for, and therefore inevitably vacates, a whole welter of possibilities immanent within political Islam. In their writing, Foucault appears utterly misguided because he failed to see, on the one hand, the inherent totalitarian core of political Islam, and on the other hand, the constitutive significance of secular democratic forces.

One of the main grievances against Foucault's sympathetic depiction of the revolution has been his gendered ambivalence toward the question of rights and civil liberties. In chapter 4 I discuss the question of feminist politics and the women's movement during the first few months after the triumph of the revolution. Foucault's critics contend that he ignored massive demonstrations of women after the revolution against compulsory *ḥijāb* (veiling) and dismissed the outpouring of solidarity offered by "global sisterhood" as another instance of Western arrogance. By scrutinizing the events of March 8, 1979, that marked the celebration of International Women's Day in Tehran, in this chapter I argue that in their critique, Foucault's detractors appeal to a universal and reductionist sense of womanhood without regard to the contingencies of postrevolutionary power struggles.

In the last chapter I examine the transformation of Foucault's conception of history and the question of the subject. A number of Foucault scholars have claimed that after witnessing Ayatollah Khomeini's *grande terreur*, Foucault retreated from his earlier fascination with *political spirituality* and sought shelter in the safe Kantian haven of the Enlightenment. On the contrary, rather than a belated liberalism, I argue that Foucault's thoughts about historical–transindividual subjectivity, the hermeneutics of the subject, and the question of ethics in his last lectures at the Collège de France were *consistent* with his depiction of the Islamic Revolution. I will demonstrate that, without speaking directly about it, Foucault reaffirmed his sympathy with the revolution without thereby endorsing its repressive aftermath.

The Danish Cartoons, September 11, and the Mishap of Relativism

On March 1, 2006, in reaction to the Danish cartoon affair,[14] twelve writers, journalists, and intellectuals of diverse political backgrounds published a manifesto called "Together Facing the New Totalitarianism." It begins provocatively: "After having overcome fascism, Nazism, and Stalinism, the world now faces a new global totalitarian threat: Islamism." The authors called for "resistance to religious totalitarianism and for the promotion of freedom, equal opportunity and secular values for all." They avowed that "the recent events have revealed the necessity of the struggle for these universal values." To leave nothing opaque, the antitotalitarian writers of the manifesto stressed that they "reject 'cultural relativism' which implies an acceptance that men and women of Muslim culture are deprived of the right to equality, freedom, and secularism in the name of the respect for certain cultures and traditions."[15]

One does not need to do more than scratch the surface of this manifesto to uncover the historical omissions that have made its production possible. They reject "cultural relativism" because they believe that is the only way to defend the rights of men and women of "Muslim culture." Who these men and women whose rights they defend are remained unfathomed. Is there such a singular phenomenon called Muslim culture? Does Islamism in its multiple manifestations form a coherent totalitarian ideology similar to fascism or Stalinism? More importantly, by turning secularism into a universal right, the twelve authors overlook the fact that the totalitarianisms they abhorred as well as the nation-building programs of the postcolonial era were all failed secular projects.

Much more intriguing than the manifesto's threadbare polemics of Universal Humanism were the names of the twelve framers of this swaggering document. It included Philippe Val (the founder of the left-ist French weekly *Charlie Hebdo*); as well as Irshad Manji, the redoubt-able neoliberal Muslim reformer (author of the best seller *The Trouble with Islam Today*); the French feminist sociologist Caroline Fourest, whose claim to fame was her controversial book *Frere Tariq* (which was an exposé of the Swiss Muslim theologian Tariq Ramadan); Ayaan Hirsi Ali, a right-wing Dutch politician of Somali origin who was elected to the Dutch parliament on an anti-immigrant platform of the right-wing VVD (her video *Submission* was widely distributed by the LPF, a Dutch neo-Nazi party); and, finally of course, the ever-present manifestation of rainbow politics, Salman Rushdie.

The alliances between the old Left and the new Right are products of a distinct historical moment in which Maryam Namazie, one of the leaders of the Iranian Communist Party, feels at home coauthoring a manifesto with Ayaan Hirsi Ali, a partisan of the American Enterprise Institute. This moment became historically distinct not only because on 9/11 a single blow had been delivered to the centers of American economic power and military might but also because it had occurred at a time of declining American hegemony. 9/11 happened at a moment when neoconservative messianic politicians entered the public arena, when Europe was finally forced to face its colonial past on the streets of its big cities, and when the Iranian Revolution of 1979 had already signaled the feasibility of an Islamic alternative.

Immediately after the 9/11 attacks, even as we mourned, a host of observers struggled to make sense of its politics and define a case for its exceptionality. Bruce Cumings, the distinguished historian of East Asia, only a few weeks after the attacks, calling the assault *infantile nihilism*, noted feverishly,

> Nothing in recent history has prepared us for such a contemptible fusion of willful mass terrorism, bloodstained earthly tragedy, and passionate, ardent conviction—the adolescent fantasy that one big bang will change the world and usher in a global "jihad," a new epoch of "Crusades," or the final solution to eight decades of history that have passed since the Ottoman Empire collapsed.[16]

For Cumings, a leading historian of East Asia who has written forcefully about mass terrorism during the Korean war, who describes the horrors of how the United States reenacted in Korea the Allies' blanket bombing of Germany and reintroduced the creation of urban "annihilation zones," who illustrates in gruesome detail targeting of civilians with napalm bombs when "oceans of it were dropped on Korea silently or without notice in America," who describes how "the U.S. Air Force loved this infernal jelly, its 'wonder weapon,'" calling the atrocity of 9/11 "unprecedented" is exceptionally bewildering.[17] He further argues: "In the past month many on the Left, in my view, have made the fundamental error of framing the terrorist attacks against the sorrier aspects of the American record abroad, when in fact nothing that has ever happened since the United States was founded could sensibly justify such wild, wanton and inhuman recklessness."[18] Cumings, along with a wide array of other historians and social theorists, inaugurated a debate on the "moral equivalency" of the 9/11 attacks by emphasizing the exceptional degree of its violence and the lack of respect for human life.[19] 9/11, they proclaimed, *defied politics.* It was either—in the language of political philosophers—an "apocalyptic nihilism, a rejection of the world as it is,"[20] or, in the messianic discourse of neoconservatives, simply an act of evil.

With the same heated sentiment of the post-9/11 reactions, the distinguished critical theorist Seyla Benhabib added her observations a few weeks after the assault:

> It has become clear since September 11 that we are faced with a new form of struggle that threatens to dissolve the boundaries of the political in liberal democracies. . . . The attacks unleashed by these groups, especially the use of the biological weapon anthrax to contaminate the civilian population via the mail,[[21]] indicate a new political and military phenomenon which challenges the framework of state-centric politics. . . . Historians always warn us that the unprecedented will turn out to have some forerunners somewhere and that what seems new today will appear old when considered against the background of some longer time span. Nevertheless to "think the new" in politics is the vocation of the intellectual. This is a task at which luminaries like Susan Sontag, Fred Jameson, Slavoj Žižek, who have seized this opportunity to recycle well-worn out 1960's clichés about western imperialism and hegemony, have failed us by interpreting these events along the tired paradigm of an anti-imperialist struggle by the "wretched of the earth."[22]

A host of other theorists have followed the same logic and have called into question the fetishization of anti-imperialist struggle and the need for a universal defense of, again in Benhabib's words, "reason, compassion, respect for the dignity of human life, the search for justice and the desire for reconciliation." In order to appreciate the lack of historical understanding of all varieties of Islamism on display here, one needs to commit a number of Feuerbachian reversals of Marx's piercing thesis eleven—namely, that *the philosophers have only sought to change the world; what is crucial, rather, is to understand it!*

"Moral outrage," as Tariq Ali points out, "has some therapeutic value, but as a political strategy it is useless."[23] Delinking 9/11 attacks from anti-imperialist struggles, and an indiscriminate use of the conception of Jihad, transforms Jihadists into suprahistorical agents motivated more by the loss of Andalusia in 1492 than any particular atrocities committed by colonial and imperialist powers of the twentieth century. Although there is an acknowledgment of the blood spilled in the centuries of political and economic domination of Western powers, those atrocities are never considered to be politically incomprehensible. The post-9/11 Enlightenment moralists argue that al-Qaeda (or at times Islamists in general) operatives do not "respect life" and do not subscribe to the accepted rules and norms of war and killing. Rather, they envision the culmination of their war against the West in total annihilation. I would point out that these writers characterize al-Qaeda's violence without temporality, as being senseless and therefore wholly unrelated to the instrumental rationality that had driven the relentless brutality of European and American imperialism.

Calling the atrocity of 9/11 "unprecedented," devoid of politics, and a mere expression of an infantile nihilism points to the ideological commitment of its proponents, who only recognize forms of violence with reference to post-Enlightenment rationalities. Indiscriminate mass murder of civilians; acts of disproportionate violence against nonmilitary targets; the use of nuclear, chemical, and biological weapons; methods of collective punishment; and all other inconceivable acts of brutality have been common features of the colonial and postcolonial world order. Then what makes the senseless brutality of 9/11 *exceptionally* senseless? I will argue later in this book that one significant point of exceptionality, what generates unease and disgust, is that the perpetuators do not legitimize their acts within the Enlightenment rationalities.

Marx was prophetically right when he wrote in the *Communist Manifesto* that "[the bourgeoisie] compels all nations, on pain of extinction, to introduce what it calls civilization into their midst, i.e., to become bourgeois themselves. In one word, it creates a world after its own image." One can take this one step further and show that the critics of capitalism and imperialism also strive to create a critical world after their own image. They create a world in which "those who are waiting for the end of the modern age," as Marshall Berman famously declared, "can be assured of steady work."[24] According to this perspective, the Enlightenment implanted a system of rational thought, as Habermas remarked, that will go on reproducing itself infinitely; its end is unthinkable unless it ushers in total annihilation. It is, indeed, the "last stage in History."[25]

In many significant ways, in their *Foucault and the Iranian Revolution*, Afary and Anderson speak on behalf of the discursive, political, and conceptual alliances that were formed after 9/11 to defend modernity against its enemies. They defend it by invoking a teleological language of progress and thereby perpetuating the structural position of the West as the sole *producer* of modernity and the non-West as its everlasting *consumer*.[26] According to this view, "The fundamental fissure in the Muslim world," as David Held proposes, "is between those who want to uphold universal standards, including the standards of democracy and human rights, and want to reform their societies, dislodging the deep connection between religion, culture and politics, and those who are threatened by this and wish to retain and/or restore power to those who represent 'fundamentalist' ideas. The political, economic, and cultural challenges posed by the globalization of 'modernity' now face the counterforce of the globalization of radical Islam."[27]

Afary and Anderson identify the "unbridled joy" of people in Kabul after the Taliban's fall in 2001 as a representative instance of the kind of historical crevice about which Held speaks. The fall of the Taliban, Afary and Anderson assert, "shocked many Islamists, as well as those Western leftists and progressives who had taken a culturally relativist position toward Afghanistan."[28] Who these Left-progressive cultural relativists are remains unexplored as well as the very fact that it was the American strategic interests that gave rise to al-Qaeda and their Taliban supporters, first to fight the Soviet invaders and then to contain the Iranian Revolution.

A whole host of liberal and Left-liberal intellectuals viewed 9/11 as an irrefutable indictment of cultural relativism. They dismissed any attempt to contemplate political roots of the assault and to think about its historical contingencies as "ethically perverse."[29] Raising questions about the context and/or political intentions of 9/11 terrorists have either been silenced by charges of "moral equivalency" or, as James Der Derian puts it, "rendered moot by claims that the exceptional natures of the act places it outside political discourse: *explanation became identified with exoneration.*"[30] The characterization of any attempt to comprehend 9/11 in its historical and political contingencies as an advocacy of "a *bien-pensant* anti-Americanism"[31] further depoliticized the event and encouraged the pervasiveness of the (non)politics of fear. A state of fear of losing "our way of life" that operates as, in Raymond Aron's words, "a primal, subpolitical emotion."[32] Those who raised questions about the political conjunctures of 9/11, particularly in its immediate aftermath, were dismissed as motivated by a "stubborn determination to inform the American people that the terrorist assault had been a response, albeit a mad and wicked one, to American power and American foreign policy."[33]

It is only through situating 9/11 terrorists outside history as evil, or residuals of a dead past, that the authors of *Foucault and the Iranian Revolution* can place the Iranian Revolution and the Islamist movements it inspired as "the specific social and political context in which al-Qaeda arose." It is only by conceptualizing Islamists of all varieties, from Ayatollah Khomeini to Osama bin Laden, as suprahistorical actors that one can take Foucault's defense of the Iranian Revolution as an indication that, had he been alive, he would have endorsed the 9/11 attacks. To show that they are not the only ones who have drawn such an erroneous conclusion, Afary and Anderson borrow from Alain Minc, the ideologue of French neoconservatism and President Sarkozy's trusted adviser. In an editorial called "Le terrorisme de l'esprit,"[34] which appeared on November 7, 2001, in *Le Monde*, Minc called Baudrillard's critique of the misguided American-led "war on terror" a theoretical extension of Foucault's defense of "Khomeinism."

In his editorial Minc illustrates the continuity between Foucault's supposed advocacy of "Khomeinism" and the value Baudrillard attributes to the symbolic and literal significance of 9/11 in exposing the vulnerability of the single-hegemon global order.[35] But using a truncated quotation,

Afary and Anderson present Minc's argument as if he were linking Foucault theoretically not to Baudrillard but to the 9/11 terrorists. Moreover, one could hardly claim that "Foucault's writings on Iran . . . continues to undercut his reputation" in France while citing his intellectual foe and a well-known advocate of market fundamentalism. I certainly doubt that Minc's disparaging remarks would erode Foucault's credibility among any intellectual community.[36]

But Afary and Anderson see in Minc and other "prominent" commentators their defense of the Enlightenment rationality against what they call "postmodern" and "postcolonial" critiques of what Fred Dallmayr once called the "Western conceit of superiority."[37] In his op-ed "Attacks on U.S. Challenge the Perspective of Postmodern True Believers,"[38] just more than a week after the 9/11 attacks, Edward Rothstein of the *New York Times* holds postcolonialists and postmodernists partly responsible for theses atrocities. This is because, he argues, the postmodernists advocate the idea that "concepts we take for granted—including truth, morality, and objectivity—are culturally 'constructed.'" In his scathing criticism, Rothstein does not even spare Thomas Kuhn, the respected sociologist and historian of science, for his role in historicizing science and scientific practice, or the pragmatist philosopher Richard Rorty, "who has challenged objective notions of truth." The attacks of 9/11, Rothstein stresses, "cry out for a transcendent ethical perspective, even a mild relativism seems troubling by contrast." He holds Kuhn and Rorty, along with other "postmodernists"(!), guilty of rejecting universal values and ideals and in turn leaving "little room for unqualified condemnations of a terrorist attack, particularly one against the West. Such an attack, however inexcusable, can be seen as a horrifying airing of a legitimate cultural grievance."

This Enlightenment rationalist fundamentalism, in the words of one of its self-proclaimed adherents, shares the commitment with *religious* fundamentalism that "there *is* culture-transcending knowledge: there *is* indeed 'knowledge beyond culture.'"[39] Both positions recognize "the uniqueness of truth" and "avoid the facile self-deception of universal relativism."[40] Indeed, we are left wondering, as James Der Derian spurns Rothstein's censure of relativism, "where would that view place fervent truth-seeking and serious enemies of relativism and irony like Osama bin Laden? Terrorist foe but epistemological ally?"[41]

This position becomes doubly absurd when Afary and Anderson situate 9/11 as the inevitable outcome of the Iranian Revolution. They recognize that radical Islamism is a diverse social and political movement but insist that they share uniform ideological commitments. They recognize that Wahhabi Saudis consider the Shi'ite Iranians to be heretics, and that the Islamic Republic almost went to war with Afghanistan under the Taliban regime, but those facts, they insist, do not change the reality that these radically different political entities form a singular movement called "radical Islamism." "Like fascism earlier, which had German, Italian, Spanish, Romanian, and many other varieties, radical Islamism has enough common features to discern it as a general phenomenon."[42] To advance their assertion, they go even as far as fabricating the fact that "the dominant conservative part of the [Iranian] government around Ayatollah Ali Khamenei condemned U.S. actions against bin Laden."[43] It is a known fact that the Iranian government railed against bin Laden and his Taliban supporters. But more importantly, the U.S. forces could not so easily oust the Taliban and end their rule in Afghanistan without Iranian logistical and political help.[44]

Islamism, as it was conceived during the Iranian Revolution, was neither an archaic form of fascism nor a traditional cultural leftover. It was rather a response to and a consequence of modern conditions. Islamism has gone through major internal transformations of its own, and its proponents have advanced important critical reassessments of its main premises.[45]

It remains imperative to understand Islamism, its technologies of debate, and its derivative political ideologies not simply through reference to the universal Enlightenment rationality and the teleological history it envisions. The Iranian Revolution triumphed ten years after the disillusionment that followed 1968 in Europe. Foucault wrote during a moment when many Europeans believed all that was revolutionary had melted into air, with all revolutionary politics being branded as totalitarian utopianism. Foucault's writings on the Iranian revolution go beyond a journalistic account of its unfolding. Foucault offers a departure from binary understandings in which the revolution was depicted in multiple ways as the struggles of the passing of traditional society in a modernizing Middle East. Although he emphasizes the religious character of the revolution, he remains skeptical of bifurcated conceptions of Islamist versus secular politics based on a temporal map of Enlightenment rationalities. The most important lesson one can draw from Foucault's essays is to regard the revolutionary moment as the realization of a condition of possibilities, rather than an instance of the reaffirmation of the internal logic of a universal History.

1

THINKING THE UNTHINKABLE
The Revolutionary Movement in Iran

> Nobody has ever seen the "collective will" and, personally,
> I thought that the collective will was like God, like the soul,
> something one would never encounter. We met, in Tehran and
> throughout Iran, the collective will of a people.
>
> —Michel Foucault, 1979

> Man gets rid of fear and feels free. Without that there would be
> no revolution.
>
> —Ryszard Kapuściński, 1982

THE MAIN THRUST OF THE CRITIQUE of Foucault's writings on the Iranian Revolution lies in the basic assumption that he failed to recognize the deep plurality of the revolutionary movement. That he was taken by a touch of "authenticity" in the naked experience of violent spectacles and dark mysticism of the *limit-experience* of revolutionary Iranians.[1] A common narrative of the revolutionary movement holds that the clergy hijacked the revolution and assumed its leadership at the expense of Left and democratic secular forces. The myth of the stolen revolution has shaped the historiography of the revolutionary movement of 1978–79 and has since become the hegemonic representation of the period. Within that frame, Foucault's support of the revolution, particularly with his emphasis on its religious tenor, appears in retrospect as a simple infatuation with a ritualistic spectacle of death and an Orientalist fantasy of the emancipatory promise of what he termed "political spirituality."

In this chapter, I demonstrate that from its earliest inception in 1977 a small but militant faction within the clergy, those who followed Ayatollah Khomeini, led the revolutionary movement that culminated in the Islamic Revolution of 1979 and the establishment of the Islamic Republic. While it is certain that many people of diverse walks of life and a variety of political parties participated in massive rallies and protests, it is also clear from the record that a religious disposition and the leadership of Ayatollah Khomeini leant this movement an uncompromising revolutionary character. In this chapter, I intend to show that Shi'ism offered a cultural context, a shared language within which a revolutionary movement could be defined, advanced, sustained, and experienced. It afforded a political milieu to spread and perpetuate a movement that massive numbers of peoples could identify with in historically complex, politically ambiguous, and, to a large extent, inexplicable ways. The purpose of the following chronology is to restore the constitutive significance of Shi'ism, both as a feature of the popular cultural endowment and as a liberation theology, in the 1978–79 revolutionary movement. Rather than a series of formal, theological, and legal principles, Shi'ism in the revolutionary context gave political expression to basic principles of justice that corresponded to what Hegel termed *Sittlichkeit*— that is, the customs, norms, and expectations inherent in the conception of the good life.[2]

Iran, the Island of Stability

Only thirteen months after the 1977 New Year's Eve state dinner in Tehran, when President Carter toasted the Shah, calling the country "the island of stability," the people's revolution closed the book of monarchy in Iran. By all accounts, the Iranian Revolution of 1978–79 appeared like a *thunderbolt from the blue*. In a conceptual universe that seemed incapable of explaining its emergence and its outcome, the Iranian Revolution was indeed "unthinkable."[3] At the time, Iran was a country ruled by an autocratic regime that allowed no public expression of dissent. The monarchy sustained its authority by perpetuating "two absolutes": the absolute and entrenched power of the state and the absolute despair of the masses.[4] President Carter's remark, therefore, did not register as something inconsistent with the general tenor of the time. No one imagined, even remotely, that the king would be toppled by the revolutionary force of millions with bare hands and open arms facing the fifth largest military in the world.

Earlier that year, the Carter administration had encouraged the Shah to adopt a policy of political openness. Iran had already emerged as a regional powerhouse, and the Shah's grip of power seemed unshakable. The monarchy enjoyed a relatively stable economy, and its radical political foes had been neutralized. The Shah had dissolved the two loyal parties in March 1975 and established a single-party system under the Resurrection Party. Soon thereafter, he reconstituted the Iranian calendar and changed its point of origin from the *hijra* (holy migration) of Prophet Mohammad to the coronation of Cyrus the Great. The Shah's Resurrection was to herald the coming of age of a new imperial power in the region with grand civilizational aspirations.

In two major operations, SAVAK (the notorious and much-feared secret police) had killed the last members of the leadership of Sāzmān-e Cherik-hā-ye Fadā'i-ye Khalq-e Iran (The Organization of Iranian Peoples' Devotee Guerrillas) first in the spring of 1975 and then in the summer of 1976, rendering the organization practically ineffective. Just a month after the establishment of Resurrection, the Shah's secret police concocted a plan to murder influential leaders of the opposition who were already serving their sentences in Tehran's notorious Evin Prison. On April 19, 1975, Bijan Jazani, a Marxist theorist and an early advocate of armed struggle, along with eight other prisoners were executed on the hills overlooking the prison complex. The next day, the headline in the state newspaper *Kayhan* read "9 Killed during an Escape Attempt from Evin Prison." The second operation in the summer of 1976 led to the killing of Hamid Asharf and the remaining members of the Fadā'iān leadership.[5]

With the decapitation of the communist opposition, in a policy informed by the Cold War, the Carter administration believed that the Iranian despot could afford a modest relaxation of his authoritarian rule. In order for President Carter's human rights policy to have any credibility, he needed to persuade the close American ally, the king of torture and unlawful imprisonment, to curb the atrocities of his feared secret police.

After the revolution it became known that the extent of these atrocities was greatly exaggerated, but at the time the Pahlavi regime had emerged as the main target of an unremitting campaign of human rights organizations. Amnesty International and other western critics of the ancien régime grossly overestimated the accounts of the brutality of the Iranian regime. In its 1975 and 1976 country reports, citing "exiled groups and foreign journalists," Amnesty International estimated the number of political prisoners in Iran between twenty-five thousand and one hundred thousand. In an article entitled "Terror in Iran," Reza Baraheni, a prominent literary and social critic, made Amnesty International's estimate widely known in intellectual circles in Europe and the United States.[6] The vast numbers of dissident Iranian students in Europe and the United States further publicized the plight of the members of the opposition inside the country.

At a time that the regime appeared to have successfully entrenched its authority, fractures began to appear in the absolute power of the state. The launching of the Resurrection Party coincided with the resurrection of a revolutionary spirit, which reintroduced Ayatollah Ruhollah Khomeini to the scene of oppositional politics. As an uncompromising leader, Khomeini had remained a voice of dissent in exile since he was forced out of the country in 1964. From his home in Najaf, Iraq, Khomeini continued to lambast the Shah for his despotism, corruption, and dependence on foreign powers. But Iranians seldom heard his voice or were allowed to utter his name in public. That changed on the eve of June 5, 1975, in the holy city of Qom. Between four and five hundred seminary students had gathered on the occasion of the anniversary of the riots that led to Khomeini's exile and defiantly called for Khomeini's return.[7] After the evening prayer, the students chanted "Long live Khomeini," "Down with Pahlavi." A large banner appeared from one of the main buildings with these words written on it in red: "Remember June 5, 1963, the day when those emancipated human beings, Khomeini and his companions, rose up against tyranny!"

The police and SAVAK attacked the seminary from their barracks outside the campus with water cannons and tear gas. They blocked the streets leading to the seminary, containing the students to the campus courtyard and preventing people on the outside from joining in. The skirmishes continued overnight. Rumors traveled throughout the city that the police had violated the sacred grounds of the seminary. More people tried to take part in the students' rescue from the police siege. One of the young students addressed the people outside the walls of the campus:

> People! We are your children. We have risen up to defend Islam and the Qur'an. We want to be free from the yoke of [the Shah's] tyranny and to be independent from the American and Israeli colonialism. We

defend the rights of the downtrodden and the oppressed. The Police! You are our brothers, our target is the bloodthirsty regime of Pahlavi, not you![8]

The students chanted "Down with the Pahlavi regime," "The divine will triumph over the evil," and "Whoever holds up a Qur'an, is sent to prison from now on." A red flag appeared on one of the domes of Imam Hossein Mosque, the tallest building on campus. Although the color red has its own significance in Shi'ite religio-political rituals, the regime publicized the act as a sign of communist infiltration. On the third day of the protests, more red flags appeared on seminary buildings and minarets. One seminary student from Isfahan proclaimed: "We want people in all corners of the city to witness that we intend to continue the path of Imam Hossein with our blood."[9]

Around four o'clock in the afternoon, Qom's police chief authorized anti-riot security and SAVAK agents to enter the campus and to end the "disturbances." Before the raid, the police chief, Colonel Javadi, addressed the protesters inside the school: "What is your real motivation for raising a red banner? Have you ever thought why the color red is used here? Do you not know what objectives those behind this follow? Bring them down and return to your quarters. No harm will be done to you if you follow our directives." The raid was brutal and indiscriminate. Witnesses reported that students were thrown off the roofs to the courtyard. The police struck the protestors violently with electric batons and punched and kicked the wounded. They arrested more than 350 people, who later reported that, while in police custody, they were beaten mercilessly.[10]

Still believing that communists posed the main threat to the stability of the regime, the state-controlled media presented the riots as a failed attempt by "Islamic-Marxists" to foment unrest in the holy city of Qom. *Kayhan*, a Tehran newspaper, reported:

The detainees [of the Qom riots] have confessed that they were distributing pamphlets published by foreign terrorist groups. They admitted that they were spreading Islamic-Marxist propaganda . . . and that they are against the principles of the Resurrection Party. The arrested protestors had put on clerical robes and infiltrated the clergy in order to advance their anti-national and subversive agenda. . . . When the security forces tried to restore order, they attacked the police with rocks and clubs. They shouted communist slogans and carried red flags.[11]

Shi'a clerics had a century-old history of political activism in Iran. Although high-ranking ayatollahs seldom violated the dominant philosophy of political quietism in the seminaries, those who did always found significant support among the younger generation of seminary students who often came from the countryside and working-class families. Despite that fact, the regime always attributed social unrest to communists. In the mind of the secret police and the regime's propaganda machine, not only did linking the protests to communist conspiracy discredit it in the eyes of the religious masses, it further justified the regime's atrocities and ensured support in the Cold War mentality of its American and European allies.

Calling the Qom protests of 1975 a communist conspiracy also forced the grand ayatollahs to issue statements condemning communism. Only one day after the seminary campus was cleaned up from days of riots, the three most influential ayatollahs tried to distance themselves from the unrest. Ayatollah Golpaygani declared: "The newspapers have published trumped up accusations against the clergy. I refute these accusations categorically. In the sacred realm of Shi'ism, there are no sympathies for communist ideas."[12] Grand Ayatollah Shari'atmadari, one of the most influential sources of emulation, also issued a statement emphasizing that "the Shi'a clergy and the seminaries have irreconcilable differences with communism and materialism. Those students arrested during the unrest in Qom have no communist sympathies. I deny all such assertions in the newspapers."[13] Fear of communist infiltration forced many high-ranking clerics to wonder about the political aspirations of the younger generation of seminary students. One ayatollah admitted that "the issue of raising a 'red flag' forced many grand ayatollahs not to take any serious steps toward securing the release of the students."[14]

In retrospect, the 1975 protests were the first signs of an emergent Shi'i revolutionary drama. Hitherto, the majority of the sources of emulation objected to the dominant culture industry that promoted the unimpeded westernization of society. But the question of monarchical legitimacy seldom entered their critical discourse. Even Ayatollah Khomeini did not question the legitimacy of monarchy until during his exile in Najaf in the 1970s. In June 1975 the grand ayatollahs in Qom and Mashhad sensed the specter of a distinct transformation. And indeed, a generation motivated by Ali Shari'ati's (1933–77) emancipatory theology was gathering force to step out of the seminary quarters and onto the unknown grounds of an emerging revolutionary movement.[15]

With the exception of Ayatollah Khomeini, all the grand ayatollahs viewed Shari'ati's revolutionary discourse with suspicion. A young Paris-educated sociologist from a famous devout family in the holy city of Mashhad, Shari'ati castigated the clergy for their inaction against tyranny. He argued that the clergy had turned Islam into a religion of superstition and deception. He advanced a theology in which prayer and politics, submission and subversion, mystical seclusion and revolution conjoin in a struggle for justice. He called his theology the *Alavid* Shi'ism, Shi'ism of action, of resistance, of martyrdom, as opposed to the clerical stagnant *Safavid* Shi'ism of the court, of the ceremonial and otherworldly concerns. The grand ayatollahs in Qom knew that Shari'ati's writing colored that red flag flying on top of the seminary minarets.

University campuses in Iran, particularly after the CIA-designed coup that toppled the nationalist prime minister Mohammad Mosaddeq in 1953, had always been a theater of student protests. These protests transformed major campuses (particularly Tehran University, Tehran Polytechnic, and Aryamehr Technical University, along with the universities of Mashhad, Tabriz, Isfahan, and Shiraz) into a battleground between dissident students and riot police. But the university security forces often would contain these rallies within the university premises, and students seldom could break out of the police blockade and spread the demonstrations out onto the city streets.

The other major organization that advocated urban guerrilla warfare against the regime, Mojāhedin-e Khalq-e Iran (Iranian Peoples' Mojāhedin), was also in disarray after a bloody internal power struggle between its Marxist faction and its Islamist faction. On June 19, 1977, Ali Shari'ati, who was claimed by the Mojāhedin as their spiritual leader, died in England of a heart attack. His death was blamed on SAVAK, and soon thereafter he would become the martyred teacher of the revolution.

The Shah now turned to his imperial ambitions of reviving the ancient Persian Empire. With the elimination of major opposition organizations complete, and under pressure from his Western allies, the Shah began a hesitant policy of political liberalization. The policy was primarily focused on improving the condition of prisons and gradually releasing those who had either served their terms or commuting their sentences. The majority of these prisoners were journalists, poets, novelists, and other dissidents with Left tendencies, mostly Marxist but also Islamist. This was to prove a major miscalculation on the Shah's part.

The Ten Nights at the Goethe Institute

The first social signs of changes happened in October 1977, when posters and fliers appeared on university campuses announcing ten nights of poetry reading sponsored by the Goethe Institute in Tehran. The newly revived Iranian Writers' Association organized the events for October 11–19. This appeared to be the first real test of the limits of freedoms that the regime was willing to tolerate. More than sixty writers and poets were scheduled to speak. The organizers, who came from various political and ideological backgrounds, assured the German director of the institute, Hans Becker,[16] that the gathering was going to be just a cultural event. The Goethe Institute had a history of sponsoring Persian poetry nights, and the organizers had no difficulty persuading Becker that they had no political intentions except asking the government for the formal recognition of their association.[17]

The Writers' Association was formed in 1968 by a diverse group of writers and social critics and commentators. The main objective of the association was to work within the legal frame of the time and defend the freedoms that were guaranteed in the constitution. When for the first time a group of writers filed for a legal status in June 1968, their application was denied based on a report prepared by SAVAK. The report concluded: "The members of this association are the same people who have been investigated before. Based on our records, they have socialist sympathies and dissident ideas. Therefore, based on section 312, the establishment of such an association with that type of membership is not recommended." In another document around the same time, SAVAK reiterates that "the Writers' Association is illegal and its members are disturbed individuals with communist, socialist, and extremist tendencies. They intend to influence the youth with their propaganda and hence we have objected to its legalization."[18]

In early 1977, with the changes in the political atmosphere, a number of writers and poets began a letter-writing campaign to revive the association. In a letter dated June 12, 1977, more than forty writers signed a petition to Prime Minister Hoveyda, demanding permission to resume their legal activities within the frame of their constitutional rights, establish a club for social gatherings, and publish a journal.[19] The letter to the prime minister was also translated and sent to reputable international literary magazines and journals with the hope that it would generate support among influential writers around the world. Although government policy toward the association did not change, the letter, published in Europe and the United States, brought attention to the plight of the Iranian writers. In a letter addressed to the prime minister, the president of PEN, Richard Howard, condemned the repressive policies of the government and asked the administration to respect the freedom of expression in Iran. The international attention forced the Iranian prime minister, who fancied himself a sophisticated man of culture, to respond in a public forum. In a speech to the Iranian radio and television club, Hoveyda declared: "We all desire to live in a country in which the freedom of expression is respected, so long as it does not undermine the very being of our nation."[20]

The prime minister's response emboldened the writers. Two weeks after his televised comments, the association issued a more poignant statement about the situation of the press and publishing in Iran. This time the number of signatories rose from forty to ninety-eight. Considering how closed public display of discontent had been since the 1953 coup, these statements generated a sense of courage and boldness among Iranian intellectuals. As Mahmoud Enayat, one of the most respected Iranian journalists, reminisced, "Although the statements were quite moderate, they left a significant mark. There was nothing radical about what those writers stated. They only protested the prevailing policy of censorship, without even criticizing the regime. But that dispassionate objection, which was unprecedented since 1953, generated passionate reverberation [among Iranian intellectuals]."[21]

In August 1977, after thirteen years of service, the Shah sacked Hoveyda and replaced him with a more technocratic and liberal-minded administration led by Jamshid Amuzegar. The changes coincided with slum dwellers' riots against forced evictions in neighborhoods in the southern and western edges of Tehran. When the city sent in bulldozers to level their accommodations, they resisted and vandalized police vehicles. Although the riots were effectively suppressed, they further revealed the discord between the Shah's discourse of Iran as the "Gate of the Great Civilization" and the realities of social and political life in the country.

It was under these circumstances that the Writers' Association seized the opportunity and stepped out of its immediate milieu to organize ten nights of poetry reading at the Goethe Institute in Tehran. By all accounts, no one anticipated the massive turnout for a few nights of poetry recitation. More than five thousand people, mostly university students, attended the first night on October 11. When the word spread that, despite heavy security presence, the grounds of the institute's garden were protected by diplomatic immunity, the crowd doubled in size for the second night. Even heavy rain did not discourage the audience from sitting in the open for hours in an anxious environment to hear a few lines of poetry and commentary. For the first four nights, every speaker respected the agreement that they would not politicize the event, instead maintaining its literary theme, albeit with marked political innuendo. The unspoken were the most important words that the crowd heard during the first nights. That, however, changed on the fifth night. Said Soltanpour, who was just released from prison as part of the new liberalization policy, broke the contract and openly condemned the tyrannical regime. One of the organizers of the event remembers that "all his poems were inspired by guerrilla warfare: bombs, explosions, and hand grenades. People were very receptive and punctuated his reading with their applause. He was agitated and showed no interest in leaving the stage."[22] Here is a passage from the first poem Soltanpour recited:

The Ghazal of Our Times

A song of blood grew in one uproar after another,
thunderous it became
The earth took another color, and time,
how colorful it became

The eyes of every seeking star, searching in blood,
A lightening of rage and a dagger in the heart of the night,

it became

[. . .]

At the night's darkness the trigger of the sun was pulled,
A mountain of fire and blood rose like a wave,
Our desire it became,

The beloved whom they call the red sedition,
Found our path in darkness of the night,
Our leader it became.[23]

Despite the increasing tension during the event, "The Ten Nights" of the Goethe Institute concluded without a major incident. Messages of support for the Writers' Association poured in from around the world. Jean Paul Sartre and Simone de Beauvoir lent their support with a letter signed by a long list of French intellectuals, including Roland Barthes, Michel Ronchant, Louis Althusser, Louis Aragon, Pierre-Félix Guattari, Hélène Parmelin, Claude Mauriac, and many others. Michel Foucault also signed the letter. This was Foucault's first encounter with the situation in Iran, an encounter that soon would turn for him into a significant intellectual and political project.[24]

The success of the Writers' Association encouraged other associations such as the Association of Iranian Lawyers and the Iranian Committee for the Defense of Freedom and Human Rights to take a measured advantage of the emerging political opening in the country. They organized letter-writing campaigns to government officials and international organizations for the recognition of their rights.

Students of different universities in Tehran organized similar events for the members of the Writers' Association on their respective campuses. The event at Tehran Technical University of Aryamehr, on November 16, 1977, became violent, and the university police arrested a number of students. The audience protested the arrests and staged a sit-in inside the athletics hall of the university. After twenty-four hours of negotiation, the police agreed to release the arrested students if the demonstrators dispersed. The crowd walked out of the university in silence, but a larger crowd joined them on the streets and turned the walk into an impressive rally of ten to fifteen thousand. The young protestors shouted "Death to the fascist regime," "Unity, struggle, victory," "Death to the Shah." A movement that began as an attempt for legal recognition of the

Writers' Association had now turned into a full-blown antiregime protest on a major street (incidentally, called Eisenhower) in Tehran.

At the same time, Iranian students in the United States staged a massive protest against the Shah's visit in front of the White House. Despite the strong police presence, the students successfully disrupted the ceremony on the White House lawn. The police used tear gas but wind blew it toward the White House and gave a number of reporters the opportunity to take pictures of the Shah and President Carter in tears. The banners in front of the White House read: "Mr. Human Rights Meets the King of Torture!"

A commonplace view considers the Goethe poetry nights to be the precursor of the revolutionary movement that began a few months later. But, as Javad Tale'ei, one of the organizers and a participant in the event recalls, "one should not forget that during the poetry reading nights, and even for months after that, we thought that the relative economic prosperity that the petro-dollar had afforded the country could not be sustained without some level of political openness. But at the time, no one could imagine that Iran would witness a revolution in a near future. During that period we wanted a reformed state structure and a guarantee of political freedom. At the time in political rallies one could not hear the name of Ayatollah Khomeini. It was the future events that change the direction of the movement toward a revolutionary path."[25]

Indeed, the revolutionary movement unfolded in a different series of events that occurred outside the milieu of political and intellectual circles whose central agenda was to restore the monarchy to its true constitutional roots. With the exception of the radical guerilla movement, whose operational capacity SAVAK had already destroyed, other political actors (i.e., the liberals of the National Front and Freedom Movement and communists of the Tudeh Party) followed the constitutional motto "Let the king reign but not govern!"

The Demise of Mustafa Khomeini and the Revolutionary Movement

The other important event in October 1977 was the death of Ayatollah Khomeini's forty-seven-year-old son, Mustafa, who was also exiled with his father in Najaf, Iraq. Like all other untimely deaths of political figures, dissident religious authorities attributed Mustafa Khomeini's death to a

Figure 1. Front page of *Resistance*, a publication of the Iranian Students Association, USA, vol. 5, no. 1, December 1977. Courtesy of Taraneh Hemami.

SAVAK conspiracy. Despite the fact that it quickly became an accepted fact that SAVAK agents had poisoned Mustafa, Ayatollah Khomeini himself downplayed the conspiracy theory in his message and treated the unfortunate demise of his son as "Divine expediency." He further called his loss "a small part of the greater misery to which the Muslim nation is subjected."[26] Mustafa's death created another opportunity for the militant clerics to mobilize the crowd in the seminaries and mosques across the country. Without exception, all the memorial services became sites of protest against the regime. A SAVAK report indicated that more than six thousand people crowded into the main mosque in Qom, chanting "Long live Khomeini." SAVAK agents filed similar reports in the cities of Yazd, Tabriz, Isfahan, Mashhad, and Tehran. In almost all cases, they highlighted the fact that the memorial services were overtly "anti-establishment" with a strong presence of "subversive elements."[27]

A high-profile service was held in Ark Mosque in Tehran. Mehdi Bazargan, the future head of the postrevolutionary provisional government, later recalled:

> No one before had seen a memorial service like this. An overwhelming crowd had packed all the prayer spaces indoors; the courtyard, balconies, rooftops of all surrounding buildings; and all the streets near the mosque. The police had given up the possibility of crowd control. But everything was orderly. All those people had responded to an invitation that was distributed a day earlier with signatures from nationalists, intellectuals, clerics, and bazaar merchants in alphabetical order

Figure 2. Mustafa Khomeini, walking behind his father (first on the left) to Imam Ali's shrine in Najaf (1965). Source: Islamic Revolution Documentation Center, *The Anniversary of Mustafa Khomeini's Martyrdom: Commemorative Photo Album*, November 2011.

without titles or designation. This was quite a meaningful and challenging task. That gathering demonstrated the willingness of many groups with different political tendencies to unite under the leadership of Ayatollah Khomeini, that militant *ruhāni*.[28]

Dariush Homayoun, the Shah's influential minister of intelligence, aptly observed that "the congregation after the death of Khomeini's son in Ark Mosque became a point of convergence between progressive liberals, the National Front, and the Left. With the exception of the government figures, every significant political personality was there. It was clear that the religious leadership had successfully mobilized all these [oppositional] forces."[29]

Whereas the 1975 riots in Qom and Mashhad failed to spread across the country, memorial services for Mustafa Khomeini in 1977 immediately became a nationwide rallying point against the Pahlavi regime.[30] Unlike the reformist undertone of the letter-writing campaigns led by the Writers' and Lawyers' Associations, these gatherings struck an uncompromising tone, holding the regime responsible for Mustafa's death. His death also brought a new form of alliance among university students (both inside and outside the country), religious institutions, and the Bazaar. A SAVAK report indicated that a minute of silence in honor of Mustafa Khomeini was observed simultaneously on major university campuses in Tehran. That kind of coordinated mobilization alerted the regime intelligence services to networks that operated undetected by their agents.[31]

In the same report, a SAVAK field agent stated that the cassette tapes of memorial sermons from different cities were now being distributed openly in the street of Qom. More than fifty thousand participated in the commemoration of Mustafa Khomeini held in Qom on the seventh day after his death.[32] An informal grassroots network called "shabakeh-ey payām-resāni nehzat Imam Khomeini" (a network distributing Imam Khomeini's messages) was formed. The main objectives of this network were to spread the name and the leadership of Khomeini, normalize public expressions of discontent with the Pahlavi regime, generate a transnational interest in Khomeini's movement, create unity under Khomeini's leadership, and intensify a campaign against the SAVAK and regime's intelligence network.[33]

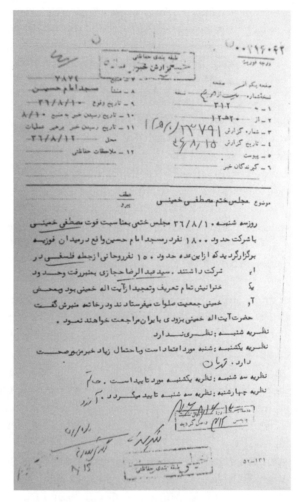

Figure 3. SAVAK report on Mustafa Khomeini's memorial service in the Imam Hussein Mosque in Tehran, October 1977. The report indicates that more than 150 members of the clergy participated in the ceremony. The speakers, it is reported, openly praised Ayatollah Khomeini to a receptive crowd. One of the speakers (A. Hejazi) promised the return of the Ayatollah soon. Source: Islamic Revolution Documentation Center, *The Anniversary of Mustafa Khomeini's Martyrdom: Commemorative Photo Album*, November 2011.

Mustafa Khomeini's death set in motion a cycle of "fortieth day mourning," which defined the basic rhythm of the revolutionary movement for the ensuing fourteen months. After the fortieth day memorial service for Mustafa Khomeini, the government sent those prominent religious figures who delivered the sermons into domestic exile in remote towns with inclement environments. But these exiles also coincided with the beginning of the month of Moharram, a month with the most symbolic significance in Shi'ite Islam for struggle against oppression and tyranny.

Every year during the month of Moharram people of all walks of life organize elaborate processions of 'Āshurā, mourning the martyrdom of Imam Hussein in Karbalā in 680 CE. Imam Hussein refused to pledge allegiance to the Umayyad caliph Yazid and revolted against his tyrannical rule. Ali Shari'ati had already rearticulated the entire history of Shi'ism based on the martyrdom of Imam Hussein as the history of struggle between the oppressed and the oppressor, between the selfless acts of emancipation against forces of tyranny and despotism. Now, Shari'ati's revolutionary theology had found a concrete expression on the streets of Iranian cities. For the very first time in recent history, with the beginning of the month of Moharram, the self-flagellating crowd of mourners in front of Hosseinieh Ershad, a lecture hall and religious complex in which Shari'ati delivered most of his fiery speeches, chanted political slogans against the Shah. On December 21, 1977, a crowd of a few hundred called the Shah the Yazid of the time and proclaimed their readiness for Hussein-like martyrdom against his tyranny.[34] In the month of Moharram, during the winter of 1977–78, Imam Hussein's historical battle of Karbala against the despotic Yazid began to be reenacted in the neighborhoods in major Iranian cities. "Every day is 'Āshurā, every land is Karbala" became the slogan that advanced the revolutionary movement's struggle for justice with a religio/transhistorical fervor. With these religious markers, the revolution unfolded like a passion play of Imam Hussein's martyrdom. The events, like those passion plays, rapidly eroded the distinction between the spectators and the actors.

Toward the end of 1977, when Jimmy Carter arrived in Tehran for a state visit, the general view was still that all that unrest was just another passing moment of discontent rather than the beginning of a sustained revolutionary movement that would soon topple the Shah. But that perception was rapidly changing.

"The Red and Black Colonialism"

Responding to the growing anti-Shah rallies and open enthusiasm for a return of Ayatollah Khomeini, on January 7, 1978, an editorial column appeared in a state-owned newspaper, *Ettelā'āt*, entitled "Iran and the Red and Black Colonialism." The color scheme of the op-ed referred to an apparent collaboration between communists and Islamists against the regime. "These days," the essay began, "during the month of Moharram, once more we are alerted toward the unity of black and red, or the old and new colonialism." The editorial asserted that Iran's unprecedented social and economic progress under the leadership of the Shah had made colonial powers scramble to restore their old influence in the country. The author, who used a pseudonym, condemned the Iranian Tudeh Party for acting in the interest of the (new colonial) Soviet expansionist ambitions. He furthermore exploited a commonplace belief about the British influence in the clerical establishment to assert that the new demands for Khomeini's return were a desperate attempt by an old imperial power to regain its lost significance.

Undoubtedly, the main objective of the editorial was the defamation of Khomeini. Highlighting the importance of the White Revolution of 1963, which instituted a new policy of land reform and woman suffrage, the author called those who rose against the reforms "reactionaries," convened under the leadership of Khomeini, who were afraid of losing their old privileges.

> This man has a suspicious background and ties with the most reactionary elements of the old colonialism. He lacked reputation among the respected clerics and was looking for an opportunity to gain notoriety through political adventurism. Ruhollah Khomeini was the perfect candidate to realize the alliance between red and black reactionaries. He was responsible for the shameful events of June 5, 1963 [which led to his exile].[35]

The anonymous columnist also claimed that "[Khomeini's] associates know him as the Indian Sayyed." The point of this baseless reference to Khomeini's Indian origins was to insinuate a British connection that had informed his political project. This calculated attack met with fierce reaction from all religious centers around the country. In two days of violent protests in Qom, and later in Mashhad, the security forces opened fire and killed scores of people. The Freedom Movement, led by Mehdi Bazargan, announced that more than 100 demonstrators were killed, 500 suffered from gunshot wounds, and more than 1,400 were arrested in two days of riots in Qom and Mashhad.[36] The bazaars in Isfahan, Tabriz, Yazd, Mashhad, Ahvaz, and many other towns closed down shops in protest of the op-ed and the ensuing savagery of the security forces. Grand Ayatollahs in Qom and Mashhad seminaries suspended their classes and demanded an apology from the government for insulting the integrity of the clergy and calling its revered personalities agents of British imperialism.

After the January 1978 riots in Qom, the revolutionary movement began a sustained expansion throughout the country. From only a few weeks earlier when voices of discontent were seldom heard on the streets of any city, now the country only existed via a revolutionary praxis. Vast numbers of Iranian students abroad turned the revolution from its early stages into a transnational event and a source of aspiration for revolutionaries around the globe.

From these very early days, it became evident that a Shi'i-Islamic symbolism had offered the movement a revolutionary ardor and turned it into an all-embracing force that perpetuated its motion through religious rites and rituals. No one understood this better than Ayatollah Khomeini. He used his folk rhetoric to weave an Islamic revolutionary sensation into the very fabric of a potent anticolonial discourse. He spoke with an inclusive tone without ever relinquishing the Islamic character of the militant movement, the leadership of which he had masterfully claimed. His message commemorating the fortieth day of the Qom massacre is just one example of how he used his effective clerical oratory to incite a revolutionary zeal.

> As I speak to you today, many big cities such as Tehran, Tabriz, Mashhad, Isfahan, have come to a standstill. Most businesses are closed and universities are on strike. The target of all these protests is one man: the Shah. People have recognized that the Shah is guilty of inflicting this misery upon the nation. They knew, but they have now found the courage to overcome that barrier of fear.
>
> . . . Today, forty days has passed from the time that they brutally massacred our devout seminarians. How many tears should our people shed over the death of their youth? Our brave nation now stands with

empty hands and sorrowful hearts united against the agents of the regime, resisting in every alley, on every street corner. Our people have proven that we are alive, not dead.

. . . Qom Seminary has revived Islam. Our respected *'ulama* have proven wrong those who believed that what we promote is the opiate of the masses, that we collaborate with the British and other colonial powers. The colonialists, the British, the Germans, and the Soviets, propagated all this that the seminaries are the place of advocacy for backwardness. They called religion the opiate of the masses, because they knew how active and vibrant Islam is.

. . . A Muslim who is oblivious toward the concerns of others is not a Muslim. . . . Islam is a religion that speaks to the problems of Muslims. . . . How can we remain silent when they kill our youth? That is not the manner of Islam. Should we be content with all these atrocities? We must change ourselves.[37]

While students at university campuses and religious centers, bazaar merchants, and sympathetic imams of major mosques around the country planned for commemoration rallies of the Qom massacre in more than ten cities, only in Tabriz did the events turn violent and riots break out in all parts of the city. Responding to an invitation by a dissident cleric and a student of Ruhollah Khomeini, Ayatollah Qazi Tabataba'ei, an estimated fifty thousand people gathered inside and in front of Mirza Yusef Mosque in Tabriz. The growing number of mourners/protestors and the radicalization of the speeches inside the mosque forced the police to open fire on the crowd. The news traveled fast around the city, and riots broke out in several neighborhoods. People torched and ransacked government buildings, banks, and police stations. In a pamphlet published a week after the uprising, Militant Muslim Students of Tabriz University claimed that the demonstrators burned to the ground 62 banks and 12 state office buildings. They further wrecked 162 government buildings and 97 banks and 7 movie theaters. Not a single place was looted. The demonstrators trashed the banks but did not touch a single bill. Many witnesses reported that in the midst of that violence and chaos an incredible discipline prevailed. The students claimed that more than four hundred people were killed during the two-day unrest. Another writer from Tehran reported that "all entrances to the city are closed, Tabriz is practically under martial law and no one is allowed to enter or exit the city. The number of the dead is now passed a thousand."[38] For the first time, after the massacre in Tabriz, the faculty of Qom Seminary issued a joint statement denouncing the massacre. Although the statement fell short of calling for the overthrow of the regime, it offered condolences to Ayatollah Khomeini, thus recognizing him as the leader of the "resistance movement."[39]

The regime continued its effort to contain the revolutionary movement by characterizing it as a communist conspiracy. Holaku Rambod, one of the main ideologues of the Shah's Resurrection Party, wondered: "It is not quite clear when and from which border the perpetrators of Tabriz sedition entered Iran." Two days later he claimed: "Known communists were responsible for dragging Tabriz into mayhem." Ja'farian, another spokesperson of the party, reiterated that "the rioters who set the city ablaze were not from Tabriz." The Shah himself remained defiant and in denial. "We will continue our policy of maximum freedom," he addressed a crowd in a stadium in Tehran one week later, "because the foundation of the Shah and the Nation Revolution is so strong that the decaying remains of the black and red unholy alliance cannot shake it."[40] However, in retrospect, the Shah acknowledged that the only conspiracy that undermined the authority of his repressive machine was the creative use of religious symbols and rituals. He wrote:

> Based on Islamic rituals, on the fortieth day of passing, the parents and close relatives of the dead would go to the gravesite of their loved one. I do not believe, before these events, anyone had exploited someone's death so shamelessly for political gains.[41]

After the Tabriz massacre, in coordinated messages, a group of high-ranking clerics declared the upcoming Persian new year on March 20 a day of national mourning. Their statement began with a quatrain:

> On the day that the Divine commandments are violated,
> there is no fest,
> On the day that our source of emulation mourns,
> there is no fest,
> On the day that thousands of seekers of justice endure torture,
> Our deserving leader bears the torment of exile,
> there is no fest.[42]

In the same statement, the *'ulama* asked the nation to commemorate the bloody day in Tabriz on its fortieth day in small and large gatherings. This time, on March 30, 1978, it was the city of Yazd that became the scene of bloody clashes between more than twenty thousand demonstrators and the anti-riot police. The opposition claimed that the security forces had shot and killed more than one hundred people. The events in Yazd marked the emergence of a new pulse in the revolutionary movement. The mourning/protest cycle had found a life of its own. City after city, town after town, marked in solidarity one another's uprisings. Each time, the slogans became more radical and less compromising. Immediately after the Yazd massacre, the newly established Association of Militant Clergy issued its manifesto calling for the overthrow of the Pahlavi regime and the establishment of an Islamic government.[43]

By the late spring of 1978, while street protests widened, workers in major industrial centers began to organize short- and long-term strikes. On April 18, 1978, workers of Tabriz Industrial Machine Factory went on strike against what they called "the savagery of the regime's agents against defenseless protestors."[44] Students at major universities around the country boycotted classes and the bazaar shopkeepers closed their doors in defiance to their respective cities' police orders to keep them open.

In his first substantive interview with a major Western newspaper, Ayatollah Khomeini explained his views of the revolutionary movement and its objectives. *Le Monde* correspondent Lucien George met with the ayatollah in his home in Najaf and described him as a determined, austere, pious leader under whose name Iranians had risen up against the tyranny of the Shah. George's description added to Khomeini's mystique as a charismatic leader, selfless and ready to accept the consequences of his action without fear and with dignity. In the introduction to his interview, he wrote:

> Khomeini's humble residence is situated in the bend of one of the narrow streets of Najaf where the houses are intricately mazelike in order to protect them from the scorching rays of the sun. This residence is like the dwellings of the poorest people of Najaf. In this humble dwelling, there is no visible sign of the authority of the leaders of rebellions or those of the opposition groups living in exile. If Ayatollah Khomeini has the power to mobilize Iranians and stage an uprising, it undoubtedly stems from his power to influence and dominate their thinking.

This power, instead of decreasing subsequent to his banishment from Iran, has increased tenfold.[45]

Despite the fact that the regime continued to blame foreign agents, communists, and "Islamic Marxists" for the unrests, the Le Monde interview provided a glimpse into the ideological intricacies of the emerging movement and its leadership. By April 1978 Khomeini had already claimed the mantle of the undisputed leader of the revolutionary movement.

In the following extended excerpt, Khomeini shows how he carefully crafted an uncompromising language that in its symbolic construct and strategic demands spoke to a vast majority of Iranians and maintained a global reach. He invented a revolutionary discourse that distressed a majority of ayatollahs whose political quietism had dominated the seminaries for decades, out-paced the reformist demeanor of nationalist and religious liberals, and was openly hostile to communists. Despite these categorical distinctions Khomeini drew between his authority and alternative oppositional politics, others found no alternative but to accept his leadership and unite under his banner.

> Le Monde: The Shah accuses you of being against civilization and living in the past. How would you answer this?
>
> Khomeini: It is the Shah himself who is opposed to civilization, and who is living in the past. . . . The Shah implements the policies of the imperialists and attempts to keep Iran in a backward and retrogressive state. The Shah's regime is autocratic. . . . It is because of these undeniable facts that the Shah is attempting to invert the matter of our opposition to his regime and accuse us of living in the past and being against civilization.
>
> Le Monde: What do you think about the term "Islamic Marxism" that the regime often uses? Do you have any organizational link with the radical leftist groups?
>
> Khomeini: It is the Shah who has used this term and his associates who repeat it. This is an erroneous concept full of inconsistencies, its purpose being to discredit and extinguish the movement of our Muslim people against his regime. Islam is based on monotheism and the Oneness of God, which contradicts all forms of materialism. The term "Islamic Marxism" is a fiction. The Shah and his propaganda machine invented this imaginary alliance between "black reactionaries" and "red saboteurs" in order to plant fear in

Muslims' hearts and sow the seeds of doubt in them. There has never been an alliance between Muslims, who are campaigning against the Shah, and Marxist elements.

Le Monde: What is your political agenda? Do you intend to overthrow the regime? What sort of regime will you install in the place of this one?

Khomeini: Our ideal goal is the establishment of an Islamic system of government. Nevertheless, our first concern at present is to topple this despotic regime. We should, at first, set up an authority that would fulfill the basic needs of the people.

Le Monde: What do you mean by Islamic government? What naturally comes to mind by that is the Ottoman Empire or Saudi Arabia.

Khomeini: The only point of reference for us is that of the period of the Prophet and of Imam Ali. . . . The type of state that we shall establish will certainly not be a monarchical regime. But what kind of government we promote is outside the scope of this interview.[46]

While the overthrow of the Shah became the main demand of strikers and demonstrators around the country, the ayatollahs in Qom continued to be cautious in their critique of the regime. In response to a German television reporter who asked whether the Shah had to step down or not, Ayatollah Shari'atmadari maintained that "it makes no difference to us one way or the other. We want freedom. We want free parliamentary elections." He repeated the old motto of the liberal constitutionalists "Let the king reign but not govern."[47] In another interview with Claire Brière of *Libération*, he struck a chord of caution, particularly against Khomeini's relentless call for the overthrow of the Shah: "We are only asking for the implementation of Islamic ordinances, justice, freedom, and an unrestricted execution of the [existing] constitution."[48]

With the exception of two organizations, Fadā'iān and Mojāhedin, that promoted armed struggle against the regime through an urban guerrilla warfare, other major political parties followed a similar reformist agenda in the earlier days of the revolutionary movement. Fadā'iān and Mojāhedin both were rendered ineffective since the last members of their leadership were either killed or imprisoned by SAVAK. Although they both enjoyed significant support among students and young urban middle classes, they lacked organizational resources to influence the direction, content, and form of the revolutionary movement. Up to the point that the uprisings around the country were still gathering revolutionary vigor, the Tudeh communist party advocated checking the Shah's dictatorship, rather than pursuing a revolutionary overthrow of his regime. Rather than reflecting the rapidly growing sentiments on the ground, the headlines and editorials in *Mardom* (The People), the biweekly publication of the party, continued to promote a reformist agenda and the expansion of Iran's relation with the Soviet bloc. For example, in the March 20, 1978, issue of *Mardom*, the editors condemned the actions of a group of dissident students who took over the Iranian embassy in East Berlin. They called it a "West German and imperialist conspiracy to damage the relation between the German Democratic Republic and Iran."[49]

By the beginning of the Iranian New Year in March 1978, it had become clear to the Shah's advisers that the growing unrest in the country was not heading toward another cul-de-sac. The movement was vast, sustained, and radical. Its leadership on the ground was inconspicuous but organized. The Shah was forced to implement a new series of political liberalization initiatives and a limited democracy project in hopes of placating and diffusing the movement. He canceled his long-awaited trip to Eastern Europe and tried to refashion himself as a religious man. He traveled to Mashhad, Iran's holiest city, to pay tribute to the holy Reza, the eighth Shi'ite imam. At the end of his pilgrimage, he told the reporters that "the source of the unrest in the country are two groups: the radical Left and extreme Right." He warned the nation that "if the government fails to maintain peace and order, the country will fall into the hands of the Tudeh party communists."[50] A week later, he sacked General Nassiri, the infamous head of SAVAK, and replaced him with the fifty-seven-year-old General Moghaddam to carry out the overhaul of one of the world's most feared intelligence and security services. To lend further support to General Moghaddam, the Shah also introduced legislation called "the expansion of democracy" to the parliament on June 13, 1978.

None of these reforms received any traction with the public or drew official notice by the religious authorities. The legislative reforms and, more importantly, the perpetual rallies and strikes, emboldened the Lawyers Guild and other professional associations to demand the expansion and implementation of their constitutional rights of assembly and freedom of expression, the separation of the branches of the government, and an independent judiciary to oversee the proposed reforms. These associations' letter-writing campaigns brought more international attention to the growing tension in Iran.

Centered around mosques, holy shrines, bazaars, and universities, large and small demonstrations continued to destabilize the regime. The dual policy of reform and suppression proved to be unsuccessful, and this failure was brought out in the open by the declaration of martial law in Isfahan on August 11, 1978. In a hastily drafted statement, the government announced:

> Last night, a few saboteurs, who had no intention but to destroy the city of Isfahan, demonstrated and vandalized public buildings and offices. Therefore, with the recommendation of local authorities, the government declares one month of martial law in order to protect the property and livelihood of Isfahan residents. The government is committed to continue its steadfast steps toward the expansion of freedoms, but it will not tolerate the anti-Islamic acts of sabotage and disturbance of the peace.[51]

Although martial law was only declared in Isfahan, for the first time, army soldiers intervened directly in suppressing rallies in Shiraz, Ahvaz, Qom, Mashhad, and Rafsanjan. While the government announced that the declaration of martial law in Isfahan needed to be sanctioned by the parliament, in reality it was already instituted in many different cities around the country. Despite the apparent allegiance of the demonstrators and their local organizers to Ayatollah Khomeini, Isfahan's chief military administrator, General Naji, continued to lay the responsibility of the unrest in the city on "a band of insurgent Islamist-Marxists whose mission is to create chaos and destruction in the country."[52]

The midsummer of rising protests also coincided with the month of Ramadan, which gave the revolutionary movement greater opportunities for mobilization and a more meaningful inspirational association with Shi'i-Islamic symbolism. Observing Ramadan festivities, for the first time since the recent movement had begun, mosques opened their doors to host gatherings with explicit political tenor. SAVAK agents reported that mosques' imams played cassette tapes of Khomeini's sermons openly to animated congregations. The intelligence field reports further frustrated the beleaguered Shah.[53] The month of Ramadan of 1978 turned mosques into places of political organization, mass mobilization, and networking. One mosque in particular operated as the clerical opposition headquarters in Tehran.

Qoba Mosque[54] is located a few blocks north of Irshād Islamic Center, where Ali Shari'ati delivered most of his fiery political sermons to a young generation of Muslim intellectuals. Shari'ati's penetrating oratory made his anticolonial rhetoric effective and popular among university and high school students. He turned Islam into a liberation theology to reclaim it from both its torpid clerical guard and modern prejudices of secularity.

The transfer of the center of Islamic resistance from Irshād to Qoba Mosque served a symbolic as well as a real purpose: that the clergy now had the desire *and* the ability to organize a mass movement to overthrow the Shah and breathe a revolutionary spirit into the soul of Islam. Qoba's imam, Mohammad Mofatteh, lacked the kind of charisma and radicalism that made Shari'ati the teacher of the revolution. But during the Ramadan (July–August) of 1978, he invited emergent political and clerical leaders of the revolutionary movement to deliver defiant sermons against the Shah and in defense of their exiled leader. Mehdi Bazargan (the future head of the provisional government), Mohammad Javad Bahonar (the first clerical prime minister after the revolution, who was assassinated in August 1981), Ali Khameneh'i (the future president and supreme leader), and many other influential figures spoke during Ramadan prayers in Qoba Mosque.[55]

The declaration of martial law in Isfahan further radicalized the revolutionary movement. Those who had hoped that the Shah could relinquish his authoritarian rule in order to save constitutional monarchy began to realize that the movement existed sui generis and was headed toward a full-blown revolution. The possibility of reform had vanished. For the first time, street battles and marches found support among industrial workers. Seventeen hundred workers in Behshahr Textile Factory went on strike, demanding better work conditions and the right of collective bargaining. The magnitude and scope of the movement rose vigorously. The grand ayatollahs in Qom and Mashhad found it increasingly difficult to invite people for calm and advocate a resolution in which the Shah could save his throne. Their dissatisfaction with Khomeini's uncompromising position, more and more, had to be kept inside the seminary quarters. In a joint statement, the three most influential grand ayatollahs—Shari'atmadari, Mar'ashi, and Golpaipani—issued a statement asking the regime to respect peoples' "legal and legitimate demands for freedom and justice." The ayatollahs reprimanded the Shah for "militarizing" the situation and leading the country toward inexorable violence.[56]

For his part, the Shah tried to strike a chord of appeasement with promises of limited political reform and a gradual expansion of democratic institutions. He hoped that he could satisfy the leadership of the liberal National Front and Liberation Movement, and the grand ayatollahs of Qom and Mashhad, with a retreat to the basic premises of the Constitutional Revolution of 1906 and relinquish his authoritarian rule in order to save his reign. Mehdi Bazargan, the head of Liberation Movement, prepared a message to Ayatollah Khomeini asking him to use his authority to slow the pace of revolutionary demands and steer the transition of power toward a more guided and controlled path. He told Khomeini: "It is better to direct the sharp edge of the attack toward the dictatorship [of the Shah] instead of his colonial supporters. We cannot win fighting on two fronts. If we provoke Americans and Europeans, it will reinforce their support for the Shah." Bazargan encouraged Khomeini to exploit the political opening that the Shah had augured and try to change the regime through electoral politics.[57] It is not clear whether Khomeini ever saw this message or not, but he remained committed to the revolutionary overthrow of the regime and tried to marginalize those who toyed with the idea of reforming the monarchy.

A few days later, on August 19, 1978, the anniversary of the 1953 CIA-backed coup that toppled the Mosaddeq administration and restored the Shah's regime, unknown assailants torched Rex Movie Theater in the southern city of Abadan. Seven hundred people were locked in and all the exit doors were blocked as the fire spread. Three hundred and seventy-seven people charred to death and the rest were severely burned. The prime minister and first deputy of the Resurrection Party, Jamshid Amuzegar, blamed the opposition and "those who are so removed from any sense of humanity, faith, and religion" for this savage act. In an unequivocal statement, Ayatollah Khomeini called the Shah responsible for this horrendous crime. "Will anyone else except the Shah and his supporters benefit from this crime? The origin of this atrocity is the same as all other mass killings of innocent people in the country."[58]

Although the true perpetrators of the Rex massacre remained at large, the event itself completely burnt down remaining bridges for compromise. While the reluctant grand ayatollahs inside the country continued their cautious support of the protests, junior clerics advanced a bolder condemnation of the regime and called for a categorical end to monarchical rule in Iran. In his statement, the revered Grand Ayatollah Shari'atmadari declared: "One can only compare this atrocity with crimes committed by the Nazis and Fascists during World War II." But he hesitated to hold the regime responsible. Instead, he chose his words carefully in the hope that he could slow down the violence that was reaching the point of no return. "We are not certain what kind of calculated scheme and devious plots are behind this tragedy. No matter who the responsible parties are, without a shred of doubt such an ugly and shameful act only shows its perpetuators' barbarity and their utter lack of conscience."[59] In Tehran, on the same day, in an intrepid move, 122 junior clerics signed their names under a statement that accused the regime of setting fire on men, women, and children. They ended their short statement by warning the regime that "the fire they have set soon will burn the oppressive regime."[60]

The Black Friday

Toward the end of Ramadan, the cycle of seventh day and fortieth day memorials had left the regime without plausible options as to how to contain the spread of protests. The vicious cycle of more killings and massive political rallies of remembrance narrowed the possibility and legitimacy of a top-down reform project. The month of Ramadan and the Shi'i rituals of remembrance also generated a remarkable space without which diverse groups of people could not participate in the revolutionary movement.

But the most important religio-political event was yet to come. Muslims celebrate the end of the month of fasting on the last day of Ramadan with Eid-e Fitr, a day of celebration and reflection. In Iran of 1978, any possibility of congregation, commemorative or celebratory, meant another opportunity for political protest. After days of negotiation with Tehran's clerical establishment and the Liberation Movement leadership, the newly appointed government of Prime Minister Sharif-Emami agreed to permit a peaceful prayer service in the Qaytariyeh area of the city's northeast. Sharif-Emami had hoped that he could invest in the Qom grand ayatollahs by persuading them that the nation was in peril and that Khomeini's path would lead to the destruction of the country. Although he found sympathetic ears in Qom and among liberal nationalists, no one had the audacity to openly support his reform cabinet. Sharif-Emami thought that he had scored a victory when the clerical negotiators for the Fitr service agreed not to allow the radical elements to turn the religious ceremony into a rally against the Shah.[61]

Ayatollah Khomeini remained undaunted and showed no concerns about the negotiations in Tehran. He issued an unyielding statement on the occasion of the Eid-e Fitr, asking the people not to comply with any conciliatory gestures. "Our Divine duties will not change," he declared, "after the month of Ramadan." "Feisty rallies toward the realization of Islamic goals are prayer rituals of all days and months. . . . Do not allow the regime to deceive you with promises of reform, do not give them that chance. . . . With your strikes and protests, make their savage acts known to the world."[62]

No one anticipated the massive crowd that gathered on the hills of Qaytariyeh in the morning of the Eid on September 4, 1978. Hundreds of army and anti-riot police trucks surrounded the hills and were positioned along the twenty-kilometer route that the demonstrators planned to march. Military helicopters circled the air, one of which carried the Shah, who personally observed the crowd of a million with teary eyes.[63] People met the soldiers with thousands of stems of carnations and roses, truckloads of which appeared mysteriously during the march down the street toward the main railway station in the southern edge of the city. These shouts shook the city:

> With Khomeini's orders, the movement continues!
> Our movement is Hosseini, our leader is Khomeini!
> Military is blameless, the Shah is shameless!
> The silence of each Muslim, is a betrayal of the Qur'an!

Estimates varied significantly of how many people marched on that day in Tehran, from tens of thousands to more than one million. One thing was undisputed: in a symbolic and literal gesture, contiguous lines of people connected the affluent north part of the city to the working-class neighborhoods by the railway station in the south. That Monday demonstration was the largest in the country's history. Word spread at the end of the rally that a second rally was planned for Thursday. The second rally grew bigger and yet more radical.

Military join us!
The movement shall continue till the death of the king!
Shame on the Pahlavi Monarchy!
Long live the path of our martyrs!

The Thursday rally, which was organized by the newly established Association of Militant Clergy, ended at Shahyad Square on the western edge of the city with a declaration that "the movement will continue until the fall of monarchy."[64] Thousands of fliers were handed out: "Tomorrow, Friday, Jaleh Square."

Sharif-Emami's cabinet would represent a fleeting attempt to inhibit the movement with conciliatory politics. Just a short two weeks earlier, in his inauguration speech, he invited all parties to "rise under the eternal guiding light of the Qur'an and the precious teachings of Islam within the constitutional law and save the nation."[65] He commuted sentences of high-ranking clerics, including Khomeini's brother, and promised that he would soon form a national reconciliation government. But now, on the eve of the second million-strong rally in one week, he abandoned his placatory discourse and, in the late hours of the night on Thursday, September 7, declared martial law in Tehran, effective immediately.

Unaware of the declaration of martial law, from the early hours of the morning people flooded Jaleh Square, this time on the east side of the city. Tanks and armored vehicles were already in place in the square. Hundreds of soldiers lined to prevent the growing mass to congregate. Army helicopters with heavy machine guns pointing to the ground monitored the situation. Military commanders ordered the people to disperse and respect the martial law, which prohibited gatherings of more than three individuals in public places. The celebratory and jubilant spirit of the two earlier marches dissipated quickly. An air of anxiety and anger overtook the square. The crowd's refusal to disperse met first with shots of tear gas and then live bullets directly fired into the densely occupied square.

Eyewitness accounts recounted the horror of hundreds being shot. The bloodshed stunned the protestors. A state of incredulity gave rise to

Figure 4. The massacre of Black Friday, September 1978. Source: Islamic Revolution Documentation Center.

rumors that "the soldiers who shot people had blue eyes and blond hair." Others claim that they overheard that "the soldiers were speaking Hebrew," and "they were Israeli soldiers who shot people from the helicopters." Many reported that they saw with their own eyes that the soldiers refused to shoot, and in a number of cases they either shot themselves or their commanders.[66] But the most important and lasting depiction of the massacre of what came to be known as Black Friday was the number of people killed during the clashes. Despite the fact that the real number of the dead was eighty-eight, the revolutionary narrative of the event was shaped by a common belief that four to ten thousand were martyred on that fateful day.

The Eid-e Fitr congregation and the ensuing rallies that led to Black Friday, on the one hand, sealed the fate of the Shah, and on the other hand, allowed Ayatollah Khomeini to establish himself as the undisputed leader of the revolution. The events of that week turned the protests into an uncompromising revolutionary movement, the demands of which were articulated and put into motion with references to Shi'i-Islamic symbols, rituals, and points of reference. By the end of the summer of 1978, Ayatollah Khomeini consolidated his leadership, and his militant disciples inside the country had taken charge of the rhythm and pace of the movement. Now confident of his incontestable authority, after the Friday massacre Khomeini issued a statement closing the door to any possibility of compromise and political solutions that were short of the abolition of monarchy. "Today," Khomeini declared, "a garden of flowers is blooming from the bosom of the Iranian nation. Today, I only see courage and jubilance in every corner of the country. . . . The Iranian nation! Be certain the victory belongs to you." With his characteristic poise, Khomeini called on the soldiers to defy their commanders and join the revolution of the people.

> The patriotic military of Iran! You witnessed the love of the nation in the way people showered the soldiers with kindness and flowers. You are well aware of the fact that in order to sustain their oppression, those plunderers have exploited you as the instruments of murder and cruelty. Join the other soldiers who have already deserted the Shah and are now fighting on behalf of their nation against his tyranny. You the great 'ulema of Islam and those political personalities who have not bowed to the Shah's intimidations and have kept fear out of your hearts, you

symbolize the resilience and confidence of our nation. In these sensitive moments, not only must you resist, you must also strengthen the spirit of the people in their struggle against their enemies.[67]

The declaration of martial law in Tehran and eleven other cities turned out to be an admission of the inability of the regime to fend off the revolutionary tide. By the end of the summer of 1978, Khomeini spoke, and was spoken of, as the uncontested leader of the revolutionary movement. And that was the movement the French philosopher Michel Foucault witnessed in Tehran. When he arrived in Tehran in September 1978, there was no contention over the leadership of the revolution. Despite their reluctance to sign on to a revolutionary struggle, the liberal nationalists (the National Front, the Freedom Movement, other prominent members of the Lawyers Guild) had already realized the irrelevance of their reformist agenda. The greatest casualty of Black Friday was the constitutional monarchy—the Shah could no longer reign or govern!

The ineffective Left, with its limited influence and marginal organizational power, found Khomeini's radicalism and his militant stance against imperialism congruent with its own political agenda. Marxists,

Figure 5. Michel Foucault arriving in Tehran, September 1978. Photo courtesy of Michel Setboun.

Figure 6. Rally in Tehran, December 1978. Source: Islamic Revolution Documentation Center.

each with different justification, promoted and recognized the leadership of Ayatollah Khomeini. With a vulgar understanding of revolutionary politics and a crude appreciation of a materialist conception of history—a crudeness borne in part, no doubt, form the history of censorship and brutal repression of their movement—the Left understood the revolution as a first teleological step toward a democratic transformation that would inevitably lead to a proletarian dictatorship.

In this chapter, I have tried to show that in contrast to narratives of "stolen revolution," Ayatollah Khomeini ascertained his leadership from the very moment that the anti-Shah protest became revolutionary in its character and in its demands. In no practical or ideological sense did other political parties and personalities enjoy the authority and influence that Khomeini exercised over the emerging revolution from his home in Najaf. The next chapter will turn to the question of how Foucault tried to make sense of the unanimity and fearless determination he saw in Tehran without subjecting it to the tropes of a linear progressive History.

2

HOW DID FOUCAULT MAKE SENSE OF THE IRANIAN REVOLUTION?

The rebellious flight of a fountain
that cannot escape the earth
and is simply trying deliverance.

—Ahmad Shamlou

FOUCAULT WAS DEEPLY ENGAGED with the prisoners' rights movement through his work with the Groupe d'Information sur les Prisons. In 1977 two French lawyers who were involved in Iranian exilic politics brought the issue of Iranian political prisoners to his attention. He also followed the news about the Iranian Writers' Association's plan to have ten nights of poetry reading at the Goethe Institute in Tehran in October 1977. He joined a group of influential French intellectuals and signed an open letter in support of the association. His growing interest in Iranian affairs coincided with his fascination with the idea of the philosopher-journalist and the challenging idea of writing the history of the present. After failing to find any traction with French papers, Foucault approached the Italian daily *Corriere della Sera* to write and edit a regular feature loosely framed as "Michel Foucault Investigates." The original plan was for him to write a series on President Carter's America. However, with his newly acquired awareness of the growing political tension in Iran, in 1978 the revolutionary events in Iran overtook this project. Foucault visited Iran for the first time at the end of the summer of 1978 and for the second time just a few weeks later in the fall of the same year.

Once he made the decision to travel to Iran, he began an intensive course of reading on Islam and Iranian history. Perhaps the most significant figure in influencing his reading list and connecting him to Iranian intellectual circles was Paul Vieille, the foremost French authority on the anthropology and sociology of Iran. Through Vieille he met Abolhasan Bani Sadr, who would become the first president of the Islamic Republic, and was encouraged to read the work of Ali Shari'ati, though at the time only a limited number of his writings were available in French or English. Works of Louis Massignon and his most famous disciple, Henry Corbin, two towering figures of the French tradition of Islamic studies, informed Foucault's comprehension of Islam. Both Massignon and (later) Corbin tried to circumvent doctrinal Islam and its interpretive legalism by emphasizing the significance of mysticism and Sufi traditions in Islam. The weight Massignon and Corbin attributed to mystic, spiritual, and ritualistic Islam left a considerable mark in Foucault's mind.

Massignon's four-volume magnum opus, *The Passion of al-Hallaj: Mystic and Martyr of Islam*, was exactly the type of scholarship that lent Foucault the ideal type of Truth-seeking revolutionary, thousands of concrete manifestations of which he later encountered on the streets of Tehran. The Persian mystic Mansur al-Hallaj (858–922) did not represent a typical Sufi master. But his execution, at the behest of Abbasi Caliph al-Muqtadir, for the alleged heresy he committed with his famous mantra *ana al-Haqq* (I am the Truth), transformed him into the very image of sacrificing life for the sanctity of truth. Following Massignon, whose rendition of Islamic mysticism greatly influenced his own view of Islam, Ali Shari'ati "sought to promote Hallaj as a typical representative of Islamic spirituality."[1] Shari'ati took an important step further in infusing Hallaj's spirituality into his liberation theology and translating it into the language of justice and emancipation. In a lecture delivered in 1968 in Tehran, and translated to French and English in the mid-1970s, Shari'ati marvels at Hallaj's burning mind. It is known that Hallaj paced the streets of Baghdad in the ninth century, holding his head between his two hands while crying, "Rebellion has taken me over, release me from the fire which is burning within me." Then Shari'ati pauses and wonders: "What if Iranian society consisted of 25 million Hallajs?"

> Such burnings are of a kind of spiritual insanity. If all of the individuals of a society were to turn into [Hallaj], there would be life and there would be liberty. There would be knowledge and learning as well as power and stability; enemies would be destroyed and there would only remain love for God.[2]

Before leaving for Tehran, Foucault was predisposed to this Islam of mystics and martyrs, despite the marginality of its practice in historical accounts of Islam. But in Tehran of 1978, ten years after Shari'ati delivered those numinous contemplations from his pulpit at Hosseinieh Ershad, the uprising of millions of Hallaj-like seekers of Truth no longer appeared as the romantic fantasy of a utopian intellectual. Foucault witnessed the reality of a nation in revolt and thus never questioned the centrality of the kind of transformative spirituality that his reading of Islam evoked.

Foucault arrived in Tehran on September 10, 1978, two days after the capital had been stopped cold by a week of massive demonstrations. The first and second demonstrations had been peaceful and drew unprecedented numbers. According to some estimates, more than one million people participated in the first, and hundreds of thousands more in the second. The third demonstration, immediately after which Foucault arrived in Tehran, known in the history of the Iranian Revolution as Black Friday, marked a turning point in the revolutionary movement. Eighty-eight people were massacred on Friday, September 8, mostly by heavy machine gun shots fired from military helicopters.

The French philosopher revealed his unexpected awe in an interview that was published in March 1979, one month after the collapse of the monarchy:

> When I arrived in Iran, immediately after the September [8, 1978,] massacres, I said to myself that I was going to find a terrorized city, because there had been four thousand dead. Now I can't say that I found happy people, but there was an absence of fear and an intensity of courage, or rather, the intensity that people were capable of when danger, though still not removed, had already been transcended.[3]

Commenting on the unprecedented presence of the masses—men, women, young, old, children, disabled, "the uprising of a *whole* population"—on the streets, Foucault describes how in Tehran he witnessed a concrete manifestation of an old abstract concept in French political philosophy:

> Among the things that characterize this revolutionary event, there is the fact that it has brought out—and few people in history have had this—an absolutely collective will. The collective will is a political myth with which jurists and philosophers try to analyze or to justify institutions,

etc. It's a theoretical tool: nobody has ever seen the 'collective will' and, personally, I thought that the collective will was like God, like the soul, something one would never encounter. I don't know whether you agree with me, but we met in Tehran and throughout Iran, the collective will of a people.[4]

Foucault turned the transformative moment he experienced during the Iranian Revolution into a reflection and commentary on history. It is not farfetched to think that he regarded himself as one of those "new men" that the revolution created on the streets of Tehran. He also turned the courage and the absence of fear he encountered in Tehran, I would like to argue here, into an impetus and a possibility of seeing the world outside the dominant progressive narratives of the March of History.

In the Iranian Revolution, he saw an instance of his antiteleological view of history. He understood the marching masses on the streets of Tehran as the embodiment of what he called "political spirituality," making history through the transformation of the self. He prioritized the act and experience of rebellion over the concerns about the outcome of the revolutionary movement.

Teleological History

Foucault rejected all forms of developmentalist discourse, Marxian or otherwise. Commonly, these views attributed the emergence of the revolutionary movement in Iran to the contradictions emanating from the Shah's modernization schemes. Rather than posing a conventional opposition between a particular past-orientation and a prescriptive future-project, Foucault defined history as a way of reinventing the present moment. This, he believed, was the distinct strength of the revolution. What attracted him to the revolution was the ambiguity within which it operated. Not ambiguity in its rejection of the Shah, but in its vision of the future, in the lack of an affirmative and precise description of its agenda. In addition to the religious character of the revolution, it was this ambiguity that generated bewildering anxiety among Western intellectuals, particularly among French observers long steeped in the national discourse of a liberating *laïceté*. In a gesture that characterized the militant secularism of most French intellectuals in 1979, Claire Brière challenged the basis for Foucault's enthusiasm for the Iranian Revolution:

The reaction I've heard most often about Iran is that people don't understand. When a movement is called revolutionary, people in the West, including ourselves, always have the notion of progress, of something that is about to be transformed in the direction of progress. All this is put into question by the religious phenomenon. . . . Now, I don't know whether you managed, when you were in Iran, to determine, to grasp the nature of that enormous religious confrontation—I myself found it very difficult. The Iranians themselves are swimming in that ambiguity and have several levels of language, commitment, expression, etc.[5]

It is in response to this common teleological view that Foucault emphasizes the idea that a nation's rebellion is a historical fact through which "subjectivity (not that of great men, but that of anyone) introduces itself into history and gives it its life."[6] Rather than making him skeptical of the nature of the revolutionary movement in Iran, Foucault viewed the fact that Iranians appeared to be swimming in ambiguity as an instance of his own "constitutive ambivalence toward history," to use Edward Said's term.[7]

Writing *history of the present* from a genealogical perspective inevitably generates moral anxieties of the Nietzschean sort. One needs to grasp Foucault's writings on the Iranian Revolution in the context of his general opposition to *any* ontology that contains teleological elements. That is to say, he would be opposed to any presentation of a present firmly rooted in a past orientation and a future projection. It is on exactly this point that he reads the Iranian Revolution as a moment when historical subjects *refuse* to subject themselves to History. Here Foucault poses the problem of history as a paradox in which a deliberately opaque quality runs through his reflections on the temporal situation of the revolutionary actor. In the revolution he saw an important affirmation of what he had already formulated many years earlier in his inaugural lecture delivered on December 2, 1970.

We must not imagine that the world turns toward us a legible face which we would have only to decipher; the world is not the accomplice of our knowledge; there is no prediscursive providence which predisposes the world in our favor. We must conceive discourse as a violence which we do to things, or in any case as a practice which we impose on them.[8]

As Michiel Leezenberg observed, Foucault turned his reports on the Iranian Revolution into a philosophical commentary on modernity. Journalism, as a way of grasping "what is *in the process of happening*," for Foucault was a means of what he called *reportages des idées*—that is, journalism about ideas that are not contained within the boundaries of the Enlightenment progressive schema. By emphasizing the significance of "ideas" and how they give rise to collective movements of revolutionary proportion, Foucault situated himself in opposition both to postmodern incredulity toward all that is grand as well as to Marxian dogma of the primacy of economy.[9] He wrote:

> Some say that the great ideologies are in the course of dying. The contemporary world, however, is burgeoning with ideas . . . One has to be present at the birth of ideas and at the explosion of their force; not in the books that pronounce them, but in the vent in which they manifest their force, and in the struggles people wage for or against ideas.[10]

In a more sociological report, originally called "The Shah and the Dead Weight of Modernity," changed by the editors of *Corriere della sera* to "The Shah Is a Hundred Years behind the Times" (published on October 1, 1978), Foucault situated the revolution not in any form of *failed* project of modernity, but rather as evidence that it is possible to transcend modernity and the spiritless world it has instituted. He writes that he had been incessantly advised that Iran was going through a "crisis of modernization," and that "a traditional society cannot and does not want to follow [its] arrogant monarch" in his attempt to "compete with the industrialized nations."[11] The revolutionary events did not signify a "shrinking back in the face of modernization by extremely retrograde elements," to which some commentators referred to as "archaic fascism."[12] But he argued that the Shah was hopelessly trying to preserve a Kemalist modernization project envisioned in the 1920s by his father to fashion the country into a European state. He ridiculed the liberal nationalists' ideas that Iran needed a *modified* modernization under a constitutional regime with the motto "Let the king reign but not govern." For him, archaic was "*modernization* itself," not the religious mode of the revolutionary expression.

> What is old here in Iran is the Shah. He is fifty years old and a hundred years behind the times. He is of the age of the predatory monarchs. He

has the old-fashioned dream of opening his country through secularization and industrialization. Today, it is his project of modernization, his despotic weapons, and his system of corruption that are archaic. It is "the regime" that is the archaism.[13]

Foucault recognized the competing interests of a variety of political parties and tendencies. But at the same time, he highlighted what he called the *paradoxical* effects of the revolutionary movement—namely, that "the revolt spread without splits or internal conflicts."[14] As he pointed out, the release of mostly Marxist political prisoners, the opening of the universities in the fall of 1978, and, most importantly, the strike of the workers of the oil industry in the south, each could introduce irreconcilable frictions into the revolutionary movement.[15] But they did not. The political calculations of competing factions remained dormant and did not find expression in what he called "the revolutionary experience itself." In that sense, Foucault turned the revolution's ambiguity and lack of any future plan from a point of unease into a source for creative possibilities.

Although Foucault endows the revolutionary movement with a "collective will" and underplays class, gender, and ethnic contradictions, he does so not at the expense of making politics effortless and uncomplicated. Quite to the contrary, he argues that something inhabits peoples' political will that is far greater and more substantive than political battles "over a future constitution, over social issues, over foreign policy, or over the replacement of officials." In a typical ironic sense, he argues that "political will is to prevent politics from gaining a foothold." Here Foucault eschews his signature genealogical method to echo the eschatological temperament of the revolutionary subject itself.[16] He argues:

> It is a law of history that the simpler the people's will, the more complex the job of politicians. This is undoubtedly because politics is not what it pretends to be, the expression of a collective will. Politics breathes well only where this will is multiple, hesitant, confused, and obscure even to itself.[17]

At a certain moment, he observes, "without precipitating social or political causes, the whole of the Iranian people were united in their opposition to the Shah." In several occasions in his reports, Foucault wondered about an "indefinable force" that had transformed life within each individual and united the Iranian body politic. "What we witnessed," he declared, "was not the result of an alliance between various political groups. Nor was it the result of a compromise between social classes. . . . Something quite different has happened. A phenomenon has traversed the entire people and will one day stop." In a romantic evocation, Foucault maintains that "there was literally a light that lit up in all of them and which bathed them all at the same time."[18]

Foucault conceptualized this phenomenon as *political spirituality*, a force that asserts itself in a continuous enchantment of history. Political spirituality appears here as an alternative to historical determinism.

> For the people who inhabit this land, what it the point of searching, even at the cost of their own lives, for this thing whose possibility we have forgotten since the Renaissance and the great crisis of Christianity, a *political spirituality*. I can already hear the French laughing, but I know that they are wrong.[19]

Foucault believed that the revolutionary movement in Iran, with its "struggle to present a different way of thinking" about society and politics, may offer the West the possibility of an exit from its own intellectual exhaustion. "We have to abandon," he conveys to an Iranian writer and social critic after his first visit to Iran in September 1978, "every dogmatic principle and question one by one the validity of all the principles that have been the source of oppression. . . . We have to construct another political thought, another political imagination, and teach anew the vision of a future."[20]

Although Foucault was right to propose that the revolutionary Iran demanded a new way of thinking about the deep connection of religion and politics, he was mistaken in thinking that the "alternative based on Islamic teachings" in revolutionary Iran had taken "nothing from Western philosophy."[21] He knew quite well that Ali Shari'ati advanced his conception of Alavid Shi'ism, to which Foucault refers a number of times, and his revolutionary historiography of Islam in dialogue with (along with references to) French existential Marxism and German phenomenological philosophy and sociology. What Foucault identifies in Iran could more accurately be defined as an idiosyncratic convergence of political and religious views that formed a revolutionary ideology without a definite association to Western conceptual commitments to History.

Political Spirituality

Although Foucault acknowledged that Shi'i Islam was the source of this political spirituality, he did not conceive of it as a *dogma* or in a *doctrinal* religious frame. He saw spirituality as a desire to liberate the *body* from the prison house of the *soul*. In this typically Foucauldian inversion, he intended to highlight the ways the body seceded from the normative docility of the technologies of the self.[22] This was not new territory for Foucault. As Jeremy Carrette has argued, he grappled with the concept of spirituality years before he encountered the Iranian Revolution.[23]

"By spirituality," Foucault explained, "I understand . . . that which precisely refers to a subject acceding to a certain mode of being and to the transformations which the subject must make of himself in order to accede to this mode of being."[24] He gives spirituality a corporeal meaning, which he directly links to the care of the self. In his discussion of the self in his later oeuvre, Foucault remains skeptical of the liberal rational subject elicited by a governable moral order. Rather, he views the care of the self as an ethical imperative wherein ethics is "the kind of relationship you ought to have with *yourself* . . . how the individual is supposed to constitute himself as a moral subject *of his own actions.*"[25] (I will expand this argument in chapter 5.)

Although in his notion of spirituality one might detect traces of Bataille's conception of *inner experience*, and its mystical intimations, this should not lead us to understand the act of transcendence inherent in Foucault's notion of spirituality and ethics merely as a transgressive *expérience limite*. Not only does such a connection discount the religious context of Foucault's discourse,[26] more importantly it *de*politicizes his conception of spirituality and ethics. Foucault's biographer James Miller promoted this depoliticized conception and transformed it into a generally accepted frame in which Foucault's enthusiasm for the Iranian Revolution was explained away by his aesthetic fascination and obsession with death rituals of the revolutionary movement.[27]

Yet, as I see it, the ethical proposition of the care of the self and the spirituality it requires for its exercise are foundationally linked to Foucault's conception of politics, particularly with what he calls "the governmentalization of the state."[28] In *The Hermeneutics of the Self*, he extends Habermas's notion of domination and argues:

> Governing people . . . is always a versatile equilibrium, with complementarity and conflicts between techniques which assure coercion and processes through which the self is constructed or modified by oneself. . . . Among the techniques of the self in this field of self-technology, I think that the techniques oriented towards the discovery and the formulation of the truth concerning oneself are extremely important.[29]

In his scheme of power, Foucault weds the state (as the instrument of coercion), religion (as an institution of legitimation), and the individual (as the protagonist of self-governing technologies), thereby "collapsing the boundaries between politics, religion and the ethics of self."[30] It is in this context that one must understand his conception of the 1978–79 revolutionary movement in Iran.

> How can one analyze the connection between ways of distinguishing true and false and ways of governing oneself and others? The search for a new foundation for each of these practices, in itself and relative to the other, the will to discover a different way of governing oneself through a different way of dividing up true and false—this is what I would call "political *spiritualité.*"[31]

Contrary to a commonplace reading of Foucault's enthusiasm about the Iranian Revolution, in his view, religion does not appear as an incidental element of the movement. Rather, it links the revolutionary movement directly to a people's general sense of their place in the world, in the creation of which religion plays a constitutive role. "So what is the role of religion?" Foucault asked. "Not that of an ideology, which would help to mask contradictions or form a sort of sacred union between divergent interests." Religion afforded the revolution a vocabulary, according to Foucault, "the ceremonial" and "the timeless drama," through which a people could redefine its existence.[32]

Although the emphasis on the religious tenor of the Iranian Revolution might be superfluous, Foucault's understanding of the connection between religion and politics was uncommon. In contrast to the skepticism of his early critics,[33] and the warnings of those whom he thought were stricken by "excessive Westernness,"[34] he objected to the argument that the role of religion in Iran was merely to provide a doctrinal platform for revolutionary intentions. The connection he sought to explore was not between religious dogma and governance. On more than one occasion,

Foucault acknowledges that "the mullahs are not at all 'revolutionary,' even in the populist sense of the term." References to "religion" in his writings on the Iranian Revolution were not to anything *spoken* by the mullahs or articulated by any other exponent of the divine text. According to Foucault, writing on October 8, 1978, *religion constituted a force that perpetuated the hermeneutics of the subject on the streets of revolutionary Iran.*

> [Religion] transforms thousands of forms of discontent, hatred, misery, and despair into a *force*. It transforms them into a force because it is a form of expression, a mode of social relations, a supple and widely accepted elemental organization, a way of being together, a way of speaking and listening, something that allows one to be listened to by others.[35]

Foucault thought Shi'ism was particularly conducive to the kind of hermeneutics that he deemed essential in the total transformation of the self. As I stressed earlier, his knowledge of Shi'i Islam, at least in its classical context, was shaped by the French scholarship advanced by Louis Massignon and Henry Corbin, both of whom regarded the quest for justice and mystical spirituality as the kernel of Shi'ism. He was also intrigued by Shari'ati's hermeneutical approach and his emphasis on the transformation of the self as the precondition of the revolutionary act. In the following conversation with Claire Brière and Pierre Blanchet in March 1979 in Paris, Foucault shifted the debate on the basis for the revolutionary movement from both Marxist economic determinism as well as an Orientalist *textual* reading of Islam.

> Whatever the economic difficulties, we still have to explain why there were people who rose up and said: we're not having any more of this. In rising up, the Iranians said to themselves—and this perhaps is the soul of the uprising: "Of course, we have to change this regime and get rid of this man, we have to change this corrupt administration, we have to change the whole country, the political organization, the economic system, the foreign policy. But, above all, *we have to change ourselves*. Our way of being, our relationship with others, with things, with eternity, with God, etc., must be completely changed, and there will only be a true revolution if this radical change in our experience takes place." I believe that it is here that Islam played a role. It may be that one or other of its obligations, one or other of its codes exerted a certain fascination. But, above all, in relation to the way of life that was theirs, religion for them was like a promise and guarantee of finding something that would

radically change their subjectivity. Shi'ism is precisely a form of Islam that, with its teaching and esoteric content, distinguishes between what is mere external obedience to the code and what is the profound spiritual life; when I say that they were looking to Islam for a change in their subjectivity, this is quite compatible with the fact that traditional Islamic practice was already there and already gave them their identity; in this way they had of living the Islamic religion as a revolutionary force, there was something other than the desire to obey the law more faithfully, there was the desire to renew their existence by going back to a spiritual experience that they thought they could find with Shi'ite Islam.[36]

In Iran, Foucault recognized the possibility in Islam of a continuous and active creation of a political order perpetuated by an individual experience of piety and the care of the self.[37] The intriguing part of his view of Shi'ism is that he does not interpret Islamic Law (capital *L*) as the source of justice; rather, in another characteristic inversion, "it is justice that made law and not law that manufactured justice." In the third installment of his reports on October 8, 1978, on the pages of *Corriere della sera*, he shows some familiarity with an old debate about the question of justice in different juridical Islamic schools. "One must find this justice in 'the' text dictated by God to the Prophet. However, one can also decipher it in the life, the sayings, the wisdom, and the exemplary sacrifices of the imams, born, after Ali, in the house of the Prophet, and persecuted by the corrupt government of the caliphs, these arrogant aristocrats who had forgotten the old egalitarian system of justice."[38] In contrast to a common Orientalist theme, which is strictly committed to the hermeneutics of Text and Law, *Foucault highlights the experience of and desire for justice in the hermeneutics of the subject.*[39] Like Shari'ati, he conceives Islam as a religion that has given people inexhaustible resources for resisting the power of the state. Accordingly, on October 16, 1978, in an essay published in *Le Nouvel Observateur,* he ponders whether one could comprehend an "Islamic government," as a "reconciliation," a "contradiction," or as the threshold of a "novelty."[40]

Foucault puts forward a conception of religion that is perpetuated in the practice of the care of the self and spirituality. He was not scandalized by the concept of "Islamic government" and rejected its suggested *inherent* link with theocracy because he understood it to be "a utopia," the terms and exact meaning of which would be negotiated in the future.

Foucault correctly refused to identify the establishment of a theocracy as the *inevitable* consequence of the religious character of the revolutionary movement. As I have shown elsewhere, the entire revolutionary movement, including its clerical leadership, shared this view that Islamic government had to be understood as an ideal, the realization of which depended on the conscious subjectivity of its practitioners. What emerged eventually as the Islamic Republic resulted not from any inherent feature of the revolution's ideological commitments, but rather from an intensely fought postrevolutionary power struggle.[41]

Foucault believed that the inspiration for an Islamic government came from faith not in legalism but in the infinite creativity of Islam. A number of religious authorities had told Foucault that although they were inspired by the principles of governance during the time of the Prophet, they did not intend to replicate it. Rather, they wanted to renew their "fidelity" to Islam without encouraging a pure "obedience." They stressed that they did not claim that the Qur'an offers precise responses to the problems of contemporary life. These problems are distinct, thus the necessity of "long work by civil and religious experts, scholars, and believers" toward their resolution. That is why Foucault understood the concept of "Islamic government" not as an "idea" or even an "ideal," but rather, as he put it, as "a form of political will."[42]

In the Iranian Revolution, Foucault observed a "displacement (and a rescue at the same time) of the tradition of modernity."[43] He predicted that his enthusiasm would scandalize the French, whose commitment to *laïcité* was fundamental to their intellectual expression. Even his friends ridiculed him. One of them, Claude Mauriac, who had been influenced by Foucault and Gilles Deleuze in the early 1970s to retreat from his earlier Gaullist politics, recalled a private conversation on November 23, 1978, in which he had expressed reservations to Foucault about his support of a *political spirituality*. He recounted their conversation in his memoirs:

Mauriac: I read your paper in *Nouvel Observateur*, but not without surprise, I must say.

Foucault: And you laughed? You are among those that I could already hear laughing.

Mauriac: No . . . I only said to myself that as to spirituality and politics, we have see what that gave us.

Foucault: And politics *without* spirituality, my dear Claude?[44]

Is It Useless to Revolt?

Foucault's enthusiasm about revolutionary politics in Iran was also informed by a fervent debate in French intellectual circles kindled by François Furet's revisionist account of the French Revolution's place in history.[45] Furet introduced a general skepticism about the significance and wisdom of revolutions in world history, consigning the French experience from a constitutive event of modern European history to an anomaly with everlasting tension between 1789 and 1793. In a post-1968 France, Furet's revisionist intervention struck a chord with the defeatist French Left and triumphant liberals, those who wanted, in Žižek's words, "a decaffeinated revolution, or a revolution which does not smell of a revolution."[46]

Not only did Foucault try to make sense of revolutionary spirituality, he also admired the fact that the Iranian masses revived the spirit of revolution, which many Europeans believed had disappeared from history. By locating the spirit of the revolution in Iran, Foucault inverted another central element of Orientalism, that of the unchanging essence of Muslim societies. Instead, he laments the stagnation of Western subjectivity and the dominant skepticism about revolutionary political spirituality.

Rather than what his biographer James Miller dismissed as an aesthetic fascination with death rituals of a violent revolution, Foucault saw in Iran a moment of creative pause in, or even negation of, his theory of power and governmentality. The Iranian masses demonstrated the possibility of resistance without participating in or perpetuating a *preconceived* schema of power. This is the single most important point that distinguishes Foucault's reflections on the Islamic Revolution from his earlier oeuvre—and indeed from every other notable observer of the events in Iran. A major theme in the revolution he identified was the forceful expression of a negation: *the Shah must go!* What made the revolution strong was the following paradox: no long-term objectives were articulated, no design for government brought forward. Simple slogans dominated popular speech. Because of this, the Iranian people expressed their "clear, obstinate, almost unanimous popular will."[47]

How far do we want to generalize from Foucault's journalism? Did witnessing revolution in Iran alter his general understanding of the means and possibility of resistance to power? Did he deviate in his observations of events in Iran from his understanding of resistance to power as an act that extends "our participation in the present system"?[48] Many early critics of Foucault, particularly in feminist scholarship, had rebuked his conception of power for its lack of recognition of the real possibility of resistance. "Foucault," Nancy Fraser once pointed out, "adopts a concept of power that permits him no condemnation of any objectionable features of modern societies."[49]

While it is debatable whether Foucault followed Derrida in negating the possibility of actual resistance to present arrangements,[50] his all-encompassing and generative notion of power troubled both the partisans as well as the detractors of his theory. Despite his sympathies toward Foucauldian ethics, William Connolly chastised him for not acknowledging that "we *can* criticize the present from the perspective of alternative ideals" without being subject to an iron law that subsumes all actions into mere reproduction or variation of the present social order.[51]

One of the most vociferous of his critics, Jürgen Habermas, also castigated Foucault for what appeared to be nihilistic apathy toward emancipatory politics. He linked nihilism in Foucault's theory to the idea of aporia,[52] which informed the pessimistic views of early Frankfurt School theorists about the post-Enlightenment world.[53] Habermas claimed that there was no critical stance in Foucault's analysis of power. If resistance simply reproduces existing relations of power, Habermas maintains, "there wouldn't be any resistance. Because resistance has to be like power: just as inventive, just as mobile, just as productive as it is."[54]

Foucault's comments such as "It seems to me that power *is* 'always already there,' that one is never 'outside' it, that there are no 'margins' for those who break with it to gambol in,"[55] seem to reaffirm the position that Richard Rorty aptly formulated in viewing Foucault as "a stoic, a dispassionate observer of the present social order, rather than its concerned critic."[56]

Foucault did attempt to avoid the categorical condemnation of all forms of resistance, which his critics read into his work. He went to considerable lengths to explain the nuances of his conception of power and governmentality. Although he developed a more cohesive theory of "counter-power" and resistance in his later work on ethics and the care of self, in earlier writings, contrary to his detractors' claims, he did *not* trivialize resistance as simply another means of participating in disciplinary power. In *Power/Knowledge*, for example, he spoke of the possibility of integrating resistance into "global strategies."[57] He identified the chief problem for intellectuals as the possibility to establish "a new regime of truth."[58]

But it is in his post-1979 writings that he carefully considers the significance of revolt as an ethical concern, in spite of the fact that it would result in giving rise to other institutions of disciplinary power. In "On the Genealogy of Ethics," Foucault responded to the charge that one can spot what appears to be quietism in his work. In reply to the question whether the Greek philosophy was "an attractive and plausible alternative" to contemporary ethics, Foucault cried out:

No! I am not looking for an alternative; *you can't find the solution of a problem in the solution of another problem raised at another moment by other people.* You see, what I want to do is not the history of solutions, and that's the reason why I don't accept the word "alternative." I would like to do the genealogy of problems, of *problématique*. My point is not that everything is bad, but that everything is dangerous, which is not exactly the same as bad. If everything is dangerous, then we always have something to do. *So my position leads not to apathy but to a hyper- and pessimistic activism.*[59]

The paradoxical notion of "pessimistic activism" captures the core of Foucault's response to the Iranian Revolution. In his very last piece on the subject, "Is It Useless to Revolt?," published in May 1979 on the first page of *Le Monde*, Foucault responded to the growing crowd of critics who ridiculed him for cheering on a revolution whose objective was the establishment of an Islamic state. In perhaps the most moving passage of his entire revolutionary *reportage*, he defended his enthusiasm without endorsing its outcome. He wrote:

Uprisings belong to history, but in a certain way, they escape it. The movement through which a lone man, a group, a minority, or an entire people say, "I will no longer obey," and are willing to risk their lives in the face of a power that they believe to be unjust, seems to me to be irreducible. This is because no power is capable of making it absolutely impossible. Warsaw will always have its ghetto in revolt and its sewers populated with insurgents. The man in revolt is ultimately inexplicable. There must be an uprooting that interrupts the unfolding of history, and its long series of reasons why, for a man "really" to prefer the risk of death over the certainty of having to obey. . . . If societies persist and survive, that is to say, if power in these societies is not "absolutely absolute,"[60] it is because behind all the consent and the coercion, beyond the threats, the violence, and the persuasion, there is the possibility of this moment where life cannot be exchanged, where power becomes powerless, and where, in front of the gallows and the machine guns, men rise up.[61]

Here, in the last installment of his revolutionary essays, we see the most Kantian Foucault where he brings to light how the noumenal dimension of revolutionary struggle transpires and "momentarily suspends the nexus of historical causality."[62] The inexplicable and irreducible rebellious subject, the noumenon, suddenly coincides in a paradoxical relation to a rational network of reality that has generated its phenomenal existence. To Foucault, this very act and experience of *becoming*, regardless of its actual consequences, needed to be celebrated. He tried to distinguish his position from the fashionable condemnations of the horrors of revolution, whether Iran in 1979 or France in 1793. For Foucault, revolts have historical significance no matter how untimely and ill-fated they are. As Deleuze, in a Foucauldian gesture, argues, "History amounts only [to] the set of preconditions that one leaves behind in order to 'become,' that is, to create something new," no matter how badly they turn out. Those who conflate the outcome of a revolutionary movement with its experience, Deleuze further explains, constantly confuse two different things: "the way revolutions turn out historically and people's revolutionary becoming. These relate to two different sets of people. Men's only hope lies in a revolutionary becoming: the only way of casting off their shame or responding to what is intolerable."[63]

For Foucault, the objectionable postrevolutionary regime could not explain the significance of the revolutionary movement in shaping the rebellious subjectivity of Iranians. One must find the manifestation of his pessimistic activism in the *inexplicable* insurrectionary individual and the *irreducible* subject. In light of the mounting evidence of atrocities perpetrated by the new regime in Tehran, his critics in France pressured him to recant his support for the revolution. In spite of being disheartened by the proliferation of violence in postrevolutionary power struggles, Foucault saw no shame in defending the revolution but insisted that "there is no reason to say that one's opinion has changed when one is against hands being chopped off today, after having been against the tortures of the SAVAK yesterday."[64]

Whereas his critics rebuked him for what they considered to be Nietzschean nihilism in his all-encompassing theory of power, now Foucault had to justify his enthusiasm about an uprising that led to the establishment of the Islamic Republic. The colonization of the uprising by realpolitik, Foucault argued, does not justify the condemnation of the revolutionary movement. What is more important from the point of view of the subject is not the level of success or failure of the revolutionary movement but in the "manner in which it was lived."

Foucault's Fanonian Predicament

The major distinction of Foucault's writings on the Iranian Revolution lies in the way he conceives the subject not as a product and producer of power but rather as the agent of resistance to it. More importantly, he avoids a common epistemic violence that turned the revolutionary movement in Iran into a legible act that conforms to recognizable historical teleologies. Foucault believed that by liberating their bodies from the prison houses of their souls, by marching fearlessly on the streets in defiance of martial law, Iranians reinvented themselves through a transformative political spirituality. A spirituality motivated and shaped by complex historical circumstances, but irreducible to it. Iranians created a new "Man" in a Fanonian sense. This new Man was inspired by a political rearticulation of the Shi'i historical drama of rising against injustice, spoke a different language (familiar but novel), invented a new way of being with others and relating to one's self, and found the transformative powers in ways hitherto thought impossible.

In the same romantic vein that Fanon believed that through the very act of revolutionary struggle the colonial subject would erase past trauma, Foucault thought that political spirituality would transpose Iranians' relation with their past. Fanon hoped that the liberated "new Man" had the capacity and the historical impulse to initiate a new beginning in a complete tabula rasa. But as the experience of Algeria demonstrated, the past easily outlived the revolution, and its weight burdened the present. Foucault tried to highlight the significance of "living the revolution," but he, like Fanon, neglected to recognize that the same magnanimous revolutionary energy could then revert into fueling a repressive state machine.

Foucault and Fanon also share something perhaps even more important, and that is their limited knowledge of the society that has given rise to the emancipatory struggle on which they each comment. In his *Dying Colonialism*, Fanon tries to reinterpret cultural practices in Algerian society outside their abstract, anachronistic context. Although he was deeply immersed in the Algerian struggle, he did not speak Arabic and had a very limited knowledge of Islam and Algerian society. He rightly points out that cultural signs are fixed neither in their meaning nor in their practice. But he fails to see how these signs, as malleable and negotiated as they might appear, exist in deeply rooted, enduring structures of domination, particularly in gender relations on which he comments in the often-debated chapter called "Algeria Unveiled."[65]

Fanon links women's "ardent love of the home" as a sign of resistance to the colonial structure that has negated reciprocal justification of interaction between the home and society at large. "The Algerian woman," he asserts, "in imposing such a restriction on herself, in choosing a form of existence limited in scope, was deepening her consciousness of struggle and preparing for combat." In reality, he further argues, "the effervescence and the revolutionary spirit have been kept alive by the woman in the home."[66] Women appropriated the cover of the veil to create an inverted panopticon against the French colonial officers. Fanon believed that the revolutionary war had offered "a dislocation of the old myths" and had transformed irreversibly gender relations in Algeria.

Fanon's perception of Islam in Algeria was informed by his deep involvement in the revolution. He lacked a nuanced appreciation of the complexity and significance of religion in Algerian society. Similarly, Foucault's view of Islam and the way it was appropriated by the revolutionary actors was greatly influenced by the political spirituality that he correctly identified as the guiding torch of the revolution. By reading Massignon and Corbin, who gave central significance to mystical Shi'ism and Sufi transcendentalism in their history of Islamic thought, Foucault was predisposed to grasp the revolution he observed in terms of the spiritual reenactment of "Seekers of the Truth." Although he correctly emphasized the significance and the hegemonic position of religion in giving rise to the revolutionary movement, he failed to see the deeply rooted networks and ethos of legalistic and doctrinal Islam that would eventually dominate the postrevolutionary state politics.

Foucault is also *too* intent to ascribe "otherness" to the Iranian Revolution. He tries very consciously not to see the revolution through the prism of a Western conceptual toolkit and thereby Orientalizes it in a worn-out discursive universe. But by doing so, he neglects to recognize "the extent to which the revolution belongs to a historical situation different from, but related to the Western context."[67] As I discuss in the next chapter, Islamic liberation theology and the emancipatory language it invented emerged from both a negation of as well as an appropriation of Western notions of justice and history. This offered the Iranian Revolution a *singularity* that could be comprehended only through an open defiance to a universal History.

3

MISREPRESENTING THE REVOLUTION, MISREADING FOUCAULT

A Revisionist History

Did the mullahs *steal* the revolution? For more than three decades, the myth of the stolen revolution has served as the master narrative of countless scholarly works as well as political treatises written by those who found themselves on the defeated side of the postrevolutionary struggle. In order to see the significance of Foucault's reading of the Iranian Revolution, I believe it is essential to set aside this myth, which is driven by a commitment to a progressive, universal History and a binary understanding of secular versus Islamist politics. Janet Afary and Kevin Anderson's *Foucault and the Iranian Revolution* is emblematic of how this myth is constructed, deployed, and disseminated. In their book, Afary and Anderson evoke this myth both to indict Foucault for his failure to foresee the looming Islamist disaster and to cast the revolution as a regressive denunciation of modernity (or modernization, they use the two terms interchangeably).

This chapter responds closely to their reading to show why it is empirically necessary to recognize the singularity of the revolution and to liberate it from the constraints of universalist narratives. Through a close engagement with Afary and Anderson's book, I intend to save the integrity of the revolutionary movement from its later outcomes. By doing so, I also try to disentangle Foucault's writings from those oppressive consequences of the postrevolutionary state-building.

Afary and Anderson claim that the originality of their book lays in the fact that they have shown that Foucault's support of Islamism and his fascination with *political spirituality* was simply an extension of his "anti-modern" philosophy. But in so doing they produce serious flaws both in their interpretation of Foucault and their representation of Islamism. In their view, Foucault's anti-modern bias prevented him from appreciating "feminist premonitions" (4) and secularist warnings about the *true* nature of Islamists as an antidemocratic and antiwoman element in the revolutionary movement. Not only did he support the reincarnation of "fascism" in Iran, more hurtfully he failed to recognize that the "Iranian people suffered under a regime for which he had helped to build support [!]" (133)."In this sense, he had no serious qualms about the way in which the Islamists had come to dominate the revolutionary movement, *displacing* the Marxist and nationalist Left."[1] The following passages depict their core argument against Foucault.

> Why, in his writings on the Iranian revolution, did he give his exclusive support to its Islamist wing? Certain modalities in Foucault's oeuvre seemed to resonate with the revolutionary movement that was unfolding in Iran. There was a perplexing affinity between this post-structuralist philosopher, this European critic of modernity, and the anti-modernist Islamist radicals on the streets of Iran. Both were searching for a new form of political spirituality as a counterdiscourse to a thoroughly materialistic world; both clung to idealized notions of premodern social orders; both were disdainful of modern liberal judicial systems; both admired individuals who risked death in attempts to reach a more authentic existence. Foucault's affinity with the Iranian Islamists, often construed as his "error" over Iran, may also reveal some of the larger ramifications of his Nietzschean-Heideggerian discourse. . . . The difference between the Foucauldian grand narrative and the liberal or Marxian ones is that Foucault's narrative privileges not modernity but the traditional social orders. (13)

Afary's earlier work on the Iranian constitutional revolution heavily informs her and Anderson's narrative of the 1978–79 revolutionary movement.[2] In that book, she begins her account of the constitutional revolution with the hanging scene of Sheikh Fazlollah Nuri, an influential ayatollah who turned against the constitutional revolutionaries. She ends it with the rehabilitation of Nuri after the 1979 Revolution. Nuri had tried to contain the judicial and legislative powers envisioned in the new constitution with references to Islamic *shari'a* and questioned the necessity of such bodies in the presence of the divine text and the clergy. For Afary, contemporary Iran is shaped by the long-term effects of the same struggle between constitutionalism and *shari'at*ism and the unresolved conflicts among secular, progressive, and democratic actors against religious, conservative "obstructionists."

If these mutually exclusive binaries remain in the background of her earlier work, in her coauthored critique of Foucault she moves this ideological device to the center of her depiction of the 1978–79 Revolution. She and her coauthor understand the revolution to be a movement against the Shah's "authoritarian program of economic and cultural modernization" (1). They emphasize the authoritarian character of the reforms under the Shah and not his project of modernization per se. While the brutal methods the Pahlavis (father and son) adopted were indefensible, their modernization objectives were a justifiable response, Afary and Anderson believe, to an irresistible historical inevitability.

They argue that in addition to Islamists, the coalition that made the revolution possible included nationalists, secular liberals, and Leftist parties. In their view, while the progressive-democratic-secular factions fought the authoritarianism of the Shah, what motivated the Islamists, the obstructionist and reactionary faction, was their hostility toward the social and cultural transformations of Iranian society that the Shah's modernization scheme opened up. "By late 1978," Afary and Anderson write, "the militant Islamist faction led by Ayatollah Ruhollah Khomeini had come to dominate the antiregime uprising, in which secular nationalists, liberals, and leftists also participated" (1).

In their historiography of the revolution, Afary and Anderson offer a narrative in which the conflict between the innately regressive Islamists and the inherently progressive secularists of all political persuasions were played out in selectively constitutive moments. The following passage summarizes their understanding of how revolutionary processes culminated in the monopolization of power by the Islamists:

> Increasingly, in the name of national unity, the secular, nationalist, and leftist demands of many of the anti-Shah demonstrators were articulated in religious terms and through the rituals that commemorated the death of [the Shi'ite Imam] Hussein. The Islamists controlled the slogans and the organization of the protests, which meant that many secular women who joined the protests were pressured into donning the veil *(chador)* as an expression of solidarity with traditional Muslims. Muharram fell in December in 1978, at the height of the uprising, and

its celebration brought a million people to the streets. By February 1979, the Shah had fled, and Khomeini returned from exile to take power. The next month, he sponsored a national referendum that declared Iran an Islamic republic. Soon after, as Khomeini began to assume nearly absolute power, a reign of terror ensued. (2)

Here Afary and Anderson misrepresent the chronology of the revolutionary movement to justify their narrative that the revolution had been initiated and led by a coalition of secular-liberal-left factions but was hijacked by Islamists in its final stage. As I illustrated in chapter 1, by the midsummer of 1978 the anti-Shah revolutionary movement was arrayed under the indisputable leadership of Khomeini. This is not to contest the fact that students of the Left largely shaped the protest movements on university campuses, or to argue against the significance of liberal lawyers' advocacy groups and other nationalists who showed dissatisfaction with the Shah's despotism. But the historiographical point here is that Khomeini's leadership was a key element of the mass *revolutionary movement* that toppled monarchy. And it was this social fact that Foucault encountered in his sojourn in Iran. Religious rituals and Islamic symbolic language were constitutive, and not incidental, features of the revolutionary movement.

Secular versus Islamist Politics

During the 1960s and 1970s, although there were marked ideological distinctions between Muslim and Marxist groups, those distinctions were not politically articulated in terms of secular and Islamist divisions. Thanks to Ali Shari'ati's legacy, for many years Muslim and Marxist revolutionaries alike regarded themselves as comrades in arms holding the same ideals, albeit with different ideologies. In his poignant defense during his show trial, Khosrow Golesorkhi, a communist poet and journalist who was tried on trumped up charges and sentenced to death in 1973, resonated with many Iranian intellectuals who saw themselves as part of an anti-imperialist and national liberation movement.

> I begin my defense with the words of Imam Hussein, the greatest martyr of the peoples of the Middle East. As a Marxist-Leninist, I searched for social justice for the first time in the teachings of Islam, and then I

found socialism. . . . I begin my words with Islam. In Iran, the true Islam has always fulfilled its duty to the liberation movements. . . . Today also the true Islam is carrying its responsibility toward our national liberation movement. There are close similarities between what Marx says—that in a class society, wealth is accumulated on one side and poverty, hunger, and misery on the other, and that the downtrodden is the producer of wealth—and what Imam Ali says, that no palace is built without the misery of thousands. This is why I call Imam Ali the first socialist in world history. . . . Being tried today in this courtroom is just another example of Imam Hussein's life. We are ready to sacrifice our lives on behalf of our country's disinherited. Imam Hussein was in the minority, and Yazid enjoyed mansions, armies, state, and power. Hussein stood up and was martyred. Yazid occupied a small corner in history, but what has been repeated in history is the legacy of Hussein and his struggle, not the rule of Yazid. Peoples' history is the reenactment of Hussein's path. As a Marxist I applaud such an Islam, the Islam of Ali, the Islam of Hussein.[3]

In his final defense, which appeared in a state-run broadcast, Golesorkhi exemplified the dissident political culture of the time by highlighting the issues of social justice as the engine of the Iranian revolutionary

Figure 7. Khosrow Golesorkhi's trial, Tehran 1973. Front row from the left: Teifour Batha'i, Khosrow Golesorkhi, Manuchehr Moqaddam-Salimi, and Karamat Daneshian, who was also executed along with Golesorkhi.

Figure 8. Still frame from a state television program broadcast on the anniversary of the Islamic Revolution in 2010. In recent years, the Islamic Republic Television has appropriated Golesorkhi's defense in which he praises Shi'i Islam as the source of his own revolutionary awakening.

movement, meaningful both for Islamists and Marxists. The ideological context of the political expression of social justice seldom became a point of contention among Iranian revolutionary organizations.

This was not only true for revolutionary organizations but also for a whole host of Left-leaning social critics, influential literary figures, and historians subscribing to the same anticolonial idea of justice and liberation politics in which they seldom highlighted the distinction between the "secular–religious" binary opposition. From the dawn of the Shah's White Revolution in 1963—the historical moment of the political emergence of Ayatollah Khomeini—until the collapse of the monarchy in 1979, these critics spoke of the Shi'i Islam of Hussein and Imam Ali as the ideological foundation of the struggle against oppression and tyranny and for social justice.[4]

In fact, it was the radical Islamists who viewed Marxists with suspicion and mistrust, not the opposite. This mistrust was exacerbated in 1975 after the Islamist leadership of the Mojāhedin adopted Marxism and cleansed the organization of those who refused to observe its so-called "ideological transformation." However, even after the new Marxist leadership assassinated one of the organization's Muslim leaders,[5] the Marxist and Muslim Mojāhedin insisted that they shared the same goals in their struggle against the Pahlavi regime and U.S. imperialism. Ideological differences, both sides maintained, must not create divisions in their united front against the Shah's tyranny. A famous letter from a Marxist member of the Mojāhedin, Mojtaba Taleqani—the son of the prominent scholar and revolutionary leader Ayatollah Taleqani, and one of the most influential clerical voices of the revolution—to his father illustrates the significance of maintaining this unified front.

After defending his "conversion" to Marxism and arguing why religion cannot offer answers to the problems of the toiling classes, Mojtaba reassures his father that regardless of his doctrinal shift, the struggle must continue against those who have been co-opted by the Shah's regime. He reminds his father that *both* of them draw their uncompromising commitment to the revolution from their unrelenting faith in the masses. He wrote,

> I do not want to flatter you, but you have so far done much for the struggle and have shown yourself to be a true son of the toiling masses and of the hard-working peasantry. You have not acted as an offspring of the powerful classes.
>
> If you did not possess these pro-mass sentiments, you would have gone the same way as the others. For to be able to resist, one must be close to the masses. In the old days, especially in the period of 1969–70, we would dismiss dialectical materialism on the grounds that if one did not believe in the afterlife one would not be willing to make the supreme sacrifice. I now realize that a communist is willing to make the supreme sacrifice precisely because his cause is that of the masses.
>
> . . . Father, I end this letter by stressing that I will resist the regime as you have done, and that I will follow your example to the end. I will try to write again soon even though I do not know when, or even if, you will receive this letter.
>
> Your Son, Mojtaba.[6]

From the earliest formative moments of the revolution, secularism never defined the point of divergence among different revolutionary organizations. Even Marxist Mojāhedin insisted that they aspired to the same objectives as the their Muslim brethren. While there were Islamist and non-Islamist camps among liberal nationalists and leftist organizations prior to the triumph of the revolution in February 1979, the question of secularism never became the defining point of divergence among these political parties. This ambivalence toward secularism had both strategic–political as well as theoretical dimensions. Politically, by the midsummer of 1978 it became clear that it was Khomeini's leadership that gave the pervasive protests around the country their revolutionary potential. Without recognizing his leadership, no political party at the time could join the rising revolutionary movement. The liberal nationalists signed on reluctantly, hoping they could use Khomeini's revolutionary alternative as a means to bargain for political reform. In their teleological view, the Left believed that revolution itself was a historical inevitability. It minimized the religious mode of the insurrection as a fleeting epiphenomenal expression of ideological superstructure.

By and large, the language of secularity was not spoken during the revolutionary movement. A secularist self-consciousness, and the democratic principle to which it referred, emerged during and after postrevolutionary struggles that led to the monopolization of state power by a diverse group of Khomeini supporters.

The Depiction of Revolutionary Events

By reading Afary and Anderson's narrative, one comes to the false conclusion that the revolutionary movement unfolded under a perpetually contested leadership struggle, suggesting that Ayatollah Khomeini became the head of the movement toward the end of the struggle through a Bonapartist political maneuvering. They also wrongly suggest that the intellectuals and political factions of the revolution engaged in intense debates about the ideological and political merits of secularism. They argue that Khomeini and his Islamist faction dominated the revolutionary movement, "*displacing* the Marxist and nationalist Left," in December 1978, only two months prior to the final victory of the revolution. This historiography sets Foucault up for failing to discern the disputing factions among the insurrectionists. Even in a chapter on how the Islamists asserted and perpetuated their leadership through "processions, passion plays, and rites of penance," Afary and Anderson make no mention of the political significance of the Shi'i ritual of mourning the fortieth day of the dead, which guaranteed the continuity and coherence of the movement in late 1977 and early 1978. This omission is critical. It distorts the fact that Foucault *indeed* witnessed a unified and not a divided and contested mass movement upon his arrival in Tehran in September 1978.

As I discussed in chapter 1, the religious expression, in its expansive rhythm and in its revolutionary soul, allowed the movement to spread so deep and so wide among diverse classes in different regions of the country. The timing, sequence, and religious idiom of these mass demonstrations do not mean that everyone who participated demanded an explicitly *Islamic* revolution. But it is essential to appreciate the fact that the Shi'i discourse of martyrdom and sacrifice—and more importantly, the provision of an extensive network of mosques and other religious sites—turned the protests into a sustained revolutionary movement. It was the language of Shi'i Islam that gave voice to the revolution, despite the fact all those who spoke it did not attribute the same meaning to its terms and concepts. Shi'i rituals afforded continuity to the movement by generating a repertoire of dissent to which a vast majority of the populace felt a deep sense of connection and familiarity.

Although Afary and Anderson acknowledge the significance of these rituals in the formative stages of the revolution (63–66), they modulate the fact that through these rituals, the clergy had already asserted its leadership by the time Foucault touched down at Tehran airport.

> In the fall of 1978, during the *early* stages of the Iranian revolution, a variety of nationalist and leftist students joined the Islamists in mass anti-regime demonstrations. Soon, however, the Islamist wing dominated. The struggle against the Shah was cast as a reenactment of the historic battle between Hussein and Yazid, and the ostensibly secular, nationalist, and leftist demands of many of the demonstrators were articulated in religious garb and through Muharram rituals. (49, my italics)

No credible account of the revolution regards the fall of 1978 as the "early" stages of the Iranian Revolution. According to their account, the Islamists took over the leadership of the revolution in December 1978, *only two months* before the final collapse of the monarchy on February 11, 1979.

Furthermore, Afary and Anderson argue that by the term "irreducible," Foucault had in mind a revolution that "was so elemental that it could not be reduced to any smaller constituent elements, such as parties, tendencies, or factions" (130). This is false. Foucault explains exactly what he means by referring to uprisings in history as *irreducible* right after he introduces the term: "This [the *irreducibility* of uprisings] is because no power is capable of making it absolutely impossible."[7] As Bonnie Honig points out, Foucault was fully aware that the revolutionary movement was far from an absolute totality. That is why he commended Pierre Blanchet and Claire Brière for their reports from Iran in which they "didn't try to break up this phenomenon into its constituent elements; they tried to leave it as a single beam of light, even though we know it is made up of several beams. That's the risk and interest in talking about Iran."[8] Honig summarizes the predicament of reductionism with an intriguing comparison with miracles.

> As the early twentieth-century theologian and philosopher Franz Rosenzweig said with regard to the miracle, of course all miracles can be explained rationally, not because miracle is not miracle but because explanation is . . . explanation. Revolution, like miracle, depends upon observers to receive it in a non-reductionist way.[9]

The point here is not that all of the factions that participated in the revolution adopted an Islamist agenda. This was true even for the revolutionary clergy themselves. Neither Khomeini nor any of his close advisers knew exactly what it meant to advocate an Islamic Republic. No one at the time knew how to translate the symbolic language of Islamic social justice into a system of governance with specific legal and political provisions. Iranians, as Foucault wrote in October 1978, were at "the threshold of a novelty." The particular form of the Islamic Republic was not the result of the unfolding of a grand scheme of the clergy toward which Foucault remained ambivalent. Although the allegorical language of Islam and its political ideology conditioned and gave voice to the revolutionary movement, Islamist governance, the centerpiece of which was *velāyat-e faqih* (the guardianship of the jurist), was the *contingent outcome* of the postrevolutionary power struggle, rather than its blueprint.

Misrepresentation of Shi'i Rituals and Ali Shari'ati's Islamist Political Ideology

Another misconception about the revolution holds that the clerical leadership knew from the beginning what type of politico-legal system they intended to establish, and that on behalf of their strategic plans they duped other revolutionary factions into accepting what appeared to be a tactical, provisional revolutionary platform. Accordingly, Afary and Anderson ridicule Foucault for his inability to fathom the "true" intentions of the Islamists. Furthermore, they turn Shi'i rituals from unifying and inspirational practices into a theater of hate and bigotry against Iranian ethnic and religious minorities. Having turned old and decisive rituals inside out, they reproach Foucault for neglecting to note these objectionable practices. "In his accounts of both Christian and Muslim rituals," Afary and Anderson proclaim,

> Foucault's omissions are surprising and troubling. He belonged to a generation that was well aware of the uses that fascist movements had made of Christian rituals of martyrdom and passion plays. Why was there no reference to any of this in his 1978–79 writings on Iran, or even in his work on the hermeneutics of religion in the 1980s, which was written later and far away from the frenzy of the revolutionary moment? These omissions were all the more surprising, given the political agenda of Khomeinism, with its intolerance toward minority religions and ethnicities, its hostility toward "atheistic" leftists and secularists, and its dismissal of women's rights. (55)

It is true that passion plays and other Muharram rituals of reenactment of the events of *'Ashura* historically had an anti-Sunni undercurrent.[10] One should not understand these ritualistic patterns in essentialist terms but rather highlight how these multifaceted practices change in diverse historical settings.[11] But by politicizing these reenactments, the Islamist ideologues of the revolution disassociated themselves from the traditionalist renditions of these events as days of mourning. By rearticulating the legend of Karbala and the martyrdom of Imam Hussein as a transhistorical battle of justice against tyranny, liberation theologians such as Ali Shari'ati de-emphasized the anti-Sunni sentiments of the reenactment rituals. In contrast to Afary and Anderson's claim, in a politicized reenactment of 'Ashura, Yazid, the second Caliph of the Ummayad dynasty against whom Imam Hussein revolted, appears as the universal tyrant. The main intention of the political 'Ashura was to unite Sunni and Shi'i, and for that matter all non-Muslims of Iran, in their struggle against the tyranny of despots, from Yazid to Mohammad Reza Pahlavi. Shari'ati in particular believed that turning 'Ashura into a reaffirmation of Shi'ism by religious rituals of self-flagellation and passion plays emptied Karbala from its universal message—that of struggle for justice on behalf of the *mustaz'afin*, the downtrodden. If there is a thread that binds Shari'ati's entire corpus it would be the transformation of "Safavid Shi'ism" from superstition and closed-mindedness into the "Alavid Shi'ism" of liberation and justice.[12]

Afary and Anderson juxtapose traditionalist and apolitical Muharram rituals with the events of the revolutionary movement and emphasize their bigotry without making any informed reference to actual anti-Sunni or anti-Semitic incidents. They criticize Foucault for failing to observe the "anti-minority" core of these rituals, without offering any evidence, with the exception of anecdotal citations, of such hostilities among the Muslim revolutionary actors. They even decontextualize their anecdotal references to advance their assertion of how, during their processions, these rituals terrorized non-Shi'ites:

> These ceremonies and processions remind non-Shi'ites and non-Muslim Iranians of their marginal and precarious status. The frenzied Muharram processions sometimes lead to violence. Often, when two rival factions *(dasteh)*, which are performing the *sinehzani* (self-flagellation rituals), come face to face in a narrow alley, neither gives the other the right-of-way. As a result, there are at times violent outbursts, resulting in injuries or even deaths, and terrifying non-Shi'ite communities.[13]

Here they not only obscure the boundary between the traditionalist particularism (Shi'i versus Sunni) and the political universalism (justice versus tyranny) of the reenactment rituals, they also disregard the context of the above narrative of violence and terror. Although processional turf war could occur during Muharram, it would be highly unlikely that what was a distinctly Lebanese communal scene could be found in the Iranian context. The composition and structure of neighborhoods and religious communities in Iran and Lebanon are distinct, each with its own subtleties. Claiming that these ceremonies remind "non-Shi'ite and non-Muslim *Iranians* of their marginal and precarious status" is a serious claim that simply cannot be substantiated by a reference to a case study of Lebanon.

Not only do Afary and Anderson fail to highlight the distinction between the traditionalist and political Muharram rituals, they distort Shari'ati's position to make it consistent with their essentialist view of Islamism as an ideology of bigotry and xenophobia. They argue that "men like Al-Ahmad and Shariati modernized the old religious narratives by connecting them to some of the themes of leftist thought, thus making them more palatable to students and intellectuals." They describe Shari'ati as an opportunistic Islamist who had an instrumental relation with the *Alavid* Shi'ism he had advanced. "He called for a revolutionary concept of Islam, one that could challenge the monarchy and bring a new generation of Muslim thinkers like him to power" (60).

Shari'ati had long been accused by his traditionalist detractors from Qom and Mashhad Seminaries of having an instrumentalist relation with Islam. At the time when he wrote his treatises on revolutionary Shi'ism, high-ranking clerics and ayatollahs organized a campaign to condemn him as an apostate for calling into question the traditional authority of the clerical establishment. A number of grand ayatollahs launched a defamation campaign against him. They asked the Shah and his secret police to stop what they called the spread of Shari'ati's poisonous words and deceptive books. They also accused him of being a SAVAK collaborator whose mission was to destroy Islam from within. A long list of ayatollahs lent their support to a petition to ban their followers from attending his lectures and issued *fatwas* condemning his heresy.[14] A number of influential clerics even highlighted the fact that Shari'ati's political Islam, what he called *Islamic ideology*, downplays differences between Sunni and Shi'i Islam. Naser Makarem Shirazi, one of his most vociferous critics, called Shari'ati's praise of the Sunni Saladin, the Muslim warrior who defeated the Crusaders and retook Jerusalem in 1187, distasteful and damaging to the souls of his young followers.[15]

Afary and Anderson's characterization of Shari'ati bears no resemblance to the man, his ideas, and the kind of contentions those ideas generated within the clerical establishment. They portray him as being yet another Islamist intellectual without distinction who promoted the same bigotry and prejudices that all fundamentalists do.

In his search for what he considered to be an "authentic" interpretation of Islam, Shariati castigated the external influences on Islam, which
had been many in over a thousand years of rich intellectual ferment
and cross-fertilization. In particular, he wished to drive out Greek philosophy, Indian and Iranian mysticism, as well as Christian and Jewish
theology. He also rejected the more *tolerant* interpretations of Islam
found in Persian poetry (e.g., Omar Khayyam), in Muslim philosophy
(e.g, Farabi, 870–950; Avicenna, 980–1037), or even in Sufi mysticism.
Finally and most controversially for Iran's leftist youth, he rejected
Marxism as a "Western fallacy," singling out Marx's humanism for particular attack. (60, my italics)

Any cursory study of Shari'ati's own work as well as the scholarship about
his contribution would show without any confusion that his project was
never about cleansing Islam of external influences.[16] As a pious man, there
is no doubt that he would have found Sartre's existentialism or humanist
Marxism profane, but in spite of the absence of the Divine in these
intellectual traditions, Shari'ati found common grounds with their *political* philosophy. Even his understanding of other world religions, Abrahamic and otherwise, could not be, by any stretch of the imagination,
categorized as being intolerant and fundamentalist.

Afary and Anderson refer to a number of essays Shari'ati wrote in
the 1970s, the English translation of which was entitled *Marxism and
Other Western Fallacies: An Islamic Critique.*[17] However, it appears as though
the book title alone gave them enough grounds to castigate him for
intolerance toward humanism and non-Islamic worldviews. Had they
engaged in a careful reading of the book, they would have found his
repeated homage to "the great eastern religions." He repeatedly declares
his admiration for their distinct comprehension of humanity's relations
with God and the world.

Just as Shari'ati professed admiration for the other Abrahamic faiths,
he welcomed secular political philosophy. Not only did he consider himself
a socialist, he called Imam Ali, Imam Hussein, and Abu Dharr Ghaffari,[18]
his revolutionary hero of the early Islamic period, "God-worshipping
socialists." Moreover, he freely appropriated key Marxian concepts,
such as "class struggle," "classless society," "imperialism," and "capitalist
exploitation," into his lexicon of Islamic ideology. The intellectual influences that conditioned Shari'ati's lifework suggest that not only was he

not an Islamic chauvinist, but he attempted explicitly and implicitly to advance an Islamic ideology that was inspired by socialist ideas of justice and diverse political liberation philosophies. He frequently quoted Marx, whose ideas he studied under a Jewish ex-communist, George Gurvitch, at the Sorbonne. He stoutly defended the anticolonial struggles in Africa and Asia and advanced his liberation theology with references to the notion of the vanguard party from Lenin, permanent revolution from Trotsky, and guided democracy from the Indonesian nationalist leader Sukarno. Not only did he not conceal his proclivities for these non-Islamic sources, he chastised the dominant clerical establishment for their ambivalence toward the predicaments of the contemporary world, especially for their response to the postwar decolonization of former imperial possessions. Indeed, Shari'ati's entire philosophy rested on the principle of the unity of all Abrahamic religions in their struggle for social justice.

When in the early 1970s high-ranking clerics accused Shari'ati of apostasy and Wahhabism, he first tried to appease his clerical critics.[19] But he was incensed by the ayatollahs' complacency in matters of injustice and tyranny. In a letter to Ayatollah Milani, who had earlier forbidden his followers from reading his books or attending his lectures, he lamented that "he still respects [the ayatollah]" and reminded him that his "presence offered hope and support to all the youth who desired a safe haven in these bewildering times." The letter that had started with a pleasant appreciation turned into an unforgiving censure of the clergy. He wrote,

Everybody is asking this question (and because of my gratitude toward you I have tried in vain to offer them a persuasive answer to them): Why is it that pious people such as yourself, who sit on the cathedral of the deputy of the Shi'i messiah *(imam-e zamān)* as a source of emulation, have not uttered a word about tyranny in this world? For eight years, the French army bloodied and massacred the Muslims of Algeria, ruined their cities, tortured their warriors, and the Algerians fought heroically. The enlightened Christian priests in France sympathized with the Algerians. The existentialist Sartre and the antireligion Ms. Simone de Beauvoir defended them and endangered their own lives for the sake of the Algerians' cause. Even the French communist Henri Alleg joined the Algerian resistance and made the atrocities of the French, their torture of the Algerian *mujahidin*, known to the world. You, one of the leaders of the Shi'ite world, did not even issue a meaningless statement of sympathy. . . . For more than twenty years now the Muslims of Palestine have suffered at the hand of the Israelis. Their atrocities are so horrific that they compelled a young Japanese man to sacrifice his life heroically in defense of the Palestinians. But our clerical leaders do not show one-thousandth of the sensitivity they display in my condemnation in denouncing the brutalities of the Israelis. . . . It perturbs me deeply to witness that a great source of emulation writes on the pages of his book that "the Prophet has advised *those who eat melon would go to the heaven!*" And then you have the audacity to call me an "unfit element."[20]

In his Sorbonne professor Gurvitch, Shari'ati found the perfect manifestation of his general theory that the primary principle of a true religious community is the struggle against injustice. In a provocative letter to his father circa 1972, demoralized by the attacks launched against him by the grand ayatollahs, Shari'ati referred to Gurvitch as "a model to be emulated." He called Gurvitch someone "who had spent all his life fighting against fascism, Stalinist dictatorship and French colonialism in Algeria . . . closer to the spirit of Shi'ism than Ayatollah Milani." He considered a Jewish man who fights for social and economic justice to be his religious brother, and denounced a pious source of emulation, who justified and upheld the exploitative and oppressive status quo, as a polytheist foe.[21]

In order to fill out their bigoted portrait of Shari'ati, Afary and Anderson distort his well-known reservations about mysticism and the rationalist school of Islamic theosophy known as the Mu'tazila. They turn Shari'ati's critique of the Mu'tazila scholasticism and Sufis' detachment from the worldly affairs into an indication of his intolerance of external influences on what he considered to be an "authentic" interpretation of Islam. They argue,

> In particular, he wished to drive out Greek philosophy, Indian and Iranian mysticism, as well as Christian and Jewish theology. He also rejected the more tolerant interpretations of Islam found in Persian poetry (e.g., Omar Khayyam), in Muslim philosophy (e.g., Farabi, 870–950; Avicenna, 980–1037), or even in Sufi mysticism. (60)

In contrast to what Afary and Anderson assert, Shari'ati's objection to those Islamic traditions had nothing to do with the question of religious tolerance. Rather, he believed that dominant interpretations of Islam had turned this religion into a lifeless belief system removed from the everyday concerns and grievances of its practitioners. He wanted to replace the antiquated Islam of inaction that was institutionalized in the seminaries with a dynamic Islam of movement and worldly engagement.

During his short career,[22] Shari'ati delved twice into mysticism and Gnostic practices ('irfan), both times as a result of political despair. The first time he turned to mystical introversion was during a period of student activism after the 1953 CIA-backed coup in Iran, which ousted the nationalist prime minister Mohammad Mosaddeq. In these years, his activism was influenced by the remnants of a short-lived movement called "God-Worshipping Socialists" (khodā-parastān-e socialist). But a general apathy toward and fear of politics in Iranian society rendered that and other political activities irrelevant. In his writings dated from the late 1950s and early 1960s, known as "desert contemplations" (kaviriyāt), not only did he see mysticism as the path to the Truth, he immersed himself in the mystical practices of solitary meditation. The kavir, or desert, both literally and allegorically represented to him the solitude that was the necessary precondition for achieving closeness to the Divine. As a young man he saw himself as a reincarnation of the great Sufi masters and poets such as Mansur Hallaj and Rumi.[23] "The desert makes a mockery of Man's material achievements," he believed.[24]

It was exactly the same solitude in Sufi practices, and not political and religious tolerance, to which he later objected. Indeed, this triggered the most important existential crisis of his life. He refuted the kind of Sufism that advocated disengagement from worldly affairs and sought certitude in the inner experiences of the Divine. The mystic experiences of desert contemplations seemed to be inimical to social responsibility. Ultimately, he felt compelled to distance himself from Sufism in order to pursue earthly justice. Furthermore, he also rejected the systematization of Gnosticism in the Sufi Orders; that is, he rejected an organizational logic in Sufism, not its embrace of the plurality of mystical experiences. During his last imprisonment, before he left the country in 1977 for the last time, Shari'ati revisited his passion for mysticism.

Ironically, at the dawn of the revolution, he considered his project a failed attempt to imagine a revolutionary Islam. He thought that the young armed activists of the Mojāhedin organization misunderstood his message of liberation. The liberation he had promoted, he later lamented, was liberation from ignorance. He thought that to end injustice and oppression, rather than taking up arms, the enlightened intellectuals must liberate Islam from the petrified clerical institutions that promoted superstition, exclusivism, and political quietism.

Not only do Afary and Anderson misrepresent Shari'ati's critique of Sufism as antipluralism, they also claim erroneously that he rejected Muslim philosophers because they were influenced by Greek philosophy. Shari'ati objected to identifying al-Farabi and Avicenna as the main defenders of the Islamic tradition not because they appropriated Greek philosophy in their Mu'tazila rationalism but because he believed that such genealogies would turn Islam into a scholastic dogma detached from the realities of Muslims' everyday lives. Through what he called Alavid Shi'ism, he intended to offer an alternative genealogy of Islamic tradition in which the defining moments were marked by *action and struggle* rather than doctrinal debates. Instead of offering a historical narrative based on philosophical discourse and theological debates, Shari'ati's history of Islam consisted of a succession of martyrs and rebellions against tyranny. He was inspired by the St. Pauls and Aarons of Islam, rather than by its St. Augustines and Maimonides; by those who chose Islam consciously; by those whose Islam was realized in exile, prison, and battlegrounds rather than in seminary quarters. Thus, he constructed an axiom of the true Islam in the idea of a movement parallel to the succession of caliphs and the great philosophers of institutionalized Islam—an Islam of Abu Dharr and Hallaj versus the Islam of Umar and Avicenna.[25]

During a roundtable discussion in the late 1960s, a historian criticized Shari'ati for reproaching traditional Islam and its institutions. The critic insisted that Shari'ati had not "rationally" and "scientifically proven" his vaunted distinction between the Islam of struggle and institutionalized Islam. The unnamed critic further ridiculed his genealogical innovation and called it far from a "neutral sociological scrutiny." Shari'ati responded:

> I am not a scientific researcher, but I feel the heaviness of centuries of torture and martyrdom on my soul. . . . This *qibla*,[26] which symbolizes emancipation from thousands of years of enslavement, has transformed into the house of oppression and ignorance, and now you demand calm and scientific research spiced by a respectful aristocratic etiquette. . . .

> The logic of Shi'ites like myself is not the same as the logic of Avicenna, al-Ghazali, of the researcher or of the Orientalist, mine is the logic of Abu Dharr. . . . O my brother, our quarrel is not over a "scientific theory," it is over the inheritance of [the caliph].[27]

In this sense, Shari'ati viewed Islam as a contested discourse the reality of which must be determined in revolutionary praxis. What he despised was the kind of orthodoxy the principles of which were discussed in the seminarian chambers or philosophers' quarters. His thought went through major transformations during his lifetime. But he never defined his project as purging Islam from "external influences."

Khomeini the Demagogue

Afary and Anderson treat Ayatollah Khomeini with the same kind of carelessness and prejudice. They portray Khomeini as a dogmatic ideologue whose philosophical, theological, and political ideas require no serious consideration. They present him as a historical residue, a product of uneven modernization, whose ideas may be summed up in a simple premodern fantasy. Like the way they describe Shari'ati, they depict Khomeini as an ahistorical actor with an unchanging political philosophy, impervious to the circumstances that conditioned his thought. The Khomeini of the 1930s, '40s, '60s, '70s, and '80s are all the same static figure with predetermined stagnant ideas, waiting opportunistically to realize his "archaic fascism."[28] For example, "As a junior cleric," Afary and Anderson write,

> Khomeini published *Kashf al-Asrar* (The Unveiling of Secrets) in 1943, a book that advocated a return to clerical supervision of the entire legal code, the return of the veil, as well as "Quranic" physical punishment. At the same time, in an innovation for clerical politics, Khomeini wished to take over rather than dismantle the state apparatus built by Reza Shah. (73)

Although they offer a number of references to justify their claim, none of those scholarly sources actually substantiate the view that in 1943 Khomeini advocated the dissolution of the state apparatus. In fact, it is commonly understood among scholars of Iran that at the time Khomeini, echoing a dominant Shi'i political philosophy, advocated a promonarchy accommodationist position.[29] For most of Islamic history, both Sunni and Shi'i theologians subscribed to the political doctrine of the primacy of order over chaos. This doctrine, whose most eloquent proponent was Muhammad al-Ghazali (1058–1111), calls for Muslims to obey their king/sultan/caliph, for he provides security for the *ummah*. In his *Kashf al-Asrār* (1943), Khomeini emphasized that "bad government is better that no government"; "we have never said that the king must be a *faqih*, or know all the conditions of the obligatory religious duties"; and "the *Ulama* always cooperate with the government if that is needed."[30]

There is convincing evidence that at the time he composed *Kashf al-asrār*, Khomeini was familiar with the idea of governance by the guardianship of the jurist *(velāyat-e faqih)*, put forward more than one hundred years earlier by Mullah Ahmad Naraqi (1771–1829). Naraqi had argued strongly for the right of the *mujtahid* (the legitimate source of religious interpretation) to act as a successor to the imam, and vested him with all the powers of the imam.[31] But despite his familiarity with Naraqi's political philosophy, in 1943 Khomeini promoted the more traditional Shi'i quietist position. He defended the principle of an advisory role for the clergy as envisioned in the 1907 constitutional amendment. Only in the early 1970s did he begin to articulate a justification for the breach of the political authority and the assumption of power by the clergy. For Afary and Anderson, however, Khomeini represents a suprahistorical fundamentalist ideology and remains the same ideologue from the time he entered the public arena to the time of his death in 1989.

In his earlier writings Khomeini adhered to the same principles put forward by the anticonstitutionalist cleric Sheikh Fazlollah Nuri (1844–1909).[32] Despite the fact that he was willing to accept the authority of the monarch, he considered all forms of constitutionalism and legislative acts to be inconsistent with the teachings of Islam. Evidently, Afary and Anderson are unaware of Khomeini's political transformations, and he appears in their critique as a transhistorical fundamentalist who planted the seeds of the 1979 revolution in his youth.

More importantly, Afary and Anderson disregard Khomeini's remarkable political transformation *during* the 1978–79 revolutionary movement. Khomeini abandoned his earlier views on constitutional monarchy and formulated a theory of Islamic governance and the rule of the jurist. He further refined his position after he was expelled from his exilic home in the Iraqi city of Najaf and migrated to Paris in October 1978. In Paris not only did he highlight the constitutional bases of Islamic government, he called for an Islamic *Republic* based on the sovereignty of the people. His radical departure from his earlier positions is evident in a declaration he issued on January 12, 1979. There he announced the formation of the Council of the Islamic Revolution, the main responsibility of which would be to make necessary preparations for the transfer of power to a postrevolutionary provisional government. The new government, he stated, would be entrusted with the following tasks:

1. The formation of a Constituent Assembly composed of the elected representatives of the people in order to discuss and approve the new Constitution of the Islamic Republic
2. The implementation of elections based on the principles approved by the Constituent Assembly and the new Constitution
3. The transfer of power to the representatives chosen in those elections[33]

Portraying Khomeini and Shari'ati as fundamentalist bigots only diminishes the significance of the historical transformations and contingencies of their ideas. By definition, fundamentalists reflexively follow doctrinal convictions that remain coherent, resilient, and resistant to changing circumstances. Throughout their book, Afary and Anderson either ignore important transformative moments in Islamist politics in Iran or misrepresent the events in order to fit the reality into their own ideological scheme. For example, they frequently remind their readers of Khomeini's and Shari'ati's anti-Semitism and their importunate hostility toward religious and ethnic minorities in Iran. These are represented as self-evident facts offered to underscore Foucault's misplaced enthusiasm for bigoted Islamist leaders.[34]

There is no question that Khomeini and the entire clerical establishment viewed Baha'ism as a heresy and considered its followers to be apostates. Moreover, they treated the question of Judaism and Christianity in classical Islamic terms, regarding Jews and Christians as the people of the Book and therefore protected under Islamic rule. In a careless generalization, Afary and Anderson invariably couple the Baha'is and Jews together as target of Khomeini's hatred. In the postrevolutionary regime, Baha'is were persecuted and in many instances executed. They were never recognized as a religious minority or accorded special protection in the new constitution. Nevertheless, anecdotal references to Shari'ati's comments about Jews or Khomeini's inflammatory conflation of Zionism with Judaism and Israel with the Jews has to be understood in the context of and in reference to the relationship between Iran and Israel along with the power the United States and Israel exercised over the political and economic affairs of Iran under the Shah. Throughout the 1960s and 1970s, a great majority of Iranian Left and liberal intellectuals used the same indiscriminate conflation of Israel with Jews. Israeli politics had become indistinguishable from Judaism.[35]

"One of the main reasons," Khomeini stressed in an interview on December 7, 1978, "we oppose the Shah is his assistance to Israel. . . . He has plundered the Muslims' oil wealth and has given it to Israel. This has always been one of the reasons of my opposition [to this regime]."[36] Not only did Khomeini make that connection during the revolutionary movement, he also made his declarations clearly in political connection with Israel even in his earlier writings. For example, in 1963, in one of his earliest political sermons against the Shah's White Revolution, although he talks about the "*Jewish* control of the Iranian economic lifelines," he made it clear that by *Jewish* control he meant the state of Israel. After a brief incarceration, he gave a defiant sermon at the Azam Mosque and repeated the point: "Our religion compels us not to reconcile with the enemies of Islam, the Quran dictates not to unite with the enemies of Islam against Muslims. Our nation opposes the Shah's accord with Israel" (1:77). And most importantly, conscious of the ambiguities in his own earlier statements, on the eve of the revolution on Christmas Day of 1978, Khomeini issued a declaration stressing that his "opposition to Zionism and Israel is a separate matter from Judaism and Jews, we must respect other religions and their followers" (4:219). And a few months later, after the revolution, he revisited the issue and reminded a group of demonstrators against Israel that "Zionism is a political and colonial project and distinct from the affairs of the Jewish community" (6:164). The point should be unmistakable: Khomeini was politically anti-Zionist, but hardly an anti-Semite. He took pains to distinguish the two, and Afary and Anderson carelessly conflate the two.

Afary and Anderson's comments on Khomeini's hostility toward *ethnic* minorities are even more unfathomable. They are troubled by Foucault's "omissions" of Khomeinist "intolerance toward minority religions and ethnicities" (54) but offer no proof of this intolerance toward minority ethnicities during the revolutionary period. It is also puzzling to think of Khomeini speaking on behalf of the Persian majority, while his entire political discourse rested on an antinationalist ideology. As I have shown elsewhere, the postrevolutionary civil war in Kurdistan and Arab, Turkman, and Azeri ethnic strife were part of a struggle motivated less by Khomeinist hostility toward ethnic minorities and more by a bloody attempt to consolidate and restore the power of the central government.[37]

Afary and Anderson invent a revolutionary genealogy in the context of which declarations of Khomeini, and the political ideology he and other Islamists represented, appear as a self-evident, homogenized, and ahistorical fundamentalism. They repeatedly misappropriate Khomeini's declarations and decontextualize them to establish a "Khomeinism" that was *inherently* dogmatic, intolerant, and fascist. For example, they cite Khomeini denouncing teachers who did not support his vision of revolution:

> If you see that your professor, your teachers, or leaders of the nation, are being diverted from their national and religious obligations, at the head of which is the uprooting of this decrepit regime, you must vehemently protest and *suggest to them the way of the nation, which is the way of God.* If they do not accept [argument], then avoid them and clearly explain their deviant ways to the innocent people. [Say] that [the teachers] are traitors to religion, to the nation, and to the country, that they want the shah and his owners, the international thieves, to continue their plundering and to keep the nation poor and backward.[38]

To make Khomeini's true intentions more deliberate, Afary and Anderson cite his interview with the BBC a few days later, in which he "hinted at the authoritarian pathway he had in mind for Iran, when he declared that he had no intention of restoring the 1906–7 Constitution. He termed it 'an old and reactionary thing,' adding, 'Islamic law is the most progressive law.'"[39] More perplexing than their romantic and idealized notion of the 1906 Constitution is Afary and Anderson's chagrin at Khomeini's categorical denunciation of it. Was the revolution not about the abolition of constitutional monarchy?

The above references to Khomeini's declarations against those who were "being diverted from their national and religious obligations" were made after the liberal nationalists appealed to him in France to accept the

Shah's concessions and allow the king to remain in power as a constitutional monarch. For decades after the 1953 coup, the Iranian secular as well as Muslim liberal nationalists (the National Front and Liberation Movement, respectively) demanded a revival of the 1906 Constitution and defended a constitutional monarchy in which they thought *the Shah must reign but not govern.* The nationalists, who remained up to that point committed to their *reformist* agenda, reluctantly situated themselves in the revolutionary camp. They tried to exploit the ambiguity in Khomeini's notion of the Islamic Government and wed it to their long-held belief in the constitutional monarchy. By the time Khomeini arrived in Paris in October 1978, the Shah's regime had unmistakably lost all legitimacy. The question then was whether to save monarchy or resume the revolution against it. In the above passages, Khomeini was not situating *his* revolutionary vision against others' revolutionary agenda. He was defending the revolution itself.

A wide range of liberal nationalists, from the reformist Ali Amini, a Shah loyalist, to Mehdi Bazargan, a Muslim reformist opposition leader, approached Khomeini in Neauphle-le-Château to arrive at a grand bargain to save the Shah's throne but strip him of all his governing powers. With millions relentlessly and fearlessly demonstrating on the streets of the Iranian cities and strikes crippling major industries and state bureaucracy, the grand bargain was dead on arrival in October 1978. No leader at the time could remain in the position of leadership by agreeing to halt the momentum of revolution. To end any hope to resuscitate the old Constitution, Khomeini declared monarchy, in no ambiguous terms and against his own previous beliefs, fundamentally incompatible with Islamic political philosophy. He repeated in a number of occasions: "The regime we will establish will have no resemblance to a monarchy" (2:47).

On October 14, 1978, only four days after the interview Afary and Anderson cite with the BBC, in response to a reporter's question, "What type of government will replace the Shah's regime?" for the first time Khomeini introduces his notion of republicanism in order to put to rest the comparisons that were being made between his conception of the Islamic government with the Saudi or Libyan systems (2:36). By introducing an Islamic *Republic,* in effect, he ended any possibility of a compromise with the regime. He made it clear, as another reporter during an interview observed, "The leadership of the revolution was not only against the Shah, but against any form of monarchy, constitutional or otherwise" (3:52). In a series of declarations and interviews thereafter, Khomeini effectively marginalized the camp that still hoped for the realization of the old constitutionalist principle that *the Shah must reign but not govern*. He stressed that "the peoples' vote will determine the shape of the next political system" (ibid.). "We will call for a general referendum on a republican system" (3:258–59). "Since our nation is Muslim and it regards us as its servant, based on that, I presume that it will ratify our proposal [of an Islamic Republic]" (3:33).

Khomeini's shift from promoting an Islamic government to proposing a specifically *republican* system was a major transformation in his political philosophy. This point is either unknown or irrelevant to Afary and Anderson. For them, these tactical shifts were made only to conceal his essentially authoritarian intentions. In consequence, observers like Foucault who took Khomeini's political maneuvering seriously were merely dupes of the cunning ayatollah.

Defending an editorial written by the influential Iranian sociologist Ehsan Naraqi in support of the liberal-nationalist concession plan, Afary and Anderson chastise Foucault for failing to appreciate the "*extremely popular wish* for a return to the 1906–7 Constitution" (91). Not a single account of the Iranian Revolution history corroborates the idea of mass support for the return of the 1906–7 Constitution at this point in time, a few months before the collapse of monarchy in February 1979. In his October 1, 1978, commentary, "The Shah Is a Hundred Years behind the Times," Foucault rightly pointed out that the liberal constitutionalist solution, "Let the king reign but not govern," had become an untenable alternative. By then, this allegedly popular wish had lost even its most vociferous advocates among the secular liberal nationalists. As Foucault reported on November 7, 1978,

> Karim Sanjabi, the leader of the National Front, had finally accepted the first point of the ayatollah's declaration, to the effect that the shah's monarchy is illegitimate and illegal. His abdication and departure had thus become a prerequisite for the reconstitution of political life. By Friday evening, the monarch lacked even indirect support anywhere among the opposition, leaving him without any room to maneuver.[40]

On numerous occasions in his interviews with the press, Khomeini was asked to draw a distinction between an Islamic Republic and other forms of republics. His response to a *Le Monde* reporter on November 13, 1978, characterized his conception of the common ground between Islam and his envisioned republic.

> *Le Monde*: Your Excellency wishes to establish an Islamic Republic in Iran. For the French people this is ambiguous, because a republic cannot have a religious foundation. Is your republic based on socialism? Constitutionalism? Would you hold elections? Is it democratic?
>
> Ayatollah Khomeini: Our republic has the same meaning as anywhere else. We call it "Islamic Republic" because the conditions of its emergence are embedded in Islam, but the choice belongs to the people. The meaning of the republic is the same as any other republics in the world. (4:479)

Khomeini took practical steps beyond his rhetorical endorsement of republicanism. He bestowed the responsibility of drafting the new constitution to Hassan Habibi, a Sorbonne-educated jurist, who later formed a commission comprising civil experts in jurisprudence.[41] Habibi was profoundly influenced by Gaullist French republicanism. Habibi's affinity with Gaullism manifested itself in the document he drafted, in which he assigned absolute executive powers to the president and called for a Guardian Council to review the constitutionality of laws passed by the *majlis* (parliament) in order to examine their compatibility with Islam.

The Revolutionary Council and the Provisional Council of Ministers under the supervision of Yadollah Sahabi, another prominent liberal politician and an advisor to the provisional government of Mehdi Bazargan, further revised the document and published the official preliminary draft on June 14, 1979.[42] This version revised the first draft by moving it closer toward a social-democratic constitution. It added provisions on women's rights—specifically the right to hold public office—and on other social justice issues it emphasized participatory democracy and further restricted the private ownership of industry. The published April 1979 version limited the power of the president and increased that of the prime minister. More importantly, it recognized municipal and provincial councils as a major source of decision-making and executive power. Ayatollah

Beheshti, one of the founders of the Islamic Republic Party and the vice chair of the Constitutional Assembly, notably advocated the issue of women's right to run for every elected office of the government (including the office of the president). Ayatollah Taleqani, one of the most influential leaders of the revolution and a member of the Revolutionary Council, championed the elevation of municipal councils as the practical foundation of governance.[43]

Not only did Khomeini trust civic jurists to draft the new constitution, on several occasions he lent his support publicly to the published preliminary draft in which no mention of *velāyat-e faqih* was made.[44] For example, in a meeting with members of the Tehran Preachers' Society on June 17, 1979, he insisted on supporting the published draft and hoped that it would be approved and instituted shortly. Indeed, until *velāyat-e faqih* was passed by the Assembly of Experts on September 12, 1979, Khomeini remained faithful to his 1978 Paris declaration of Islamic republicanism, in which *ruhāniyat* (the clergy) was to assume an advisory role in the guidance and proctorship of the state.[45] According to Hassan Habibi, the Revolutionary Council approved the published version of the constitution with the direct blessing of Ayatollah Khomeini, who had only expressed minor concerns about the consistency of the document with Islamic jurisprudence in matters of women's rights and the relationship between the Shi'ites and minority Sunnis. In an interview with the *Kayhan* daily, Habibi argued that Khomeini believed that "the realities of our society do not allow a full appreciation of *velāyat-e faqih*, our society is not ready to accept this."[46]

Whereas Foucault saw in the phrase "Islamic government" an ambiguous notion oscillating between "a utopia" and "an ideal" that would eventually open a contested politics of governance, Afary and Anderson see the unfolding of a preordained fundamentalist clerical order. For Foucault,

[Islamic government] is something very old and also very far into the future, a notion of coming back to what Islam was at the time of the Prophet, but also of advancing toward a luminous and distant point where it would be possible to renew fidelity rather than maintain obedience. In pursuit of this ideal, the distrust of legalism seemed to me to be essential, along with a faith in the creativity of Islam.[47]

At the time he wrote these lines in October 1978, the same revolutionary spell that had mesmerized millions of Iranians might have enchanted Foucault. But nevertheless, he rightly repeated the caveat that a religious authority pointed out to him that "it would require long work by civil and religious experts, scholars, and believers in order to shed light on all the problems to which the Quran never claimed to give a response."[48] For Afary and Anderson, Khomeini and the other clerical leaders of the revolution appeared to adhere to medieval dogma, oblivious to the predicaments of the contemporary world. Afary and Anderson's commitment to their own modernist ideology rendered them incapable of recognizing that Khomeinism was not, as Ervand Abrahamian put it, simply "a religious crusade obsessed with scriptural texts, spiritual purity, and theological dogma." Khomeini was a shrewd and flexible populist, conditioned by and responsive to the historically distinct, socially specific political and economic grievances of the Iranian people.[49]

The Atrocities of the Islamic Republic

The historical events that offer the most compelling material for Afary and Anderson's interpretation of the Iranian Revolution lies in the immediate postrevolutionary period, which eventually led to the "reign of terror" of the 1980s. They argue that the following acts: the dissolution of family protection laws, the brutal suppression of the Kurdish (and later Arab) demands for the right of self-determination, instituting mandatory *hijab*, the executions of prominent figures of the ancien régime, and, soon thereafter, the indiscriminate mass executions of members and sympathizers of the opposition parties, *all* showed the conspicuous continuity in and internal consistency of Islamism. Rather than acknowledging the postrevolutionary contingencies of power struggles, they identify the "reign of terror" as the foreseeable unfolding and inevitable manifestation of Khomeinism.

The fact of the terror is indisputable. It remains a defining and brutal moment in the history of the young Islamic Republic. Tens of thousands were imprisoned, executed, and assassinated by the state. The state took repressive measures to curtail the short-lived liberties and democratic institutions. The critical question, however, is *why* and *how* the postrevolutionary moment degenerated into bloodshed and oppression. To reduce such events to the unfolding of the internal logic of Islamism hinders deeper understandings of the mechanisms by which revolutionary moments of collective political participation give way to the power struggles of state-building.

In Afary and Anderson's chronology, there are no words of the contingencies that informed the policies and politics of the new republic. In their narrative, actions of the postrevolutionary state were motivated by its ideological commitments rather than being shaped by the demands and realpolitik of state-building. I do not use state-building here as a euphemism to conceal the brutality with which it is associated. Rather, I want to emphasize that one needs to contextualize the consolidation of power not as a signifier of the fascist core of Islamist *ideology*, but as concrete responses to *particular events*. In March 1979, Afary and Anderson write, "[Khomeini] sponsored a national referendum that declared Iran an Islamic Republic. Soon after, as Khomeini began to assume nearly absolute power, a reign of terror ensued" (2). Or, in the conclusion of the book, they simply declare that "Khomeini moved quickly to repress feminists, ethnic and religious minorities, liberals, and leftists—all in the name of Islam" (163). They also mention that during this period, from 1979 to 1988, more than twenty thousand political prisoners were executed (301n128).

In their narrative, this repression operates like a self-propelling machine. There is no mention that on June 28, 1981, an opposition group blew up the headquarters of the ruling Islamic Republic Party and killed more than seventy of its founders and members of the parliament. Among the dead was Ayatollah Beheshti, who served as the chief justice at the time. Two months later, on August 30, 1981, President Ali Raja'ei and Prime Minister Mohammad Bahonar were assassinated by another bomb blast. In a period of two years, from 1981 to 1983, the Mojāhedin organization carried out countless assassinations against key personalities of the clergy, members of the parliament, influential Friday Prayer Imams, members of neighborhood militia forces, and those who were suspected of cooperation with the regime. Hashemi Rafsanjani, then the speaker of the parliament, and Ali Khamenei, then the president, both were injured during assassination attempts. None of these justify a policy of indiscriminate execution of young members and sympathizers of the opposition parties. However, it demonstrates that the atrocities committed by the Islamic Republic were not simply the realization of Khomeinism.

Foucault's early critics compared him with intellectuals who defended fascism and Stalinist totalitarianism. In a scathing commentary, Claudie and Jacque Broyelle, who appeared to be rehabilitating themselves from their Maoist past, called on Foucault to "acknowledge his errors" like a good reflective intellectual and confess: "I was mistaken. Here is what was wrong in my reasoning: here is where my thinking is in error."[50] In reply, in addition to pointing out their complete misunderstanding both of the revolution and the historical significance of political Islam, Foucault rebuked them for calling on him to acknowledge his error. This was "a maneuver," he spat, "whose form and content I detest." Frustrated by the intolerance of those who found his conception of political spirituality an errant aberration in the French tradition of anticlericalism, Foucault refused to participate in a polemic the basic premise of which was "You are going to confess, or you will shout long live the assassins."[51]

Afary and Anderson hardly mask their glee in their description of how the French ridiculed Foucault. For them, not only was the comparison of Foucault with those who defended fascism and other totalitarianisms legitimate, but more importantly, they argue, time had proven the truth of the fascist core of Islamism. In the epilogue of the book, after nodding to the ideological and political diversity of Islamism, they conclude: "Nonetheless, like fascism earlier, which had German, Italian, Spanish, Romanian, and many other varieties, radical Islamism has enough common features to discern it as a general phenomenon" (163).

They provide a number of references to substantiate the claim that Islamism indeed exists as an ideologically unified general phenomenon. The two scholarly authorities whom they cite on this point, John Esposito[52] and Fred Halliday,[53] however, contradict their thesis. Neither Esposito nor Halliday consider the varieties of Islamist movements, from the Taliban to the leadership of the Iranian revolution, to be parts of a single phenomenon. On the contrary, they emphasize the social context of the different Islamist movements in order to highlight their distinctions and distinctiveness, not their uniformity.

Paul Berman is the only authority they offer who advances a theory of Islamo-fascism and a direct correspondence between Islamism and totalitarianism.[54] But Berman, who defended the American invasion of Iraq and who advocates a messianic American interventionism for the promotion of democracy around the world, could hardly be a credible expert on Islamism or offer a justifiable alternative to what Afary and Anderson call "Western cultural relativists."[55]

They enumerate a number of instances, from Khomeini's *fatwa* against Salman Rushdie, whom they call "a man of the Left [!]" (164), to the Taliban's destruction of the Buddha statues in Bamyan to highlight the internal consistency and fascist core of Islamism in spite of its regional, social, and cultural diversity (164–67). To further prove that Islamists of all kinds form a united front regardless of their differences, they even claim, without substantiation, that the Iranian supreme leader and the "conservative part of the government . . . condemned U.S. actions against bin Laden" (173). This, of course, is erroneous. The collapse of the Taliban regime was made possible by the indispensable help and strategic planning of the Islamic Republic. During the war, "members of the Iranian Revolutionary Guard Corps even cooperated with the CIA and the U.S. Special Operation Forces in supplying and funding the commanders of the Northern Alliance."[56] Even the Bush administration's special envoy, James Dobbins, stressed that the Islamic Republic's assistance was crucial during the war, and more importantly, in reaching an agreement at the December 2001 UN-sponsored conference in Bonn, Germany, on the transitional government of Afghanistan.[57] Nevertheless, Afary and Anderson conclude that "the unbridled joy with which the population of Kabul greeted the fall of the Taliban in late 2001 shocked many Islamists, as well as those Western leftists and progressives who had taken a culturally relativist position toward Afghanistan" (165).

Misreading Foucault

Afary and Anderson draw on their facile, uniform picture of Islamism in order to make self-evident the flaws of Foucault's view on the Iranian Revolution. "It is relatively easy, from the vantage point of the twenty-first century," they point out, "when militant Islamist movements have caused immense destruction not only in Iran, but also in Algeria, Egypt, Afghanistan, and the United States, to see substantial flaws in Foucault's writings on Iran" (136). But Foucault's ultimate sin was not his ignorance of Iranian history, they argue, but something deeper that has also motivated a whole generation of intellectuals in the West: he adopted a romantic idealization of premodern societies. They argue that Foucault, and by association other so-called cultural relativists, cheered on the revolution because he discerned a manifestation of his poststructuralist critique of modernity in the supposedly antimodernist chants of Islamist radicals on the streets of Tehran!

> Both [Foucault and Islamist radicals] were searching for a new form of political spirituality as a counter-discourse to a thoroughly materialistic world; both clung to idealized notions of premodern social orders; both were disdainful of modern liberal judicial systems; and both admired individuals who risked death in attempts to reach a more authentic existence. Foucault's affinity with the Iranian Islamists, often construed as his "error" over Iran, may also reveal some of the larger ramifications of his Nietzschean-Heideggerian discourse. (13)

With his Nietzschean view of history, they argue, Foucault saw in Khomeini an *Übermensch* who could persuade "millions to risk their lives in the struggle against the Shah" (14). Poststructuralists (they never make it clear who else besides Foucault they have in mind) and leftists (namely Howard Zinn and Noam Chomsky) were so mesmerized by Islamist anti-imperialist discourse and preoccupied with their critique of the "secular liberal or authoritarian modern state and its institutions" that they allowed "retrogressive movements," such as Islamism, to flourish (136).

Is what they claim true? Did Foucault privilege a romantic premodern social order over modern governmentality? Did his generative and relational theory of power call for rescuing the modern subject by returning to an "authentic self," as they argue? Did Foucault combine "an admiration for the Orient with a certain nostalgia for the aristocratic" in order to cope with the modern "callous form of individualism?" (18). It is only through a perfunctory reading that one can argue that Foucault's affinity with the Iranian Revolution stemmed from his nostalgia for the past. Afary and Anderson offer such a reading of Foucault with out-of-context quotations and puzzling misinterpretations. For example, they attribute Foucault's "blissful" ignorance of the "hierarchical traditions" that regulated relations between "adults and youths, men and women, and upper and lower classes" to his fascination with "silence" as a mode of expression. Here they cite Foucault:

> Silence may be a much more interesting way of having a relationship with people. . . . I think silence is one of those things that has unfortunately

been dropped from our culture. We don't have a culture of silence; we don't have a culture of suicide either. The Japanese do, I think. Young Romans or young Greeks were taught to keep silent in very different ways according to the people with whom they were interacting. Silence was then a specific form of experiencing a relationship with others. This is something that I believe is really worthwhile cultivating. I'm in favor of developing silence as a cultural ethos.[58]

Afary and Anderson do not acknowledge that he made these comments in an interview in 1982 discussing his experience in a Japanese Zen temple. For them, in this passage, Foucault is privileging "the silence of mostly youth, women, and the lower classes in premodern social orders . . . as a preferred mode of discourse."[59] They interpret Foucault's contemplation on silence as an expression of his Orientalist prejudice through which he constructs a binary history of submissive and irrational East versus assertive and discourse-oriented West. Although, they assert, "Foucault was probably [!] an Orientalist" (20), unlike other Orientalists, he sympathizes with the Orientals' "pre-technological lifestyle" and their victimization by Western imperialism.

Although Foucault's use of silence in his work is at times ambiguous and confusing, it is hard to imagine that any of these ambiguities would lead one to interpret his assertions as a defense of the *silencing* of the subjugated. Indeed, Foucault is aware of the operational varieties of silence in society. As he remarks in a 1982 interview, "There [are] many different ways of speaking as well as many forms of silence."[60] In his work, Foucault divides silence into two general forms.

The first, more evident in his earlier work, particularly in his *Archeology of Knowledge* (originally published in 1969) is a mechanism through which the normalizing and disciplinary powers of religion and science manage the *silenced* body. In this case, all the powers of discourse and speech exist in a binary opposition to silence. Foucault viewed silence as the "broken dialogue" of the mad (*Madness and Civilization*, 1961), the silent observation of the prisoner (*Discipline and Punish*, 1975), the *imposing* silence of confessional technologies (*History of Sexuality*, 1976).[61] With these metaphors, he positioned silence as a "mechanism of exclusion," an instrument in the service of domination. In this first instance, he regards silence as a coercive normalizing technology as a means of manipulating and controlling the *silenced* self (in "cloister, prison, school, and regiment").[62]

In the second instance, developed in the first volume of his *History of Sexuality* (1976), and later with his concept of political spirituality, Foucault points to the hermeneutic significance of silence in the disciplinary apparatus of confessional technology. Here, silence is situated not in a binary opposition to speech acts, but itself as a mode of communication. This is the point he stresses in his comment on Zen Buddhism.[63]

In his later work, however, he introduces a new conception, what he calls "pedagogical silence."[64] Here Foucault distinguishes between "being silent" as a pedagogical strategy and "being silenced" as an exclusionary practice. Pedagogical silence could be traced back to Stoicism with its "practices of the self, . . . emphasized and laid down by the Pythagoreans."[65] Stoic Silence was an alternative to the Platonic discipline of learning by dialogue. In short, Foucault's treatment of silence in both cases, as a behavioral discipline borrowed from Zen Buddhism or as a pedagogical principle of the Stoics had nothing to do with justifying or approving the repression (the silencing) of the oppressed.

In a footnote, Afary and Anderson recognize that in the *History of Sexuality* Foucault adopts two "seemingly contradictory attitudes" toward the concept of silence—one as a strategy of resistance and the other as a repressive imposition. And they conclude: "What [Foucault] misses is that premodern silences are also imposed and forced, especially on women" (280n3). They emphasize Foucault's inattention toward the plight of their transhistorical conception of women, because they want to illustrate that his gendered ambivalence was a central feature of his defense of Islamism. More importantly, in his historiography, Foucault carefully avoids these types of binary oppositions between modernity and premodernity. To say that he endorses a premodern silencing of women or other oppressed groups while he is critical of silencing practices of modern disciplinary technologies is, to say the least, a gross misunderstanding of Foucault's genealogical history.

Neither does Foucault's antiteleological genealogy romanticize the past, nor his theory of disciplinary technology and discursive power privilege pastoral or ancient modes of being and subjectivity. One can appreciate the anxieties that Foucault's genealogy generates when he aims to "record the singularity of events, outside of any monotonous finality."[66] But a plausible concern for a Nietzschean nihilism one might detect in Foucault's radical genealogy is far from a caricature of him defending the premodern against modern relations of power. Even a superficial reading of Foucault's lectures at Collège de France on *Security, Territory, Population,* delivered a few months before his first trip to Iran, shows the absurdity of the claim that he felt affinity with the Iranian revolution because of its promise of the return of a repressed past![67] In those lectures, Foucault clearly argues how pastoral (priestly) power is diffused in modern techniques of governmentality and disciplinary regimes. He links governmentality genealogically with Machiavellian state philosophy of *raison d'etat* and ultimately to the medieval church and Christian pastoral authority. It is the idea of the priest as the shepherd, the guardian and guide of the flock, and its mixing with the Greco-Roman techniques of self-examination that, according to Foucault, shaped the effective core of the modern governmentality. Given Foucault's distinctive genealogy, it is difficult to imagine how it would be possible to think conceptually that he privileges premodern formations over modernity.

Afary and Anderson's misinterpretation of Foucault relies on a common liberal view of the transcendental individual. They reject what they perceive to be Foucault's despairing view of modernity and its all-encompassing disciplinary technology, and argue that he disregards the greater freedoms that liberal democracy has afforded the individual along with the same technologies (90). Foucault's foundational blunder, in their view, becomes self-evident in response to the question: *Is the freedom of the modern subject not greater than that of the premodern individual?* Afary and Anderson's affirmative response resides in their teleological view in which they project the modern subject back onto the premodern individual, an individual who experiences love, belief, freedom, privacy, and other proclivities of the modern subject within the oppressive confines of the premodern order.

More importantly, Afary and Anderson's entire project rests on a series of mutually exclusive dichotomies, on the one side of which they locate anything modern, and on the other retrogressive residual premodernity. In a brief note on contemporary Iranian history, they recapitulate their approach to a century of revolutions in Iran:

> To Iranians and those familiar with the country's history, the revolutionary uprising of 1978–79 was part of a series of turbulent events stretching back to 1906, in which the themes of democracy versus autocracy, nationalism versus imperialism, socialism versus capitalism, secularism

versus clericalism, and women's emancipation versus tradition had played themselves out at several key junctures. (72)

To put it bluntly, this appealing historical narrative is far removed from the interactions and relations of significant actors of the two revolutions and Iran's decades of contested politics. The turbulent twentieth century in Iran generated ambiguous alliances between different social groups and political parties. There was not a single historical moment in which the dichotomous distinctions such as "democracy versus autocracy" or "secularism versus clericalism" described the real distinctions on the ground between the premier political actors. This history is marked more by actions of secular autocrats, clerical democrats, Westernized nationalists, and traditionalist defenders of women's equality than by the coherent efforts of one side of those Manichaean configurations against the other. The *ideal types* that Afary and Anderson construct to justify their progressive teleology hardly reflect the careers and political affinities of actual historical actors in Iran.

A binary history curtails in significant ways our understanding of the dynamics of the revolutionary movement in Iran. The revolutionary movement of 1978–79 did not spread along the line of a secular versus Islamist binary narrative. A multifaceted theology of discontent, a religious emancipatory language, and a symbolic appropriation of Islamic rituals gave the revolutionary movement a voice with which a diverse group of revolutionary actors identified. Leftist students' movements, the impressive reception of poetry nights at the Goethe Institute in the fall of 1977 in Tehran, riots of shantytown dwellers, the letter-writing campaigns of human rights lawyers, and the indispensible strike of oil workers never posed an *alternative to* the revolutionary movement that emerged under the leadership of Ayatollah Khomeini.

The 1977–79 movement was primarily motivated by issues of social justice and dignity in which the explanatory significance of binary devices such as secular versus religious were at best limited. The bifurcated misrepresentation of the revolutionary movement also ridicules Foucault further for his inability to see what must be evident to any observer. That there were two factions in the revolutionary movement—one progressive, secular, and democratic and the other reactionary, religious, and tyrannical—and Foucault chose to endorse the latter. It is in this context that Afary and Anderson link Foucault's politics not only to his ignorance of the Iranian situation, but also, and more importantly, to his theoretical commitment to a critical stand against the Enlightenment rationality. It might be true, they propose, that Foucault was unaware of the long history of secular and religious frictions in Iran, but he supported Islamism because of his romantic awe of the premodern.

One of the major flaws in Afary and Anderson's analysis of the revolution and Foucault's interpretation of it is that they assume, as Norma Claire Moruzzi argues in her insightful review, "that the Iranian revolution was not only a failure but a disaster, and they, therefore, are appalled that Michel Foucault wrote excitedly about it while it occurred."[68] Indeed, whether a revolution is a failure or a success within itself is an ideological question the answer to which involves many different aspects of social and cultural life and might not be known for generations. Was the Chinese Revolution a success or the Russian a failure? Was the Haitian Revolution a failure judged by its legacy of repressive regimes or a success reckoned through its overturning of slavery? How many generations passed until historians began to speak of the French Revolution as a triumphant marker of modern Europe? The Iranian Revolution has gone through many conflicting periods and has not followed a straight path along the lines of Brinton's *The Anatomy of Revolution*. The initial hopes and moderation coexisted with a *reign of terror*; and the period of *terror and virtue* proved incapable of eliminating the strong roots of the Thermidor spirit. But the long eight-year Thermidor period under President Khatami (1997–2005) led to a return of the soldiers of virtue and the proponents of terror. And now in 2015, the spirit of moderation and hope returns. To borrow from Foucault, "These days nothing is finished, and the dice are still being rolled."[69]

Afary and Anderson argue that the blunder of Foucault's romantic and culturally relativist views (which are somehow also poststructuralist) is the most manifest in gender and sexuality politics. Foucault, they stress, is blind to the Islamist antiwoman outlook because of his theoretical shortcomings on feminist politics and Orientalist fantasies. I will elaborate on this point in the next chapter.

4

THE REIGN OF TERROR, WOMEN'S ISSUES, AND FEMINIST POLITICS

The veil will fall, from Tehran to Casablanca!

—Women protesters in Paris, March 1979

ON NOVEMBER 6, 1978, *Le Nouvel Observateur* published the following letter, called "An Iranian Woman Writes," by Mme. Atoussa H. The letter castigated Foucault for his failure to acknowledge the oppressive *nature* of Islam and reprimanded "the Western Left" for romanticizing the Iranian revolution without regard to its oppressive ideology.

> Living in Paris, I am profoundly upset by the untroubled attitude of French leftists toward the possibility of an "Islamic government" that might replace the bloody tyranny of the shah. Michel Foucault, for example, seems moved by the "Muslim spirituality" that would advantageously replace, according to him, the ferocious capitalist dictatorship that is tottering today. After twenty-five years of silence and oppression, do the Iranian people have no other choice than that between the SAVAK and religious fanaticism? In order to have an idea of what the "spirituality" of the Qur'an, applied to the letter under Ayatollah Khomeini's type of moral order, would mean, it is not a bad idea to reread the texts. Sura 2 [*sic*]: "Your wives are for you a field; come then to your field as you wish." Clearly, the man is the lord, the wife the slave; she can be used at this whim; she can say nothing. She must wear the veil, born from the Prophet's jealousy toward Aisha! We are not dealing here with a spiritual parable, but rather with a choice concerning the type of society we want. Today, unveiled women are often insulted, and young Muslim men do not themselves hide the fact that, in the regime that they wish for, women should behave or else be punished. It is also written that minorities have the right to freedom, on the condition that

they do not injure the majority. At what point do the minorities begin to "injure the majority?"

Spirituality? A return to deeply rooted wellsprings? Saudi Arabia drinks from the wellsprings of Islam. Hands and heads fall, for thieves and lovers. . . . It seems that for the Western Left, which lacks humanism, Islam is desirable . . . for other people. Many Iranians are, like me, distressed and desperate about the thought of an "Islamic" government. *We know what it is.* Everywhere outside Iran, Islam serves as a cover for feudal or pseudo-revolutionary oppression. Often also, as in Tunisia, in Pakistan, in Indonesia, and at home, Islam—alas!—is the only means of expression for a muzzled people. The Western liberal Left needs to know that Islamic law can become a dead weight on societies hungering for change. The Left should not let itself be seduced by a cure that is perhaps worse than the disease.[1]

Mme. Atoussa H.'s remarks offer an iteration of what has become a familiar trope in twenty-first-century political debates over headscarves and the vulnerabilities of Muslim women.[2] There is nothing new about the kind of textual essentialism based on which Mme. H. castigates Foucault's sympathies toward the Islamic revolution. For Atoussa H., an unvarying transcendental Islam informs Islamist politics that steers the genuine revolutionary impulses of the masses toward its inherently oppressive project. In that picture, the divergent Islamist tendencies in Iran, the Saudi Wahhabism, Indonesian Islam, and Pakistani postcolonial state all share the same common repressive core. Unlike Atoussa H.'s claim, Foucault remained as one of the very few voices to defend the revolutionary movement not despite but because of its religious mode of expression.[3] But her letter offered a new impetus to French intellectuals to call on Foucault to reconsider his position and acknowledge the pitfalls of defending the Islamic Revolution.

The apparent Orientalist prejudice that guided Atoussa H.'s critique of Foucault did not disturb Foucault's critics. The depiction of "Islam" as a historical actor, extirpated from the cultural and political contingencies of its practitioners, and Islam as a world view that shapes and homogenizes different cultural practices and discursive traditions has always been a hallmark of classical Orientalism. As Abdallah Laroui, the Moroccan historian and public intellectual, and an early critic of Orientalism, once wrote, the problem of the Orientalist historiography lies in the way it creates a closed cultural system, the fundamental features of which are perpetuated by textual theological references, regardless of time and space. Laroui further argued that for Orientalists, "There are no differences between classical Islam and medieval Islam or simply Islam. There is, then, only one Islam: an Islam that mutates within itself when tradition takes shape on the basis of a reconstructed 'classical' period. From that time onward the actual succession of facts becomes illusory; examples can be drawn from any period or source whatever."[4]

By contrast, Foucault showed more sensitivity toward the Orientalist proclivities that informed Atoussa H.'s comments.[5] In a short response, he reminded Mme. H. that he did not come up with the idea that a "Muslim spirituality would advantageously replace dictatorship." Rather, he was impressed by the *historically contingent* fact that millions of Iranians had dared to shout "Islamic government!" while being chased, beaten, arrested, and killed by squads of soldiers on their cities' streets. He pointed out that one should be true to the "elementary obligation to ask oneself what content was given to the expression and what forces drove it." Foucault rightfully identified Atoussa H.'s hostility toward the Islamic Revolution not in her misreading of his own views and the events of the revolution but in her merging together "all the aspects, all the forms, and all the potentialities of Islam within a single expression of contempt, for the sake of rejecting them in their entirety under the thousand-year-old reproach of 'fanaticism.' . . . The problem of Islam as a political force is an essential one for our time and the coming years. In order to approach it with a minimum of intelligence, the first condition is not to begin by bringing in hatred."[6]

More than three decades after the revolution, it is now self-evident that the situation of women in Iran, despite patriarchal policies of the postrevolutionary regime, is hardly explicable with a few references to the Qur'anic verses. It is certainly true that the Islamic Republic instituted a new regulatory regime that hindered women's social mobility and incessantly tries to constitute a gender-segregated public sphere. But it is also true that the same policies generated conditions for an unprecedented participation of women with religious commitments from divergent social classes in public life. Development indicators released by the World Bank and UNICEF show that in the areas of education, employment, life expectancy, and health, women's situation in Iran improved significantly compared to the years of modernization under the Pahlavi regime.[7] An ahistorical textual invocation of Islam simply cannot account for the complex field of gender politics in postrevolutionary Iran. Instead, as with the revolution itself, an analysis of gender politics requires a careful attention to the specificities of events and contingencies of ideas that inform it.

A cursory look at the historical changes in Shi'i discourse on gender relations shows the heterogeneous and at times contradictory practices it has engendered both before and after the revolution.[8] In contrast to the "feminist premonitions" of Atoussa H., Parvin Paidar illustrates, the revolutionary movement in Iran significantly altered the position of the clergy on women's political and social participation. Although this unprecedented change did not advance an anti-patriarchal awakening, it did signify a remarkable transformation in gender relations in Iran. With her utterly reductionist view, Atoussa H. invited Foucault to give primacy to a truncated passage in the Qur'an at the expense of the lived experiences of Iranian women who participated in demonstrations by the millions. But the question of the role of Shi'ism, as Paidar shows, in the position of women must only be addressed within the political contingencies and various historical conjunctures of its exponents. Far from being fixed and predetermined, Paidar asserts,

> the political agenda of Islamic forces was set throughout [the past] century in response to and as part of an interaction with other political forces. This was why Islamic gender policies put forward within various historical conjunctures were indeed heterogeneous and at times contradictory. An example of this was the way in which some of the gender policies of the Islamic Republic, such as women's right to vote, contradicted previous positions adopted by Shi'i clergy under the Qajar and Pahlavi regimes.[9]

More often than not, ideological commitments, even if they remain impervious to political circumstances, generate unintended social realities.[10] Foucault was more concerned with the revolutionary *movement* and the realities that it was generating in its wake. He insisted that one should not draw an unmediated connection between the Islamic dogma and a literal reading of the Qur'an with real-life and revolutionary experiences of the ordinary masses. This is plainly historical thoughtlessness.

This kind of reductionist generalization envisages women's status with reference only to formal/legal institutions—which in any event are diverse and contradictory, particularly on "the woman question"—and ignores the lived experiences of women and the hermeneutics of power and authority outside the scripture.

The postrevolutionary struggle for the consolidation of power by the Islamic Republic and its ensuing reign of terror afforded more credibility to warnings, such as Atoussa H.'s, about the inherent repressive character of Islamism. If Foucault failed to see the wisdom in Mme. H.'s prudent warning on the antiwomen *essence* of Islam, his later critics observe, he should have faced the fallacy of his misplaced enthusiasm about the revolution's "spiritual" élan and the tableau vivant of "men rising up" in the postrevolutionary brutalities committed by the Islamists, particularly against women.

Foucault's detractors warned him that his idea of political spirituality, which he romanticized as a new mode of revolutionary expression, was nothing more than an ideological foundation for a religious tyranny. They stressed that the Islamic Revolution, unlike what Foucault imagined, did not stand at "the threshold of a novelty," but rather it set in motion a giant leap backward toward the creation of a brutal theocracy. Without a doubt, the reign of terror that ensued after the establishment of the Islamic Republic added considerable currency to the contentions of Foucault's critics. The execution of more than four hundred military commanders, intelligence officers, and torturers, along with a number of key ministerial members of the ancien régime, added further evidence to the backwardness of the postrevolutionary regime and its religious ideology. Human rights organizations and Western governments condemned the Islamic Republic for its speedy trials and executions, despite the fact that an overwhelming majority of revolutionary parties supported and encouraged those acts of swift justice.

Foucault repeatedly delinked his notion of political spirituality and the significance he attributed to Shi'i Islam in the revolutionary movement from the establishment of an Islamic government. But his detractors continue to insist that the philosopher failed to acknowledge the *inherent* authoritarian and repressive characteristic of political Islam. A repressive state, they argued, was the *inevitable* consequence of the Islamic revolutionary ideology.

From the Revolution to the Reign of Terror

In *Islam and Dissent in Postrevolutionary Iran*, I have shown, through careful examination of the events and debates that led to the final ratification of the constitution of the Islamic Republic, that the clergy did not follow a master plan after the assumption of power in 1979. It is true that Khomeini and his followers promoted an Islamic state, but they remained uncertain about how exactly such a regime was to be created and what its establishment entailed. As much as the revolution itself was "unthinkable," as Charles Kurzman argues in his thoughtful monograph, the postrevolutionary state-building also unfolded along inconceivable lines with unpredictable outcomes.[11]

Neither the provisional government nor the Revolutionary Council, both appointed by Ayatollah Khomeini, appeared to be committed to the kind of radical and fundamental changes that would satisfy the militancy that had consumed the revolutionary spirit of the masses. A diverse group of parties saw the provisional government incapable of the radicalism that the postrevolutionary reconstitution of society required. Three major communist groups, Tudeh Party, Fadā'iān, and Peikār,[12] in addition to a host of radical Islamist parties, both inside and outside the revolutionary government, exhorted the provisional government to advance a radical platform of social transformation and deliver swift revolutionary justice against the remnants of the ancien régime.

Only one week after the collapse of Pahlavi Dynasty, the provisional government announced that it was working on a frame to issue a general amnesty for high-ranking officers of the military and SAVAK agents who were not directly involved in the torture and murder of political dissidents. In response, the most influential communist organization in Iran, the Fadā'iān, issued a piercing statement on February 16, 1979, under the heading: "General Amnesty, A New Year Present to Counter-Revolution!" In their statement, they called the action of the provisional government "an open animosity toward the revolution."

FELLOW REVOLUTIONARY IRANIANS!

While the blood of tens of thousands of our martyrs, who sacrificed their lives for the liberation of oppressed peoples of Iran, still drips from the walls; while the majority of the bloodsucking mercenaries and villains of the old regime under the guidance of the CIA are busy plotting against the revolution; while, based on the admission of the Provisional Government, the SAVAK agents are still busy slaughtering people and conspiring against the revolution, what does issuing a general amnesty mean? Is it not a gift to the enemies of our nation?[13]

The more the provisional government tried to contain the revolutionary vigor of competing political parties and the militant drive of neighborhood and professional associations, the deeper it fell into a crisis of legitimacy. In their revolutionary political discourse, the Left and militant Islamists understood respect for human rights and deference to formal legal procedures only as liberal jargon appropriated by agents of colonial interests in order to suppress the revolutionary tide. Together, they shut down early attempts of Prime Minister Mehdi Bazargan and his allies, including a number of influential members of the clergy, to advance an Islamist political philosophy congruent with a democratic political discourse. Bazargan believed that his administration was forced to resign after only nine months through a "revolution against the revolution," which was primarily motivated by a Marxian-inspired philosophy of "permanent revolution."[14] And it wasn't only Marxist parties who promoted perpetual radicalization of the revolution. Militant Islamists, who were influenced by Shari'ati's liberation theology and Khomeini's uncompromising antiestablishment fervor, spoke openly about the significance of "permanent revolution" as a core principle of their revolutionary ideology.[15]

Ultimately, in its first attempt the government failed to resist the expansive radicalization of revolutionary demands. In Kurdistan, Leftist and nationalist Kurdish parties occupied government buildings and demanded regional autonomy. After a failed attempt at negotiation, the new revolutionary government responded with massive air strikes, which eventually led to a bloody war in Kurdistan. In Turkman Valley, in northeast Iran, land distribution disputes led to a full-fledged armed conflict between the Fadā'iān-led resistance and the newly formed Revolutionary Guardians of the Islamic Revolution. With massive support and encouragement from all political fronts, the revolutionary courts handed down execution orders in summary trials.

When Habib Elghanian, a well-known Jewish entrepreneur and an ardent supporter of Israeli interests in Iran, was executed by firing squad on May 9, 1979, the communist paper *Peikār* celebrated his execution in these lines:

THE SACRED WRATH OF THE PEOPLE!

Once more, the flames of the sacred wrath of the people devoured another group of spies and villains in the revolutionary courts. Those ignoble and deceitful creatures who presided over the pillage and plunder of our toiling people with a pharaonic authority, showed a despicable and nauseating display of begging for their lives and to continue their shameful existence. How blind and ignorant are those who believe that the people will forget the blood of their martyrs and the dreadful agony they suffered during those oppressive years. And how blind and ignorant are the masters of these reprehensible criminals in the West and Israel, whose tears for the violation of "human rights" now drips on their filthy faces to show sympathy for the bloodsucking "humans" like Elghanian. They think that they can shake the unwavering determination of the people for the annihilation of those traitors who protected their colonial interests for decades. Let them dream! Our people will destroy its enemies and no power in the world may stop them.[16]

In a resolution authored by Senator Jacob Javits, the U.S. Senate passed a resolution condemning the increasing number of executions in Iran, particularly that of Elghanian, as human rights violations. A coalition of Iranian communist organizations called a massive rally against the continuing American intervention in Iranian affairs. In addition to the call for the nationalization of all Iranian industries, the organizers declared their full support of "the executions carried out by the revolutionary courts" and asked for a *further expansion of the scope of the executions*. The declaration, signed by eleven communist organizations, generically called "The Unification Conference," also demanded the "establishment of labor camps for the rest of SAVAK agents and other guilty members of Pahlavi security and police forces and government bureaucracy."[17] The Fadā'iān issued a separate but similar declaration, wondering: "What does the wicked American imperialism object to? The very fact that the Americans are defending these criminals is a proof that they were guilty and their sentences could be nothing less than execution."[18]

Rather than a simple manifestation of "political spirituality" and a plain evidence of the inevitable consequences of Islamism in power, the atrocities that were committed after the revolution were the outcome of a conflict between two tendencies, on both sides of which Islamist and secular actors fought to advance an agenda. One side remained committed to an anticolonial and anticapitalist program and advocated a "permanent revolution" for the reconstitution of the entire society based on competing conceptions of social justice. The other side called for the institutionalization of the revolution through legal and formal procedures and called the incessant radicalization of postrevolutionary politics a "revolution *against* the revolution."

Foucault's critics saw in Islamism and what Foucault celebrated as *political spirituality* simply a bridge to totalitarianism. His critics identified in the postrevolutionary power struggle, particularly in the form of gender politics and the imposition of new restrictions on women's mobility, an instance of the fallacies of abandoning Enlightenment rationality and its immutable universal referents. The influential French Marxist Orientalist Maxime Rodinson wrote:

> Michel Foucault, part of a line of radically dissident thought, placed excessive hopes in the Iranian Revolution. The great gaps in his knowledge of Islamic history enabled him to transfigure the events in Iran, to accept for the most part the semi-theoretical suggestions of his Iranian friends, and to extrapolate from this by imagining an end of history that would make up for disappointments in Europe and elsewhere. . . . The "political spirituality" that had inspired the revolutionary movement—covering over the more material motives for the discontent and the revolt—had at a very early stage shown that it operated by no means in the humanist sense that had been attributed to it, very naively, by Foucault.[19]

To his detractors, it is more puzzling that the philosopher of gender and sexuality saw no spirituality in women's protests against mandatory *hejāb* during the first postrevolutionary celebration of the International Women's Day on March 8, 1979. If Foucault could dismiss Atoussa H.'s lone plea as a disgruntled Westernized woman, how could he ignore the voice of thousands of Iranian women marching on the streets to mark the International Women's Day in March 1979? How could he dismiss a global feminist movement that supported them, both by taking part in rallies in Tehran and mobilizing women in Paris, New York, Milan, and London?

Did Foucault's silence on the "imposition of chador"[20] and Ayatollah's Khomeini's order to abolish family protection law further confirm feminist skepticism of his theory of power? How could Foucault remain unfazed in the face of what *Le Monde*'s Jean Gueyras described on March 14, 1979, as the "insults and jeers" of Islamic militants who hounded the women with charges of being "agents of the SAVAK, instruments of imperialism . . . tools of international communism, . . . [and] defenders of the Pahlavi dynasty"?[21]

Liberation, Women, and the Hejāb

Since the time leading up to the Constitutional Revolution of 1906, the issue of *hejāb* has been one of the key signifiers of modernity in Iran. Both symbolically and literally, *hejāb* in Iran represents the embodiment of nationalism, citizenship, colonialism, culture, and class. Gendered trajectories of modernity in Iran have always generated social formations that, more often than not, defy simple binary distinctions between the traditional versus the modern or the religious versus the secular. Modernist discourses motivated by such schemata perceive *hejāb* as the means of women's subjugation, a patriarchal device for the prohibition of women's public life. Not only did the revolutionary movement in Iran negate this modernist assumption, more importantly, the unprecedented rise in the literacy rate and economic participation of women under the postrevolutionary regime demonstrated the ambivalence of *hejāb* in relation to women's participation in public life.

Although during the revolutionary movement women of the Left did not wear a headscarf to cover their hair, they shared an ideological commitment and a cultural affinity with Muslim women activists in believing that a modest dress signified an anti-imperialist conviction. An overwhelming majority of men and women of the Left who joined the revolutionary movement regarded the *hejāb* as the site of a continuous and contested debate over issues of class, gender, and nationalism.[22]

In that context, *hejāb* never signified a distinction between secular and Islamist revolutionary parties. It indeed was a shared view, on the one hand, of a majority of Iranian men whose *gheirat* (masculine pride) was vulnerable to what seemed to them to be the real force of emasculation (namely, colonial penetration), and on the other hand, by women who saw their dignity threatened and their body objectified by the encroachment of Western capitalist consumer society. Not only was the female body a location of patriarchal exercise of authority, but also, and more generally, it was a site of negotiating modernity and its boundaries in Iran. Afsaneh Najmabadi aptly conceptualized this Iranian feminist view as being "modern-yet-modest."[23]

As much as competing political parties have contested the significance and boundaries of modernity, they have also questioned the meaning and manifestation of modesty. The concept of *gharbzadehgi* (westoxication), which was popularized by the influential social critic and novelist Jalal Al-e Ahmad (1923–69), captured this gendered sense of alienation that allowed "a common thread to unify a diversity of prejudices."[24] Between the inauguration of the White Revolution in 1963, which laid the foundation for land reform and industrialization, and the revolutionary movement of 1977–79, more than ever women emerge as the very embodiment of *westoxication*. For both the secular as well as the Islamist Left, Iranian women appeared to be a double Other: "the enemy within, *fitna* [sedition, immorality], and the enemy without, the West." Such a conceptualization paved the road for both secular and Islamist oppositions to Pahlavi capitalist reforms "to sing in unison condemnation of the 'super-Westernized' woman."[25]

Although from different standpoints, both the Islamist and the secular Left generally considered this "super-Westernized" woman to be the signifier of a plague that had imperiled the integrity of the Iranian society. "In its crudest form," to borrow again from Najmabadi,

> She was identified with a woman who wore "too much" make-up, "too short" a skirt, "too tight" a pair of pants, "too low-cut" a shirt, who was "too loose" in her relations with men, who laughed "too loudly," who smoked in public. Clearly, it signified a subjective judgment; at least to some extent it was defined in the eyes of the beholder. . . . Yet, both [the Islamic militant and the radical secular] felt comfortable in denouncing *gharbzadeh* and the *gharbzadeh woman* in a single voice.[26]

Many of the earlier critics of *gharbzadehgi* believed that under capitalism women had been exploited both as laborers and frivolous consumers. "The promised equality of men and women," Al-e Ahmad lamented in 1962, "was only limited to a coercive unveiling. We opened the doors of a few schools to them and after that? Nothing! That was enough for them. . . . What have we done in reality? We have allowed women to appear in public: a mere hypocrisy, a pretense. We have dragged the woman who is the guardian of our tradition, family, and bloodline to the street and compelled them to become lascivious and spread depravity and debauchery. We encourage them to be vain, aimless and devoted to fashion."[27]

There is no doubt that during the revolutionary movement women's dress became a site of political struggle. To exercise their political dominance, vigilant Islamist operatives harassed, and on many occasions attacked, women who appeared in rallies without headscarves. In the final months of the revolution, Muslim militants chanted the demeaning and misogynistic slogan *yārusari, yātu-sari* (cover your hair or have your head whacked). On numerous occasions Islamists targeted women without *hejāb* during anti-Shah rallies. Moreover, reports appeared in Tehran dailies that these vigilantes had beaten nonobservant women and even in a number of cases thrown acid on women's faces. Although influential members of the clergy tried to emphasize that *hejāb* means modesty in dress and not a particular form of cover, attacks on women without a tight headscarf grew exponentially. In an interview published in *Kayhan* newspaper on the same day that the Shah left Iran, Ayatollah Montazeri, who was just released from prison, told a French reporter that "Islamic *hejāb* does not mean wearing a veil and being socially insulated. The goal is to not see women naked [*lokht*] in society in such a way that they become the object of lust."[28]

Although not pervasive before the revolution, these incidents raised enough concern for Khomeini to declare in an interview with the Lebanese paper *Amal*:

Today Muslim women participate in political struggles and rallies against the Shah. I was informed that in different Iranian cities women have initiated political meetings. Under the Islamic system, women and men enjoy the same rights, the right of education, the right to work, the right of ownership, the right to vote and get elected. . . . However, there are instances for both men and women that they are prohibited from engagement in sinful acts that would lead to corruption and decadence. The desire of Islam is to protect the dignity of men and women. In Islam, men must not objectify women. This is mere propaganda that

Islam allows violence against women. This is a conspiracy to taint the face of Islam.[29]

But the assumption of political power introduced a new frame within which the militant Islamists began to institutionalize their politics of gender. Women's issues and gender politics became particularly central to radical Islamists because it constituted an important marker that could distinguish their anticolonial "revolution in revolution" from the Marxist Left.

Six Days in March: Women's Protest without Women's Movement

On February 26, 1979, only two weeks after the victory of the revolution, Ayatollah Khomeini annulled the Family Protection Law of 1967 and its 1975 amended version.[30] Khomeini knew that the unity and uniformity that his leadership afforded the revolutionary movement would not remain uncontested for long after the triumph of the revolution. He knew that the spirit of Islam and the symbolic revolutionary language with which it inspired millions of Iranians of many creeds and classes needed to be translated into a body of institutional projects of postrevolutionary state-building.

Despite the popularity of his revolutionary Islam and the indisputable charismatic leadership he had enjoyed during the revolutionary movement, Khomeini's political philosophy and his brand of liberation theology remained marginal within the seminaries. Therefore, he asserted his authority over gender politics and women's issues so soon after the revolution not only to stress the Islamic character of the revolution against liberal and communist contenders of power (as it is often highlighted in the literature) but also to reestablish his authority among the seminarians, by placating the conservative clerical establishment in order to consolidate his power. The abrogation of the long-disputed Family Protection Law, which had limited and later eliminated the authority of the clergy in matters of marriage, divorce, custody, and alimony, sent a strong signal to both possible sources of contention.

One week later, on March 3, Khomeini also declared that women could no longer serve as judges in civil or criminal courts. But what brought Khomeini's serial declarations on women's issues to the general attention in newspapers and political parties was his announcement about *hejāb.* On March 6, 1979, addressing a group of seminary teachers and their students, Khomeini criticized the persistence of westoxication in the country even in government offices. "I am told," he proclaimed, "that in our government offices the old ways continue, the way things were under the Shah. Sinful acts should not be committed in the Islamic state's ministerial offices. Naked women should not appear in ministerial buildings; women should go, but they must respect *hejāb.* They should go and work, but with *hejāb.*"[31]

In spite of those overt assaults on women's rights, women's issues continued to be addressed in the frame of revolutionary politics, nationalism, class struggle, and anti-imperialism. With the exception of the National Front, the oldest liberal organization in Iran, and small Trotskyist groups, the members of which had mostly returned to the country from Europe and the United States, Left and liberal parties remained ambivalent about women's issues. In a manner typical of so many radical political movements of the time, they considered it to be a diversion from the "essential" objectives of the revolution.[32] The majority of women's organizations operated as an appendix to different political parties to further anti-imperialist struggles and demands for social justice.

On March 29, 1979, after the first few weeks of protests, the main women's organization, the National Union of Women, declared its establishment with a statement that began with tribute to the "women martyrs of the revolution," who all belonged to armed guerilla resistant fighters. In their mission statement, they further explained that they would not cooperate with "organizations with links to China or the Soviet Union." The statement continued: "We will cooperate neither with those groups that assemble women against revolutionary forces nor with those reactionary groups who mobilize women during these sensitive times around divisive and digressive issues. . . . *We consider the struggle against imperialism to be our most essential goal.*"[33]

Even influential independent public intellectuals and literary figures who published the literary and political magazine *The Book of Friday (Ketāb-e Jom'eh),*[34] who did not follow a particular party politics, used the same frame of anti-imperialist struggle for justice to address women's issues. In a special issue celebrating the International Women's Day on March 8, 1980, while different authors criticized the patriarchal policies of the new regime, they also emphasized that the revolution failed to achieve its "deep anti-imperialist objectives." One author called "the uprising of Siahkal," the birthplace of the communist Fadā'iān guerilla organization, the "most glorious moment in the Iranian women's movement." The Left-leaning intellectuals of *Ketāb-e Jom'eh* even discussed the Family Protection Law and its nullification in relation to capitalist development and colonial ambitions. A commentator with the pseudonym Diana wrote:

> The Shah and his imperialist planners introduced the Family Protection Law, and other articles of the "White Revolution," in order to strengthen the foundations of capitalism. After successive defeats of the global imperialism, their strategists began to advance plans to expand capitalism's reach through new programs in the Third World. They implemented a series of social reforms in order both to impede the inevitable rise of liberation movements and to ease the expansion of capitalist market economy. The land reform initiatives in Iran as well as laws such as "Family Protection" were examples of this new policy. In reality, the Family Protection Law was designed to release women from family bonds in order to satisfy the needs of capitalist relation of production for cheap labor.[35]

Even those who openly challenged the abrogation of the Family Protection Law in February or made their dissatisfaction known about compulsory *hejāb* regarded these decisions as *diversions* from the true objectives of the revolution. One of the most famous women writers and a secular social critic, Homa Nateq, a respected member of the Writers' Association, called the entire project of women's emancipation of the Pahlavi era "cosmetic." In a speech she delivered at a rally at Tehran University on February 8, 1979, she declared that "women's liberation is an indispensable part of the emancipation of the entire society. Women will be free when the revolution is realized."[36]

In a series of essays in the main Tehran newspaper, *Kayhān*, titled "Iranian Women and the National Revolution," Nasser Takmil Homayun, one of the influential leaders of the National Front, a self-proclaimed secular liberal party, began his first installment with the title "They Wanted the Iranian Woman to Be a Western Doll." Further, he chastised those who "exaggerate" the issue of women's right in Islam and called that a "source of divisionary politics among the revolutionary forces." He ridiculed Pahlavi-era policies on women's affairs, calling them a plot to Westernize Iranian women. He concluded his article by stressing:

> Under the pretense of women's emancipation from the medieval dungeons, the goal of this destructive, predatory, and dissolute group [the Pahlavi regime] was to pave the road for the Westernization of women's social life, particularly with its most degenerate cultural expressions. Fortunately, with the blessing of our nation's colossal social and political movement, and with the massive participation of the brave women of our subjugated people, this conspiracy failed. Undoubtedly, the new national struggle and cultural self-reliance will terminate the calamity that once threatened the Iranian family.[37]

Despite earlier assurances, on the eve of March 8, Ayatollah Khomeini called on the provisional government to uphold Islamic dress codes in its offices. His pronouncement scandalized many who played a significant role in the revolutionary movement, including a number of members of his own Revolutionary Council. This was the second time, after the abrogation of the Family Protection Law, in three weeks that issues of women's rights had become a point of contention in the postrevolutionary power struggle. That was the reason why the festive preparations for the first postrevolutionary International Women's Day turned into a rally with specific women's rights demands such as the recognition of women judges and, most importantly, a call against compulsory *hejāb*.

The main newspapers in Tehran carried Khomeini's caution against "naked women"[38] in government offices as their front-page headline with responses from government officials, high-ranking clerics, and a diverse group of political personalities. Plans for the March 8 rallies, one of the first mass events after the young revolution, were thrown into confusion when the rallies unexpectedly turned into a protest against compulsory *hejāb*. Thousands of women gathered in Tehran University and the next day in front of and inside the hallways of the Ministry of Justice chanting, "In the spring of freedom, absent is the rights of women."

Although the liberal provisional government endorsed Khomeini's remark on the necessity of *hejāb* in government offices, it also tried to highlight the distinction between *hejāb* and *chādor* (the veil). State-owned newspapers tried to temper their reportage of the women's rallies with assurances that the leader's proclamation was not tantamount to a new law. While defending Khomeini, in an op-ed in *Kayhān*, Hojjat al-Islam Eshraqi, his son-in-law, called for calm and respect for the Islamic codes of ethics. He wrote,

> It is true that we are obliged to follow Islamic regulations, but we need to consider that *hejāb* does not mean the *chādor*. We ask women to appear with dignity in covering their body and hair. *Chādor* is a common and respectable way, but there are other ways of decency that correspond to the nature of the work women do and that must be respected.[39]

Three days later, after streams of rallies in Tehran and a number of other cities around the country, *Kayhān* published an interview with Ayatollah Taleqani, the most revered religious and political authority after Khomeini. The front-page headline read: "Ayatollah Taleqani: *Hejāb Is Not Compulsory.*" Taleqani, using the language of benign paternalism, tried to introduce *hejāb* in a cultural context rather than a religious obligation. He compared it with the Indian sari and encouraged women to look at it as a matter of identity and national pride. "There must be no coercion even on Muslim women [to observe the *hejāb*]. This is not what Ayatollah Khomeini suggested; he offered his fatherly guidance like a father who advises his child, nothing more."[40]

In order to defuse the rising tension and violence on the streets, Mojtahed Shabestary, an advisor to the director of the National Radio and Television, added a political dimension to Taleqani's cultural twist. He connected the Iranian struggle to the utility of the veil during the famous Algerian liberation movement. "Let us not forget," he remarked, "that it was the same veil that was a cover to hide our weapons from the view of the SAVAK."[41] And finally, while stressing the significance of *hejāb*, one of the most respected sources of emulation, Ayatollah Mahalti, condemned any form of violence against women.

While the religious establishment and political leaders of the republic tried to give the *hejāb* a national and political significance, political parties and independent actors on the Left continued to accentuate national unity against imperialism , referring to issues such as *hejāb* detrimental to the revolutionary energy that had just toppled the monarchy. On March 10, 1979, next to her *hejāb*-less photograph, *Kayhān* published a commentary by Simin Danshvar, an influential writer and Jalal

Al-e Ahmad's widow, entitled "Let's Build Our Wrecked Iran." After already three days of unrest and women's protest on university campuses and in front of the Ministry of Justice, Daneshvar exhorted the opponents as well as the advocates of compulsory *hejāb* not to give the counterrevolutionaries excuses to derail the revolution. The following lengthy excerpt captures the core of the way the majority of Left and liberal intellectuals who defended the revolution perceived the question of the *hejāb* and the protests triggered by Khomeini's declaration at the time.

I did not intend to write solely about women, because I consider women, men, and children a single unit of human family. In our country this family has been subjected to colonialism, exploitation, and powerlessness, we have all experienced this oppression together. Many times women of divergent groups have invited me to join their women's organization. Their rationale was that women were subjected to double oppression. I did not accept their invitations. My reasoning was that if a just regime is established, men, women, and children will enjoy its protection. The problem of patriarchy must be addressed directly with men with the hope that together we reach a common understanding. These are our husbands, sons, and brothers, and exclusive women's organizations might appear as a mobilization against them. I hope that these organizations will not cause divisions, especially during this time that what we need is unity *(vahdat-e kalameh*[42]*)*. I fear that these associations would distract the people and cause dispersion and confusion. I fear that it would throw a wrench into the wheel with the power of which the revolutionary justice, independence, and freedom turns.

[. . .] I regard Ayatollah Khomeini, the leader of the Iranian peoples' revolution, as the very essence of justice. I consider him to be a man who has stepped into the field of battle with his word and with it he has destroyed an unparalleled arsenal. I know him as a man of a new history, a new air, a new morality, a man who believes in what he preaches.

[. . .] But unfortunately, visible and invisible hands are at work to muddle the pure face of the people's revolution with unwarranted divisions and trepidations. And which division would be better than the separation of vast groups of toiling women and intellectuals from the revolution? What kind of schism would be greater than spreading doubts and despair in their hearts and pushing them toward extremist ideas of the Left or Right?

[. . .] Let me put everyone's mind at rest. *Hejāb* in the form of a *chādor* is not an Islamic but a traditional issue. Our sisters stepped into the arena of revolution with that particular cover because they considered it as a signifier against servitude to consumption and the insolent dolls of the Pahlavi era. But those privileged women with bottomless dollars of their supporters escaped this land and now we are left with those who enjoy to make something out of nothing and to turn a whisper into a scream.

[. . .] Any time we were able to rebuild this ruined house, sort out its economy, take care of its agriculture, establish the rule of justice and liberty, whenever all of our people have a safe roof over their heads, enjoy universal education and health, then we can busy ourselves with unessential issues and matters of jurisprudence. Then we can sit in a home with solid foundations and think with ease about the way women appear in public.[43]

Meanwhile, protests continued on March 10 and 11. An estimated fifteen thousand women gathered inside and in front of the Ministry of Justice building, asking the provisional government to guarantee the right of women to work with equal pay without compulsory *hejāb*. Groups of club-wielders and militant supporters of the new regime attacked women protesters. Four women were hospitalized for injuries they sustained after they were assaulted by knife.[44] Two key liberal/Left figures addressed the crowd at the Ministry of Justice, the respected historian and public intellectual Homa Nateq, who a few weeks earlier had castigated the Pahlavi-era women's emancipation as a "cosmetic" reform, and Hedayat Matin-Daftari, the grandson of Mohammad Mosaddeq, the founder of the newly established National Democratic Front, one of the most vociferous advocates of democratic rights during the early postrevolutionary period. Both speakers, however, struck a conciliatory tone and reiterated that the "women's question" should not distract the revolution from its "main" responsibilities. Nateq began her address with these words:

Rather than weakening the provisional government, my intention is to strengthen it. . . . Revolutionary struggle is gender blind. In recent years, many women, from the *Fadā'i* or *Mojāhed* organizations, have been jailed and endured torture. They did not fight or lose their lives because of women's issues, they struggle on behalf of the Iranian people. We have no separate demands from those of the toiling classes; at least I don't. . . . We believe that women's emancipation cannot be achieved independently from the emancipation of all toiling classes, and Imam Khomeini is a defender of the toiling classes. . . . We have heard that they say that we are counterrevolutionaries; that we are anti-*hejāb*; that we are defending the old constitution; that we incite division. We reject all these accusations. We have never denounced *hejāb* . . . . We are against coercion of any kind, Reza Khan's coercion to remove the *hejāb*, and coercion to reinstitute it.

Those who assaulted us on the street were agents of the old regime and the defenders of the Pahlavi monarchy. We hear that they say we have arisen on behalf of the old Family Protection Law. That law was one of the most reactionary laws of the Pahlavi era. Women do not need these kinds of safeguards. If we are equal we don't need a family protection law. We shall not defend this law.

They have reported that we visit the government offices "naked." I ask you who can go to these offices naked in this cold winter? Introducing the woman question in this period is a diversionary tactic. Under current circumstances, we must not have a question called the woman's issue. They said something about the *hejāb* and took it back immediately. We must not create friction over this. We must accompany the *Mojāhedin*, even at the expense of wearing a headscarf. We need to know that no one will conspire on our behalf in order to bring back the monarchical order. We protested for two days and I believe that we have achieved our goal.[45]

The other speaker, Matin-Daftari, a human rights lawyer, had earlier split from his grandfather's organization, the National Front, because he believed that its leadership had betrayed the organization's founding liberal principles. For him, and for many other activists of the earlier generation, the experience of the 1953 CIA-led coup against Mosaddeq was fresh and pertinent. Despite his reservations about the emerging changes in the judicial system, Matin-Daftari also tried to lessen the tension and steer the rally toward a quick resolution. "In my political and social lexicon," he told his strident audience, "there is no specific topic under 'women's rights.' From a social, political, and spiritual standpoint, I see no difference between men and women."

In this period, we need unity more than any other time. We need to maintain the same kind of solidarity that we had achieved during the revolution. We should not forget that our main, deceitful, and cunning enemy is vigilant. They are the same counterrevolutionaries whose presence we have seen during these past few weeks. What could the plan and strategy of the imperialists be? They intend to create domestic conflicts, conflicts between brothers and sisters, fathers and sons, and comrades against comrades.[46]

Islam Kazemieh, a leading secular figure in the Writers' Association and one of the main organizers of the famous poetry nights at the Goethe Institute in 1977, added his voice in a scathing critique of those who prioritized *hejāb* and women's issues. He dismissed the idea of the primacy of women's issues as "an intellectual exercise far from the needs and traditions of common Iranian women." Furthermore, he repeated others' denunciation of Pahlavi reforms as a phony *(qolābi)* charade *(namāyeshi)* that led to nothing but turning women into "Western dolls."[47]

In her book on the women's rights movement in Iran, Eliz Sanasarian, who witnessed and interviewed women during the same period, reported that during the months before and after the revolution, even the members and employees of the Women's Organization of Iran (WOI), the main office of women's affairs under the Shah, joined the revolutionary movement. These women did not view Khomeini, Sanasarian writes, "as contradictory and vague figure, but as a savior, a solution to the Iranian dictatorship." A WOI official confided to her that "it was a real movement and we couldn't help but to think the best of him, all the groups were trying to give him the best of credits."[48] In her encounters with educated women, Sanasarian discovered that they viewed with skepticism the rumors that Khomeini and other religious leaders were anti–women's rights. "They thought such rumors were a plot to null women's support of the revolution." She further noted that all of the female university students she interviewed "supported the revolution and Khomeini's leadership."[49] And these were not only daughters of the underprivileged who attended public universities. This was a political attitude also shared by elite Westernized women. "I still recall," Sanasarian continues, "the comments of an upper-class woman who told me, two months before the Shah's overthrow, that she would sacrifice herself at Khomeini's feet. Indeed, an outlandish comment from a woman whose wardrobe consisted of the latest European fashions!"[50]

On March 10, 1979, at the conclusion of a rally of more than fifteen thousand people at the Ministry of Justice in downtown Tehran, the provisional government issued its official new policy on *hejāb*. Its spokesperson, Amir Abbas Entezam, released a short statement that "the Prime Minister and other gentlemen in the government firmly believe in the Qur'anic verse *la ikrāha fid-Din* (there is no compulsion in religion). Thereby, the government will not issue an order for mandatory *hejāb*."[51] The provisional government's statement ended six days of women's rallies, from March 8 to March 13, which were mostly centered in Tehran. In an editorial in *Kayhān*, one of the leaders of the women's protests, Badri Taher, wrote:

> Now that all the revolutionary leaders have declared the official position of the government in regard to the Islamic *hejāb*, and even have called those who assaulted the protesting women counterrevolutionaries, the continuation of rallies is meaningless. The truth is that the ousted Pahlavi regime yearns for dividing the county into "religious" and "nonreligious," it wishes to foment a civil war . . . Loudly, and with all sincerity, we must declare that if women's rallies were justifiable and correct till yesterday, under present circumstances, they are unacceptable and wrong. To continue the rallies is tantamount to treason, yes, treason![52]

While the leaders and many of the participants of the *hejāb* rallies believed that the issue was put to rest by mid-March 1979, the revolutionary leaders continued to view the issue as an instrument of the consolidation of power. In the summer of 1980, after Ayatollah Khomeini delivered another critical sermon on the official policy of *hejāb* in the country,[53] the government announced that its offices will no longer admit women visitors and employees without the observance of proper *hejāb*. What the government considered "proper" was unspecified. What was clear then was that women were not allowed to wear short-sleeve dresses and at the least were required to cover their hair with a headscarf. It took another three years before, in the summer of 1983, the parliament finally passed legislation codifying *hejāb* and banning women from entering any public spaces without observing it.

While navigating the postrevolutionary political landscape and negotiating the demands of all those who participated in the revolutionary movement, a great majority of political parties considered the stability of the provisional government to be an important feature of the continuity of the revolution. Rather than a mere conspiratorial abstraction, all those who had invested in the revolutionary movement considered the threat of a coup or a counterrevolutionary resurgence to be a concrete historical possibility. The majority of political parties of the Left and the women organizations they had established immediately after the revolution either refused to support women's rallies or participated in them reluctantly. None put forward a platform in which women's issues were articulated independently from the general issues of social justice or anti-imperialist demands. It was that very context to which the global solidarity movement that spread in Tehran, Paris, and New York in March 1979 remained inattentive.

White Women's Burden: Kate Millett Goes to Iran

After the collapse of Pahlavi monarchy, in late February and early March of 1979 a spate of women organizations surfaced. With the exception of professional associations, such as the Association of Women Jurists, these organizations were the an extension of their respective parties and operated as their "women's branch."[54] The Women Organization of the Tudeh Party, the Iranian Women's Association (Jam'iat-e zanān-e Iran), the Revolutionary Union of Militant Women (Ettehādieh-ye enqelābi-ye zanān-e mobārez), the Association of Women's Awakening (Jam'iat-e bidāri-ye zanān), the Provisional Committee for the Celebration of the International Women's Day, the Association of Militant Women (Jam'iat-e zanān-e mobārez) were among the newly established organizations that entered the postrevolutionary political theater. None of these organizations emerged inside the country during the revolutionary struggle. Despite the fact that a great majority of these organizations' founders had just returned from the United States or Western Europe, they failed to articulate a feminist politics outside the binaries of objectified versus militant women, Western blasé dolls versus modest committed revolutionaries, the champions of embourgeoisement versus the defenders of toiling women.

Those who wished to advance a feminist politics set their sights on the first International Women's Day after the revolution, March 8, 1979. They hoped to turn the celebration into a day of solidarity between European and American activists and their Iranian "sisters." The key organizers of the Provisional Committee for the Celebration of the International Women's Day were members of the Socialist Workers' Party (SWP), a

Trotskyist group with a meager influence in the Iranian Left. Members of the SWP also had just returned from Europe and the United States where they had successfully forged relations with feminist writers and activists. They had generated these connections through another organization they established in the mid-1970s called the Committee on Artistic and Intellectual Freedom in Iran (CAIFI). CAIFI organized press conferences and actions in the defense of the Iranian Revolution and generated sympathy among American writers and other intellectuals, among them Kate Millett.

The author of *Sexual Politics*, a key text in American second-wave feminist literature, and an influential figure in women's rights activism, Millett was originally invited by the CAIFI office in New York to speak at a Women's Day rally in Tehran. "The phone rang," Millett recalls the day the CAIFI organizer conveyed to her, "Kate, your sisters in Iran need you."[55] The controversy over *hejāb* only two days before March 8, however, complicated her trip and its main objective. Suddenly, the plan to deliver a message of solidarity to the Iranian women at a rally in the

Figure 9. Kate Millett, still image from the short documentary *Mouvement de Libération des Femmes Iraniennes, Année Zero*. Directed and produced by Sylvina Boissonnas, Claudine Mulard, and Michelle Muller.

Figure 10. Kate Millett, Claudine Mulard, and Sylvina Boissonnas at a press conference in Tehran, March 11, 1979. Associated Press Photo.

university, turned into a mission to rescue the Iranian sisters from the emergent *hejāb* oppression. Millett documented her ordeal in Iran in a hastily produced book called *Going to Iran*.

In her book, far from a feminist with a clear message of solidarity, Millett appears fraught with doubts and confusion. "I was scared," she writes, "I was angry nobody was there [at the airport to greet us], after traveling all this way, all that trouble. . . . There we were, stranded, hopeless. Helpless" (55). Unlike Foucault, who claims no particular role in advancing the causes of the revolution and writes his essays as a self-described philosopher-journalist, Millett declares: "I am not in fact going to Iran as a journalist. . . . I'm going on a mission to and for my sisters in Iran—and I want that designation" (39). By and large, the American media reflected the same sentiment and offered significant coverage to her trip, which was cast as "Kate Millett in Iran to Aid Feminists."[56]

But with her first encounter with those Iranian sisters at the airport the colonial roots of her mission to Iran surfaces with almost predictable Orientalist mockery:

> The first sight of them was terrible. Like black birds, like death, like fate, like everything alien. Foreign, dangerous, unfriendly. There were

hundreds of them, specters crowding the barrier, waiting on their own. A sea of *chadori*, the long terrible veil, the full length of it, like a dress descending to the floor, ancient, powerful, annihilating us. . . . Look at them and they do not look back, even the friendly curiosity with which women regard each other. Still wearing the cloth of their majesty, they have become prisoners in it. The bitterness, the driven rage behind these figures, behind these yards of black cloth. They are closed utterly. The small, hardly visible men in their suits have absolute control here. (40–50)

It is highly unlikely that she had encountered a sea of *chadori* women at the airport. Keeping in mind that it was only four weeks after the revolution, there could have not been many women with full *chador* present at the airport. Muslim women who took part in security operations at the time were mostly young women who wore baggy pants, long-sleeved loose dresses, and headscarf. Perhaps there was a small number of *chadori* women greeting their relatives returning to the country. The fact that the women she encountered at the airport generated the kind of oppressive anxiety she expresses in the above passage only shows how ill-prepared she was for this trip. Millett saw the revolution through her unwavering white Western feminism, colored by the influence of the Iranian Trotskyists who had arranged her trip. In her mind, the armed militia of the Revolutionary Committee, which had assumed the security of the airport and the city, represented the "counterrevolutionary" forces who had *stolen* the revolution and with Khomeini's leadership were successful in exploiting the failure of the Left to "snatch away the triumph of the insurrection" (56).

Millett's account typifies the kind of dated feminism whose mission was to save "brown women," in Gayatri Spivak's words, "from brown men."[57] Western women have interpreted the local and heterogeneous practices of the veil in the societies of the Middle East and South Asia as direct, incontrovertible evidence of women's subjugation. They straightforwardly link women's liberation with unveiling.[58] Millett claims a privileged insight into the subjugated *chadori* woman's consciousness, a privilege afforded by her feminist standpoint.

I saw the women in veils afraid to talk to us—that woman I asked a question, actually just how to use the telephone. Waiting for her husband who'd gone off for a moment and was coming back. She was afraid to death of being seen with me. *Yet there's a silent kind of communication: she knew that I knew she was intimidated.* And when she left she snuck me a little glance and a smile. Like, *"forgive me, I can't manage any more than this now."* It's familiar, isn't it? From home, from women everywhere. (57, my italics)

With the familiarity Millett expresses with the *chadori* woman's plight, she situates herself as an insider, albeit without any comprehension of cultural, class, and colonial complexities that shaped the revolutionary politics in Iran and, more specifically, that fleeting moment at the airport. She speaks of a common oppression, "from home, from women everywhere," without realizing that "it was primarily bourgeois white women," as bell hooks observes, "both liberal and radical in perspective, who professed belief in the notion of common oppression."[59] Perhaps there is no merit in my scrutinizing Millett's disregard of the historicity of her position or how she disguises the true character of women's varied and complex social realities. Many feminist scholars since the mid-1970s have been exposing and exploring the problems with the essentialization of women's experiences. As Donna Haraway so aptly remarks:

> There is nothing about being "female" that naturally binds women. There is not even such a state as being "female," itself a highly complex category constructed in contested sexual scientific discourses and other social practices. Gender, race, or class consciousness is an achievement forced on us by the terrible historical experience of the contradictory social realities of patriarchy, colonialism, and capitalism.[60]

It took a few days for Millett to realize that the invitation she received to join feminist Iranians was extended to her by the CAIFI office manager in New York without careful coordination with his Iranian feminist comrades. "I feel I am running after feminism in Iran," she writes on the third day of her visit, "despite their invitation, I have yet to meet even one sister. . . . I want to stay with women, feminists, sisters. Where are they?" (68–69). After she finally meets her handler in Iran, Millett realizes that she represents a very small group of women, mostly expatriates, who are desperately trying to make their presence known to other, more established, parties inside the country. "We may get nothing and so we might be forced to tail on to a big rally of the Communist Party held tomorrow," Kateh Vafadari, the leader of the group, informs Millett.

Millett disagrees with their strategy after one day of knowing the group: "That would be terrible. . . . It wouldn't even be doing it on the right day, tomorrow's the seventh, International Women's Day is the eight. Why can't *we* celebrate our day the right time; why isn't there anything in the whole city for women?" (72).

Although critical of their strategy, Millett goes along with the plan and realizes that in order to attract a crowd they needed to invite a famous poet, "Sylvashore Khasroe [*sic*]," (presumably she means Siyavosh Kasrā'i). "He's very popular," they tell Millett, and will draw a good crowd. Even when she develops an affinity toward her feminist comrades, she adopts the patronizing language of *approval*. They are naïve, but sincere; young, but committed. Here she talks about Vafadari's skills and devotion to the cause:

> And her optimism is infectious. I find myself persuaded as well as charmed. Part of me also thinks she's daft to trust the deals she's made; I smell betrayal already, they will say yes and then say no. But how can you resist her rejoicing? Or frown on her achievement, for that matter? This has been a heroic struggle. . . . There is something about this young woman that is heroic, that commands respect. Something commanding in her, even; you know she's a leader. She carries that when she speaks to you, a certain authority she's won, worked for, suffered for during years of apprenticeship in CAIFI [in the United States]. Now here, among women, she wears her years in the other cause with modesty, but also with certain assurance; she is a foundress. Years abroad in exile, in danger and under threat of solitary confinement should she return. . . . *And now she has nearly alone, with only ten or eleven comrades, dared to establish a women's liberation movement.* (79, my italics)

Millions of Iranian women marched on the streets during the revolutionary movement. Yet in Millett's mind, their liberation now hinges on the imported, daring actions of an expatriate who is a seasoned veteran of apprenticeship in a meagerly influential political cell based in the United States. Good material for a romantic revolutionary novella with a sympathetic heroine, objectionable when used as a historical point of reference.

As Millett's narrative unfolds, increasingly *Iranian* women's role in this international day of solidarity fades. Finally the day of the rally arrives. She remembers a 1970 rally in Bryant Park on the fiftieth anniversary of women's suffrage. Thousands of people "in a good mood sitting on the grass as the dusk came over the Park." That was a "fete, a true celebration." But this one, she seethes, "is no festival, no celebration. This is an unpleasant paranoid mass, and I am a foreigner whom they would hardly enjoy in good mood, or with good feelings between nations. But translated, female, inferior to them—male, overwhelmingly make, and what women there are attached to a male as by a cord" (98). She becomes ever more cynical as the event progresses. The affinity she felt on her arrival at the airport with the *chadori* woman, whose oppression she sensed, gives way to sarcasm and a sense of unconcealed civilizational superiority.

> But the women so ruled, even as they sit and listen; next to the man, leaning to instruct now and again. How all the language of their women's bodies is deference; the very headscarf, nunlike, modern—worse than a chador, updated and without the ancient beauty. *These are women closed to us.* To see them is to feel defeated. Hard to believe that this patriarchal bullying atmosphere could even associate with revolutionary, socialist ideas. In fact, it doesn't. The "revolution," in this place, is only a word for tribal patriotism, tribal patriarchy. Revived in the fierce arrogance of the men, *the frightened docility of the women.* (99, my italics)

The more days Millett spends in Tehran the more alienated she feels from the intense postrevolutionary political landscape. Vafadari and others also begin to realize the awkwardness of the presence of Millett and other foreign feminists. She shows reservations about the wisdom of feminist delegations from France, Germany, and Scandinavia joining the rally at the Ministry of Justice. Simone de Beauvoir is to lead the delegation. "What impression," Vafadari wonders, "will it make among people here?" (152). The foreign dignitaries and Vafadari and her comrades debate whether they should grant an interview to Claude Servan-Schreiber, the editor of *Effe* ("a slick magazine, chic"). Once more Vafadari objects: "It's insufficiently political. They might just come for a story, as reporters, or as superfeminists, to colonize." Millett responds: "I argue uselessly for sisterhood. I am alone, pumping away for international feminism, an idea which has brought us all together and whose full ramifications I still hardly grasp" (153).

Finally signs of self-doubt appear more pronouncedly in Millett during the press conference in which Iranian women presented their case to the world on March 8, 1979. She enters the press conference thinking about the words of a woman who has asked her earlier that everyone must know that "the women are denied their right, that at the very moment when they had won their freedom, it is being taken from them. That American women, that women in every country in the world must hear this. Must see it on television. 'Tell all the women for us. Keep telling it.' 'I will.'" Vafadari arrives late to the press conference without her comrades. She is torn, Millett observes, between being angry and being scared. Two of her comrades were arrested outside Tehran University and others were afraid to participate. Nervously, Vafadari reads her group's statement. "We," Millett confesses, "are looking a bit stupid now; the purpose of this farce was to introduce the world press to Iranian feminists, a few international feminists being done the honor of acting as go-between— and *we can only produce one Iranian feminist*" (158–59).

Nevertheless, Millett remains unperturbed about the absurdity of the international sisterhood in solidarity with the overwhelmingly absent Iranian women. "Miss Mill*ett* [she makes sure to register the mispronunciation of her name]," an American reporter forces the issue, "given the fact that the revolution was to overthrow the Shah, it was also to repel foreign interests and influences, including American influences and interests; given the *delicate* state of affairs here—do you feel it proper for you to involve yourself in an Iranian issue?" But with the contradictions she has witnessed, the fact that her own Iranian comrades insist not to introduce her as an American, but only generically as a "foreign" dignitary, Millett seems unmoved and pays no heed to the significance of the question. "We chuckle along the table—the man himself is an American; the hypocrisy of this question is wonderful. . . . Here is the emissary of an American capitalist corporation, a major television network, rebuking me for being in Iran at the moment of its emancipation" (172).

Vafadari rises above the ruckus to defend her comrade: "Kate Mill*ett* (even she does it) [Millett's comment] came here for the eighth of March. And we were glad to have her here." But that does not satisfy the audience. To Millett's chagrin, the few Iranian women in the conference room, who have been critical of the whole event, object. "It's not a question of loving her," the Iranian woman challenges Vafadari, "how many people *know* Kate Millett?" ("Oddly enough," Millett interjects here, "she pronounced it correctly.") "How many women here know Simone de Beauvoir? We don't."[61]

During the same news conference, a veteran reporter pressed her to take a position on Ayatollah Khomeini. The next day, in their coverage of the news conference, one of Tehran's newspapers quotes Millett as calling Ayatollah Khomeini a "male chauvinist." The day after, the members of the Revolutionary Committee carried out a deportation order issued by the provisional government for Millett and her companion Sophie Keir, whose photographs later would illustrate Millett's book.

In a variety of ways, Millett's mission recalls the colonial anxiety of *différance*. She does not shy away from situating herself as a part of an "internationalist" movement that began in the nineteenth century. "It is interesting," she says in response to the question of foreign intervention in Iranian women's affairs, "how international the women's movement has always been historically; in the nineteenth century and in this century as well" (173). Alas, she derives her internationalism from the naturalization of the "not-to-be-veiled" female body, universalizing Western, white, and professional middle-class life experiences, and rendering all other forms deficient. Such a stance has authorized interventionism of Western feminism and imbued them with confidence in their position.[62] Through such interventions, not only do Western feminists reaffirm their own emancipation but, more importantly, they universalize the cultures and values that inform those experiences as the point of reference for the *universal, essentialized,* and *singular* liberated woman.[63]

This feminist interventionism, particularly in that contested moment, further reinforced the spurious choices between working-class politics, Islamism, anti-imperialism, feminism, and counterrevolutionary Westernized elitism. "This moment of cross-cultural feminism," Naghibi observes, "was overdetermined by the colonial history of the international feminist project."[64] As Millett's narrative shows, this interventionist feminist ideology further marginalized Iranian women despite their momentous role in the revolutionary movement. It forced on them a fictitious choice between enduring patriarchal nationalisms or liberal-Western feminisms. An overwhelming majority of Iranian women were absent subjects in the feminist universe in which Millett and her contacts in Iran resided. Millett's Orientalist feminism did not allow her, and other international feminist interventionists, to recognize the intricate assemblages of revolutionary politics, anticolonial sensibilities, nation-building, and religious sentiments within which women's issues were articulated.[65]

"Thanks, But No Thanks," Iranian Women's Groups Tell Foreign Feminists

During her two-week stay in Iran, Millett's polarizing presence made even those who were actively involved in demonstrations uneasy.[66] In an interview published in the *New York Times*, four women who participated in the rallies told the *Times* reporter that they did not appreciate the interference of feminists from other countries. All four women (Mrs. Mirmajlessi, a set designer, married to a physician and mother of two children; Farideh Garman, an architect who had just returned from fourteen years in Italy; Nasrin Farrokh, a musician, stage director, and opera singer; and a chemist who preferred to remain anonymous) agreed that they made their discontent known to the government about the possibility of compulsory *hejāb* and now wanted a return to calm. "I think we made too big a thing of the demonstrations," Garman said. "We made our point and received the answer we sought, but then it began to look like the women were against the Imam [Khomeini]. Now is not the time for a split here. We should keep what we have gained and strengthen it, not weaken it."[67]

They all also agreed that the issue is not the *hejāb*, "We have spent enough time talking about the *chador*," the chemist said, and everyone agreed. "If anyone tries to [take away] our rights, women will fight again." In this fight, they insisted, they do not need the interference of feminists in other countries. They singled out one name: Kate Millett. "I think she has no right to talk for Persian women," the chemist said. "We have our own tongues, our own demands. We can talk for us." The set designer Ms. Mirmajlessi echoed the same sentiment: "She and no one else who is not Iranian can say anything that we should listen to about Iranian women. She does not know us. I do not know what she is doing here."[68]

Despite reports about the dissatisfaction of Iranian women who participated in the March 8–13 rallies, most Western media depicted Millett's sojourn as a valiant act of feminist solidarity. The *Washington Post*, in its Style section, printed the story of how Millett's visit was marred by divisions among Iranian feminists who lacked proper understanding of women's rights. The *Post* reported that "American feminist Kate Millett yesterday ran into her stiffest opposition since arriving here a week ago. Paradoxically, the trouble came from the embattled Iranian women *she's here to help* in their fight for equality."[69] The article featured a photograph of the pensive Millett, with thick black-frame glasses and a distant gaze, smoking a cigarette, under a picture of *chador*-covered women in an unspecified demonstration to highlight the stark contradiction between a forward-looking feminist defender of women's rights and backward defenders of tradition.

A group of "hecklers," the article reports, contested Millett's and her Iranian sponsors' credentials during a press conference in Tehran and

Sexual Politics in Iran
Kate Millet Finds That Tehran's Feminists Are Not United

Iranian women demonstrating in Tehran; below, Kate Millet; above photo by Associated Press

By *Jonathan C. Randal*

TEHRAN—American feminist Kate Millet yesterday ran into her stiffest opposition since arriving here a week ago. Paradoxically, the trouble came from some of the embattled Iranian women she's here to help in their fight for equality.

At a news conference Millet organized to introduce her Iranian feminist friends, women hecklers contested their credentials and right to speak in the name of Iranian women.

The often confused proceedings were suffused with an underlying hostility. It appeared directed more toward Millet's thesis of international feminist solidarity than her presence here as a foreigner—and a suspect American at that—in these xenophobic post-revolutionary times.

Democratically, she asked the hecklers to join her and her friends at the speakers' table, but they declined.

Talking out problems—and the techniques of consciousness-raising—have not caught on in Iran, where many of the Western-educated women leaders are split among orthodox com-

munist, Maoist democratic and Trotskyite tendencies.

Particularly upsetting to the hecklers was Millet's insistence that Shah Mohamed Reza Pahlavi had done nothing for Iranian women—an assertion that the dissenters, although no friends of the departed monarch, felt flew in the face of reason.

But Millet drew no rejoinder in asserting that because of the threat of Islamic fundamentalism, "our rights of education, abortion, child-care, divorce, employment in the professions —all the things we have fought for since the commencement of the women's movement in 1847—are in great jeopardy in this society."

Earlier in private conversation Millet, the author of "Sexual Politics," had denounced the general atmosphere: "It is not only the women who are fed up, but vast numbers of people, about the abrogation of civil justice, the executions, the puritanism, the general joylessness, the narrow ecclesiastical and antidemocratic tone."

"Women," she asserted, "will lead the protest in Iran against all curtail-

See MILLET, B5, Col. 1

Figure 11. "Sexual Politics in Iran: Kate Millet Finds That Tehran's Feminists Are Not United," *Washington Post*, Monday March 12, 1979, p. B1.

their right to speak in the name of Iranian women. "The often confused proceedings were suffused with an underlying hostility. It appeared directed more toward Millett's thesis of international feminist solidarity than her presence here as a foreigner—and a suspect American at that—in these xenophobic postrevolutionary times." Here the reporter's conclusion is illuminating, speaking about a nation that just three weeks earlier had toppled the Pahlavi regime, he opines: "Talking out problems—and the techniques of consciousness-raising—have not caught on in Iran, where many of the Western-educated women leaders are split among orthodox communist, Maoist, democratic and Trotskyite tendencies."[70]

Despite numerous occasions that Iranian women involved in protests told Western reporters that they support Khomeini and their intention was not to instigate unrest and division in the ranks of revolutionary forces, the headlines continued to depict the rallies in Tehran along the line of "Women March against Khomeini."[71] Frustrated by foreign feminist interventions, in another interview with a *Baltimore Sun* correspondent, Nasrin Farrokh calls these visits "embarrassing and provocative." A graduate of the University of Florida in music, Farrokh reiterated that "the government has so many serious problems to sort out that to present them with fresh demands at this stage is stupid."[72] Nevertheless, the rallies were naturalized as a part of the inevitable transformative women's universal politics. "The confusion confronting Iranian women," an op-ed piece in the *New York Times* declared, "is the same confusion that confronts most of us. Refusing the veil is a first step on the long road to liberating women from being responsible for everyone else's behavior. . . . American women may feel further along this road than Iranian women, but, in the historical context, that distance is not very significant. . . . We who care obviously hope that the 'modern' women of Tehran will prevail."[73]

Many commentators, both inside and outside academe, now brushed aside the justification of *hejāb* as a signifier of protest and revolutionary politics. Now that the revolution has triumphed over tyranny, they argued, those instrumental apologies for the *hejāb* had to give way to an explicit defense of secular-modern-democratic politics. "Now that the revolution has been achieved," a respected historian of modern Iran advised "the Iranian woman" in the pages of *Newsday*, "the *chador* reverts to its earlier symbolic meaning: her subjugation."[74] The illustration that accompanied the op-ed left nothing opaque about the standpoint based on which feminists of the global sisterhood viewed the events in Iran. An oversized man in a suit, with his upper body outside the frame, pulls the leash of a woman, covered in the *chador*, who follows him submissively.

In words and images, the conflict between "modern" and "traditional" women became the centerpiece of the feminist solidarity politics in the West. A small number of professional, open-minded, secular, Western-looking, cigarette-smoking women in Iran became the vanguards of an

Figure 12. Illustration by Gary Viskupic. *Newsday*, March 29, 1979, p. 94.

emancipatory politics, which might fail without the help of their Western sisters. In ten days, from March 12 to March 21, different women's organizations organized rallies in defense of their Iranian sisters in New York, Paris (and ten other cities in France), Madrid, Barcelona, Rome, Milan, and Montreal.

On March 15, 1979, in New York, two hundred women demonstrated in what the *New York Times* dubbed "the first large-scale [!] show of solidarity with those agitating for women's rights in Iran." The report mentioned that the demonstration was held at a time "when all sides in the Iranian revolution are sensitive to suggestions of Western influence in the new Government." But that caution was qualified by Gloria Steinem's assertion that "American feminists had sought assurances from women's rights leaders in Iran that support from Americans was welcome."[75] Steinem made the assertion in the midst of her own legal battle against Random House to prevent the publication of a chapter in Redstockings' *Feminist Revolution* titled "Gloria Steinem and the CIA."[76]

On the same day, in a crowded hall in Paris, Simone de Beauvoir announced the formation of the Comité International du Droit des Femmes (CIDF). She declared that the main inspiration behind her initiative was the struggles of Iranian women and their postrevolutionary plight. She also told the audience that a delegation of feminist activists was planning to depart for Tehran in a few days. During the meeting, a group of Iranian activists objected to de Beauvoir's plan and argued that such a mission was ill-conceived and that the time for such an intervention by Western women was not right. De Beauvoir responded angrily, "I've seen many revolutions in many different countries. Whenever we talk about defending women, we are told that 'the time is not right.'"[77]

After Kate Millett's controversial visit, a number of Iranian women contacted the Comité and asked them at least not to include any Americans in their delegation. The Comité agreed and sent one German, one Egyptian, one Belgian, one Italian, and fourteen French women on a mission to Iran. The Egyptian member of the delegation was Laila Said. Although she was not a Muslim, being from Egypt could offer more legitimacy to the visit. "On March 8, 1979," she wrote a few years later in her memoir, "a demonstration against the obligatory wearing of the veil was staged in Iran, and some of the demonstrators were imprisoned or put under house arrest." Yet this memory was based on rumor, not fact.

Figure 13. Simone de Beauvoir (with Elisabeth Salvaresi) announcing the formation of Comité International du Droit des Femmes, in response to "the Iranian situation." Paris, March 1979. Photo by Martine Franck. Courtesy of Magnum Photo.

The news of the rallies in Tehran had spread through feminist networks with particular inaccuracies to make the foreign intervention imperative and indispensable. At the time, no one was arrested; no one was under house arrest. But the situation in Iran appeared to be critical. "Urgent pleas for help were sent to Western feminists," she recalls. "Simone de Beauvoir was mobilized as was Gloria Steinem, who called to see if I would join the delegation that was leaving for Tehran from Paris. I did not hesitate to say yes."[78]

Inside Iran, women who participated in the rallies continued to object to foreign feminists' instrumental appropriation of their demands. Rather than being concerned with the clergy stealing the revolution, they began to fear the might of their international "sisters." These Iranian women protestors were concerned that "their sincere efforts may be undermined by foreign women who have aggravated the conflict by joining their demonstrations and shouting anti-Khomeini slogans."[79] One of them, Minou Moshiri, drafted an open letter to Simone de Beauvoir's committee on route to Tehran for another solidarity visit. "Please stop worrying us," Moshiri wrote, "and please try to understand that women's liberation, Western-style, is irrelevant, inapplicable, unacceptable and distasteful in our country. . . . No moral support, no economic support, and above all, no delegation of hysterical females to enlighten us, if you please."[80]

Iranian women's reservations for these solidarity visits created a rift in the French delegation and changed the objective of the trip from helping their Iranian sisters to a fact-finding mission. Instead of organizing press conferences or participating in rallies, the delegation limited its work in a three-day visit to meeting with a number of women activists and journalists, the provisional prime minister, and clerical leaders of the revolution, including Ayatollah Khomeini. The majority of members of the delegation objected to the visit to Qom, where Khomeini resided at the time. They argued that wearing a headscarf to visit Khomeini would defeat the purpose of their visit. After four hours of debate, and after consulting with de Beauvoir in Paris via telephone, only four members of the group decided to make the two-hour trip to visit the undisputed leader of the revolution.[81]

Claire Brière, who reported for *Libération* during the revolutionary struggles in 1978, made all the arrangements for these high-level meetings for the CIDF delegation. In an interview with Mahnaz Matin in

2008, Brière recalls how unprepared and ignorant of the situation in Iran the members of the committee were.

> I thought they were a group of journalists who were interested in reporting the news from Iran. But they intended to do some kind of political work, which did not leave a good mark. Even Kate Millett's work was not good. Iranian feminists were worried about her presence. Because of being an American, she should not have gone to Iran. She should have thought about what she could really do for Iranian feminists; not just go there and give lectures! The French delegation also had the same problem. They were egotistical Parisians who went there just to say *here we are*. A number of them belonged to affluent and even aristocratic classes. They had no idea what was going on in Iran, how the poor and the religious lived in Iran. Their predicament was not Iran! They did not care about the social environment there.[82]

Brière describes how puzzled she was when members of the committee argued that they were not willing to meet with Khomeini if they were required to observe the *hejāb*.

> They said, "Why should we comply with this? Iranian women are struggling against the *hejāb*, why should we observe it?" Some were saying that we will go to see Khomeini with the *hejāb*, but will take it off in front of him! The German reporter, Alice Schwartzer, said: "We will take off our pants!" I asked them: "Do you take your panties off when you meet other dictators? Why do you want to do this in front of Khomeini? Not only is this kind of act disrespectful, it is also blasphemous. They would kill you." They said that they would call and ask Simone de Beauvoir. Right in front of my eyes, they called Paris and talked to her. And she agreed with that plan. Can you believe that? I told them that such a behavior would harm Iranian women, because they will say that this is what women demonstrating on the streets are asking for, the same thing that these European women do: to take their panties off! They could not understand this issue. They did not know that in a religious town like Qom, the issue was not only the Ayatollah, the concern comes from the entire population.[83]

By the time the French delegation arrived in Tehran, women's demonstrations had already been dissipated. The provisional government reassured women that there was no plan to institute a regime of compulsory *hejāb*, at least not in the near future.[84] No one intended to jeopardize the increasingly tenuous unity of the revolutionary movement, neither those ayatollahs who saw an opening to advance their patriarchal and at times misogynistic readings of the *shariʿa* law nor those who feared that the new gender restrictions might only be the beginning of a total consolidation of power by the clergy.

Western media reported women's retreat with chagrin and amusement. Two months later, the *Chicago Tribune* reported: "The demonstrations stopped. Not so much as a whisper came from the feminist camp. 'And what of the women?' a friend writes me from New York. 'From here, they seem to have disappeared completely.'" Now that the excitement of rallies was over, the French and American feminists were back home writing books about their Iranian ordeal, the Iranians had to see with sober eyes their social and political role in the postrevolutionary Iran. They rightfully "feared that counterrevolutionaries would exploit the women's issue. Having made their point, they fell into quiet discussions. . . . There is no single person who speaks for the women of Iran, nor is there a formal group one can learn upon to check the movement's direction. *'Movement' might even be stretching a happening.*"[85]

For the first time, outside the milieu of the opera singer, the set designer, and the chemist, Goli Dahri also appears in the pages of the *Tribune*. An illiterate woman, "as are about three-quarters of the 17 million women in Iran," who lives on the southern edges of the city in a rented room with her family of eight. She makes daily trips to a nearby street gutter to wash dishes and the apparel of her family, carrying her infant in a sling across her bosom. "She wears the *chador*, but not when she is washing. It would get in the way. When she is washing, she wears a scarf. She could not care less about the heavily publicized struggle for women's rights in this country, and in that regard, she is in an overwhelming majority. Her highest hopes are for more food, more income, and more than a single room in which to live out her life. These are the common goals of that majority."[86]

By contrast, Susan Kamalieh, who studied the arts in Michigan and at New York University, sees the reason for the plight of women in Iran in Iranian men's sexuality. "The real truth is that Iranian men haven't had enough women," Kamalieh remarked. "The tradition, the customs, lead to a high level of sexual frustration." After maneuvering on a downhill slope of the Alborz Mountains on the outskirts of northern Tehran, ahead of two male skiing companions, she informs the interviewer that she has "made up her mind to quit her job at the cultural center in the city and to move with her Iranian boyfriend to Paris, where they will live together. She may be gone for two months; she may be gone for good."[87] Kamalieh and other women whose ways of life had turned them into strangers in their own land faced an existential predicament.

The Right to Speak, the Right to Represent

In his essays on the Iranian Revolution, Foucault intended to introduce the possibility of thinking outside the universal referent on questions of governmentality and power. This is not to suggest that he was inattentive to the questions of rights. Quite the opposite, he was more concerned with how issues of rights and authority could be articulated from a standpoint particular to the Islamic-Shi'i-Iranian experience. Unlike Kate Millett and other feminist internationalists who disregarded in toto the particularities and contingencies of the Iranian experience, Foucault believed it was crucial to highlight the weight of the Iranian actors and, correspondingly, to downplay the importance of what *Westerners* regarded as the "proper" objectives for Iranian aspirations. He began his open letter (April 14, 1979) to the provisional prime minister, Mehdi Bazargan, in objection to the postrevolutionary summary trial with these words: "Today, many Iranians are angry that they are being given such noisy lectures. As to their rights, they showed that they knew how to make them prevail, they alone."[88] He ends the letter by reminding Bazargan that he does not address him as a Frenchman who possesses the right of criticism bequeathed to him by the project of the Enlightenment. "Mr. Prime Minister," he wrote in utter contrast to de Beauvoir, Millett, and other feminist interventionists' patronizing language, "I do not have any authority to address myself in such a manner to you, except the permission that you gave me, by helping me understand, at our first meeting, that for you, governing is not a coveted right, but an extremely difficult obligation. You have to do what is necessary in order that the people will never regret the uncompromising force with which it has just liberated itself."[89]

We hear muted voices from Iran in the chorus of international condemnation of the treatment of women in Iran. While the main actors of the March protests emphasized the nuances and cultural complexities of gender politics, major newspapers in Europe and the United States and feminist publications, such as *Des femmes en mouvement, Ms. Magazine, Choisir, F Magazine, Histoires d'elles,* and others, continued to represent the rallies as women's struggle "to control their own lives," as a pamphlet published in *Libération* (March 14, 1979) claimed, "and against an Islamic normalization."

In Paris, on March 21, 1979, Gisèle Halimi, the editor of the popular feminist magazine *Choisir,* announces the rise of a new "feminist internationalism" that has grown from the solidarity with Iranian women. A month later, *Histoires d'elles* declares: *In Iran, the Chador Goes On, in Paris It Burns.*[90] In Tehran even the Trotskyist associates of Kate Millett, women and men who had recently returned from exile and, in their own words, were few in number and limited in influence, tried to distance themselves from foreign interventions and the kind of feminism that the internationalists advocated. In Iran we see an evolving tale of navigating across the plains of revolution, nationalism, anti-imperialism, women's rights, and class politics. Whereas in Paris, in total disregard and frank ignorance of this cautious negotiation of gender politics, feminist interventionists rallied to burn the veil as an act of liberating women's shared essentialized body that somehow could be extricated from the contingencies of history, culture, and politics. In order for this interventionist approach to legitimize itself, its proponents constituted an individual female subject outside history, one who is not only an autonomous individual but, as Spivak once observed, also individual*ist.*[91]

The dominant feminism of the Second Wave during the 1970s situated the female body as the universal referent for women's emancipatory politics. If women's actions or beliefs appeared to be inconsistent with this normative construct, they were construed either as emanations of false consciousness or coerced words and deeds that subverted their true interests. In all the numerous reports about the March 1979 protests in Iran, the same selected few (the opera singer, the set designer, the chemist, the architect) appeared, whether in the *Irish Times* or the *New York Times,* the *Guardian* or the *Washington Post,* representing the voices of Iranian women. But one could not hear even those voices in feminist proclamations of solidarity with Iranian women. Something novel was happening in Iran, something to which Foucault called attention and feminist internationalists utterly dismissed: *women sought to legitimize their gender politics with references to nonpatriarchal interpretations of Islam.* They situated their demands in a culturally specific and historically contingent frame.

Unlike their feminist sisters from the West, they tried to look at the question of *chador* not merely as a signifier of oppression but more from a sociological and historical standpoint. Nasrin Farrokh, the opera singer, insisted that women's rights could and should be derived from the teachings of Islam. "Under Islam, women are economically independent. If a woman gets married, she can keep her own wealth . . . she can keep her own name. She does not have to breast-feed her babies if she does not want. It's time for these things to come out." Mirmajlessi, the set designer, followed up, "The Koran gives us freedom, but we were never told this."[92] They all disputed the past understandings of Islam and its prescribed views on women and believed that the revolution had called for a new reading of religion. The unnamed woman, the chemist, reiterated that "during the time of Mohammad, there was no *chador.* In many of our villages today no one wears the *chador.* The women work with men. The *chador* is an urban thing about 100 years old. Poor women put it on when they came into the city to conceal the rags they were wearing. Somehow it became a fanatic thing with religious leaders." "The *chador*," Farrokh said, adding more class analysis to the chemist's historical view, "became a part of life for poor women."[93]

"Feminist Premonitions" and Women's Status under the Islamic Republic

In practice, during the past three decades since the revolution, gender politics and policy under the Islamic Republic have been far from the mere enactment of literal readings of the Qur'anic verses or a replication of the repression of women in Saudi Arabia on which those "feminist premonitions" had originally relied. There is no doubt that for the consolidation of power, the postrevolutionary regime instituted formal and legal apparatuses in order to constitute a *Homo Islamicus.* But at no point in its history was there a consensus among the ruling elite on what determines the Islamicity of their subjects, particularly in regard to gender relations. Issues of women's education, employment, access to abortion, inheritance, public participation in the arts, sports, and many other activities in civil society foment heated discussions in the legislative and executive branches of the government.[94] More importantly, these policy and legislative issues encouraged serious hermeneutical engagement with Islamic theology, prophetic tradition, and Iranian Shi'ism.[95] And they opened up debate about the content and meanings of Islam to the people through the electoral politics of the new republic. In its realpolitik, the Islamic Republic negated the essentialist "premonitions" that it would implement a literal reading of the Qur'an and expunge women from the public and restrict them to the domestic sphere.

Second Wave feminists have always argued that education and employment are the two most important material conditions for women's "autonomy and liberation."[96] But the interdependent and meritorious principles of autonomy and liberty as the indicator of women's status in any particular society must be understood within the historical trajectories and cultural contingencies in which the very notions of womanhood, autonomy, domesticity, and public sphere are meaningfully construed. Despite the fact that feminist theory locates the differences between men and women in a social context, and not in biological distinctions, by and large it remains essentialist and monocausal. Second Wave feminist theory was primarily based on a common distinction between public and private spheres. Ignoring the cultural and historical conjunctions that give rise to the meaning and significance of domesticity, it advanced a general theory of patriarchy in which it linked women's oppression directly to their activities in the domestic sphere. "In effect," as Nancy Fraser and Linda Nicholson aptly observe,

> the theory falsely generalized to all societies an historically specific conjunction of properties: women's responsibility for early childrearing, women's tendency to spend more time in the geographical space of the home, women's lesser participation in the affairs of the community, a cultural ascription of triviality to domestic work, and a cultural ascription of inferiority to women. The theory thus failed to appreciate that, while each individual property may be true of many societies, the conjunction is not true of most.[97]

Not only did this universalist approach fail to appreciate the historical conjunction and specific revolutionary moment that shaped gender politics in 1979 Iran, it continues to disregard major changes (and women's political role in propelling those changes) that have occurred since the time of the revolution in the status of Iranian women in relation to education, health, employment, artistic and cultural production, and civic engagement. These changes were not the result of top-down state policies but rather the consequence of a contentious engagement between different factions within the polity, the women's community and civic institutions, and political parties and activists.

During the first two decades of the Islamic Republic, despite a devastating eight-year war with Iraq, which claimed half a million lives on both sides, the literacy rate among women rose from 35 percent in 1976 to 74 percent in 1996. By the year 2006 only 4 percent of young women remained illiterate. Women made up 60 percent of the incoming class of university students for the school year 2006–7, and that trend continues. The conservatives of the Eighth Parliament introduced legislation for affirmative action for men to catch up with women in higher education. As part of the new legislation, which was partly ratified, women who use resources of free public universities had to commit to a ten-year employment (public or private) after graduation.

Between the years of 1986 and 1996, women's employment also rose sharply. The percentage of female employment as a portion of the total female population rose 6 percent from 19.8 to 26 percent and another 7 percent by the end of the next decade.[98] Women's health and prenatal care has seen the most dramatic change. Women's life expectancy rose from 57.60 on the eve of the revolution to 72.12 by 1999. Infant mortality decreased more than fourfold in 15 years from 109 per 1000 to 25.[99] An aggressive family planning and population control program was also instituted in 1989. The program successfully reduced the population growth rate from the high of 3.4 percent in 1986 to 0.7 percent in 2007. During the same period, the fertility number per family dropped from 6.5 to less than 2. Although the Islamic Republic repealed the family planning and protection laws of the old regime soon after assuming power, in a significant shift, in 1988, the government introduced and carried out one of the most efficient family planning programs in the economically developing world. Before his death in 1989, Ayatollah Khomeini endorsed the new program, thus affording religious legitimacy to this ideological revision. As Homa Hoodfar argues, without national consensus-building, a massive mobilization of women (both by government agencies as well as nongovernmental agents), effective religious justification, an efficient delivery service in birth control and contraceptives (such as distribution of free condoms), and premarital sex-education programs, this ambitious family planning project could not have been realized.[100]

The purpose of this sketchy report is *not* to draw a sanguine picture of women's conditions in contemporary Iran. The complexities of how governmental and nongovernmental actors interact on these issues, how the expansion and containment of state power shape the social realities of women of different classes and ethnicities, or how religious doctrines and convictions hinder or facilitate women's mobility cannot be fully appreciated here. Nor is it to deny the claims of those Iranian women today who experience the *hejāb* as repressive and find the dominant Islamic regulations an obstacle to their mobility. My overriding purpose here is to show that it was through an engagement with, rather than an abandonment of, religious text and lived traditions that a vibrant gender politics emerged in postrevolutionary Iran. I mention these changes in women's status in Iran to illustrate how historical, political, and cultural contingencies (the interaction between different political actors of the postrevolutionary period), and not a transhistorical Islam *inherently* hostile to civil liberties and women's rights, determined the outcome of the revolution.

What happened in postrevolutionary Iran was not far from what a high-ranking cleric told Foucault in one of his visits in October 1978. "A religious authority," Foucault wrote, "explained to me that it would require long work by civil and religious actors, scholars, and believers in order to shed light on all the problems to which the Qur'an never claimed to give a precise response. . . . In pursuit of this ideal, the distrust of legalism seemed to me to be essential, along with a faith in the creativity of Islam."[101] Foucault recognized this moment of historical rupture that opened up possibilities of new forms of social and historical engagement. He also realized that the dignity of revolutionary actors and the formation of historical subjects, in contradistinction to subjects of history, could only materialize by retreating from the Enlightenment's universal referent. In the next chapter, I will demonstrate how Foucault rereads Enlightenment and a subject-centered history through what the Iranian Revolution taught him.

5

WAS IST AUFKLÄRUNG?
The Iranian Revolution as a Moment
of Enlightenment

Enlightenment is man's release from his self-incurred tutelage.
—Immanuel Kant

Argue as much as you will, and about what you will, only obey.
—Frederick II

The movement through which a lone man, a group, a minority,
or an entire people say, "I will no longer obey," and are willing
to risk their lives in the face of a power that they believe to be
unjust, seems to me to be irreducible.
—Michel Foucault

FOUCAULT REVISITED THE QUESTION of enlightenment *not* because of a late conversion to humanism but because his experience of the Iranian Revolution offered him a novel context to rethink it. Rather than a sign of remorse from his defense of the revolution, Foucault read the Iranian Revolution *back into* Kant's *Was ist Aufklärung?*

In his letter to the provisional prime minister, Mehdi Bazargan, Foucault made it clear that he was under no illusion that the postrevolutionary state would be the agent for the realization of the spirituality of the revolutionary uprising. Whereas the opposition was scandalized by the very notion of an *Islamic* Republic and tried to draw an indubitable link between the Islamic nature of the new regime and the atrocities committed by the supporters of Ayatollah Khomeini in the course of consolidating their power after the revolution, Foucault distinguished himself by confessing to Bazargan: "Concerning the expression 'Islamic government,' why cast immediate suspicion on the adjective 'Islamic'? The word 'government' suffices, in itself, to awaken vigilance. No adjective—whether democratic, socialist, liberal, or people's—frees it from its obligations."[1]

But Foucault's haphazard and rather aimless critique of the newly born regime did little to satisfy his querulous detractors who continue to call upon him to acknowledge his errors. They turned a misunderstood and misappropriated rendition of the spirituality he found in the revolutionary movement into an indictment of his radical philosophy. "No," penitent former Maoists Claudie and Jacques Broyelle wrote in March 24, 1979,

> the philosopher is not responsible for the blood that flows today in Iran. It is not he who invented Islam and the ayatollahs." It is not he, sitting cross-legged in Qom . . . like Mao, not long ago, [who issues] "supreme directives." The philosopher contents himself with painting and offering images, holy images: the abridged illustrated imam, sequel to the hurried marabout of people's justice. . . . The philosophers of "people's justice" should say today, "Long live the Islamic government!" and it would be clear that they are going to the final extreme of their radicalism. Or they should say, "No, I did not want that, I was mistaken. Here is what was wrong with my reasoning; here is where my thinking is in error." They should reflect. After all, that is their job.[2]

Fresh from their own recantation and disillusionment with Maoism, the Broyelles showed the same carelessness and historical negligence in their interrogation of Foucault as they demonstrated in their condemnation of Maoist China. In *Deuxième rétour de Chine*,[3] originally published in 1977, they detail how their life experiences in China from 1972 to 1975 spoiled their earlier enthusiasm for the Chinese Revolution. The Broyelles and their coauthor Evelyne Tschirhart taught French in Beijing and helped the Chinese official publishing house in editing French texts. Their passion began to fade as they tried to navigate the impenetrable, meandering bureaucratic halls in which their hosts expected them to operate. In *China: A Second Look*, one learns in a succession of anecdotes about the cultural incompatibilities of three French intellectuals frustrated by the restrictions imposed upon their movement by the government. They also write with a sarcastic wit about the Chinese idiosyncratic understanding of Marxism and their peculiar revolutionary ideas, albeit without knowing Chinese or through a meaningful engagement with Chinese history. As one reviewer suggested, "Broyelle, Broyelle, and Tschirhart are perhaps most profoundly upset by the failure of the Chinese to implement the authors' own European notion of what a proper revolution should be."[4]

The general tone of Foucault's critics reflected the same kind of unease among French intellectuals who remained indifferent about the cultural particularities and historical contingencies of the Iranian revolution. The editors of *Le Matin* invited Foucault to respond to the mounting critique of his writings on the Iranian revolution. In a short piece, he declined their invitation. "I am 'summoned to acknowledge my errors.' This expression and the practice it designates remind me of something and of many things, against which I have fought. I will not lend myself, even 'through the press,' to a maneuver whose form and content I detest. 'You are going to confess, or you will shout long live the assassins.' Some utter this sentence by profession, others by taste or habit." Similar to his response to Atoussa H., he reminded his critics that "Blanchot teaches that criticism begins with attention, good demeanor, and generosity."[5]

Foucault's critics castigated him for thinking about the possibility of a transformative politics and mode of living in and relating to the *present* outside of Enlightenment teleological schemes. They misconstrued his notion of political spirituality to be an endorsement of theocracy. Similarly, they regarded his refusal to condemn the Islamic Revolution to be an expression of his ambivalence toward the formal and institutional recognition of rights.

Yet Foucault saw in revolutionary Iran an instance of what he perceived to be the essence of Kant's definition of enlightenment: "Man's release from his self-incurred tutelage."[6] Through their revolt, Iranians put forward an example of what he considered to be a true critique—namely, "the art of voluntary insubordination, that of reflected intractability."[7] Moreover, the revolution he had witnessed, and tried to understand, had a transformative effect and shaped his rereading of the project of Enlightenment in his later work.

The hostility and sarcasm of Foucault's critics compelled the philosopher to abandon any direct engagement with the topic after his last piece, "Is It Useless to Revolt?" appeared on May 11, 1979, in *Le Monde*. In it, he characterized the French intelligentsia as being trapped in a form of enlightenment that enclosed them in a tribunal of Reason, of "setting rational limits on what we can legitimately know."[8] In later years, on a number of occasions, he evoked his displeasure with the way he was derided and decided to close the book on the Iranian Revolution. A year later, in April 1980, *Le Monde* asked him to participate in a series of interviews with philosophers on the condition of intellectuals in France. He accepted the invitation with the proviso that he remain anonymous. With a mask of anonymity, he returned to his grievance against the French intellectuals, castigating them for turning the practice of critical engagement into a vogue of condemnation, judgment of guilt, and attempts to silence and ultimately to destroy the object of criticism.[9]

"I can't help," the masked philosopher lamented, "but dream about a kind of criticism that would try not to judge but to bring an oeuvre, a sentence, an idea to life." He criticized the ambivalence of those intellectuals who failed to imagine the consequences of their destructive criticism in "reality." "When they 'criticize' someone," he pleaded, "when they 'denounce' his ideas, when they 'condemn' what he writes, I imagine them in the ideal situation in which they would have complete power over him. I take the words they use—*demolish, destroy, reduce to silence, bury*—and see what the effect would be if they were taken literally."[10] In a romantic tone, more reminiscent of Whitman than Foucault, he yearned for a critical discourse that

> would light fires, watch the grass grow, listen to the wind, and catch the sea foam in the breeze and scatter it. It would multiply not judgments but signs of existence. . . . Criticism that hands down sentences sends me to sleep; I'd like a criticism of scintillating leaps of the imagination. It would not be sovereign or dressed in red. It would bear the lightning of possible storms.[11]

Earlier, in another essay first published in *Le Nouvel Observateur* on April 23, 1979, ten days after he wrote the open letter to Prime Minister Bazargan, Foucault underlined his discontent with the arrogance of "wanting to impose one's law on others." Speaking without reference to the way he was chastised by the critics, he noted, "God knows, police patrols of ideology are not lacking; one hears their whistle: right, left, here, move on, right away, not now. . . . The pressure of identity and the injunction to break things up are both similarly abusive."[12]

Foucault's unwillingness to revisit his essays on the Iranian Revolution by no means signals an implicit renunciation of his earlier critique of Enlightenment rationality. Rather, I argue that neither did the Iranian revolutionary movement negate his earlier conceptions of the subject nor did the postrevolutionary atrocities force him to reconsider the consequences of his radical antihumanism or retreat to the bosom of the liberal or existential fold.[13]

In his later writings, Foucault shifted the historical context of his theory of the subject from the post-Enlightenment to antiquity. His lectures on *The Hermeneutics of the Subject* at the Collège de France (1981–82), his extensive writing and lectures on the "care of the self" and ethics, and more broadly on what he called "the critical ontology of ourselves," show a distinct emphasis on the historical significance of the subject, which, I propose, *is* a reflection of the Iranian Revolution in his later writings.

How to Reconcile the Early and Late Foucault

Many scholars regard Foucault's earlier work through the lens of his haunting evocation on the vanishing of mankind's historical authorship in the final passage of *The Order of Things*: "Like a face drawn in sand at the edge of the sea."[14] A commonplace reading of Foucault, particularly among feminist theorists, found his theory of invasive disciplinary power and networks with constitutive authority over the subject to be impermeable to the possibility of resistance. Although he stressed that power also produces resistance, that haphazard nod never satisfied his most ardent critics.[15] For them, as Alain Badiou writes,

> [Foucault's] problem then became that of accounting for the source of such resistance. If the subject—right down to its most intimate desires, actions, and thoughts—is constituted by power, then how can it be a source of independent resistance? For such a point of agency to exist, Foucault needs some space that has not been completely constituted by power or a complex doctrine on the relationship between resistance and independence.[16]

The Cambridge Companion to Foucault, published in 1994,[17] was largely conceived on the premise that Foucault's thinking swerved markedly in the late 1970s and early 1980s. Roy Boyne locates this shift between the first and second volumes of *The History of Sexuality*. Whereas in his earlier writings, "genealogies of power/knowledge seem to exclude all notion of truth, enlightenment, self-understanding or effective political strategy," in his later work, this doctrine "gives way to a sense of renewed ethical and social engagement. . . . There is the suggestion of a certain Utopian residue."[18] Many feminist theorists also questioned Foucault's concern in his later writings with subjectivity as puzzling and even embarrassing. His new position appeared on the surface, as Jana Sawicki opined, to "fly in the face of his earlier proclamation of the death of man and his anti-authoritarian predilections for anonymous authorship." Sawicki then raises the question: "Had Foucault, the notorious post-humanist, recanted?"[19]

There is no doubt that Foucault was (and I will argue later, remained) critical of Kantian Enlightenment and the humanist tradition it inspired. In his view, humanist rationality presupposed an autonomous (or authentic, in the case of Sartre) subject with inherent abilities and natural impulses for emancipation from the domination of others. How could a subject *constituted* by normative rational disciplinary technologies suddenly instigate resistance *constituting* new subjectivities and seeking the transformation of his or her own existence and the world he or she lives in? Foucault's docile bodies that are generated through a microphysics of power, it has been generally believed, are incapable of and impervious to emancipatory politics.

Foucault's impassioned support of the Iranian Revolution did little to cast skepticism on such an interpretation of his genealogical method as subject-less history. His detractors continue to emphasize the nihilism they perceive to be at the center of his critical stand against normative universalism, transcendental Reason, and the autonomous individual as the source and the point of reference for all oppositional politics.

It is precisely here that Foucault's writings on the Iranian Revolution offer a possible clue that can help resolve the irreconcilability of the "Man in revolt" with the docile subject of disciplinary power. In a number of interviews in the 1980s, he tried to correct this misconception of his earlier works by explaining: "I am far from being a theoretician of power,"[20] and "Thus, it is not power, but the subject, that is the general theme of my research."[21]

What his critics failed to detect in Foucault's genealogical scheme was not the very possibility of politics but a *political project with a normative and universal Referent.* He understood modern disciplinary power as being ubiquitous but not inescapable, so long as the exit routes were envisaged on the outer boundaries of the possibilities in the present. In other words, the subject could not emancipate herself by deriving the principles of her politics from the same rationality that has constituted the conditions of her subjugation. This position does not *necessarily* lead to political defeatism or philosophical nihilism. Did Foucault "raise a question whether or not there is such a thing as a way out?" Charles Taylor answers his own question, "Foucault's analyses seem to bring evils to light; and yet he wants to distance himself from the suggestion that would seem inescapably to follow, that the negation or overcoming of these evils promotes a good."[22] Although Taylor analyzes Foucault from a more sympathetic position, he voices a general consensus that a critical standpoint is not credible unless it relies on what Habermas calls a "normative yardstick."[23] A whole host of critics follow the same logic: namely, that without the introduction of normative notions of right and wrong, as Nancy Fraser argues, one *cannot* oppose "the modern power/ knowledge regime."[24] Nancy Hartsock expands on this idea and further situates Foucault as part of a repressive patriarchal system, which writes from a position of male domination and, with his theory of ascending power, condemns women and other modern subjects to perpetual oppression. Despite his objection to the project of Enlightenment, Foucault remains, Hartsock stresses, within its boundaries because he fails to put "anything in its place."[25]

The novelty of Foucault's critique of the Enlightenment and universal Reason coincides with the same point that his critics identify as his failure. He did not imagine the exit from modern disciplinary power as being a strategy of escaping from the prison house of one epistemic regime (i.e., the Enlightenment) into the haven of another. He found in the ambiguity he encountered in the Iranian Revolution—its nonprogrammatic discourse of negation, and the unfamiliar concept of an Islamic government—a historical illustration of his genealogical project. "The revolution," he wrote in February 13, 1979, two days after the collapse of monarchy, "showed, at certain moments, some of its familiar traits, but things are still astonishingly ambiguous. . . . Maybe its historic significance will be found, not in its conformity to a recognized 'revolutionary' model, but instead in its *potential* to overturn the existing political situation in the Middle East. . . . Its singularity, which has up to now constituted its force, consequently threatens to give it the power to expand."[26] In Iran he found a revolutionary movement that instantiated the critical attitude he associated with enlightenment, an attitude with a *singular* universality and a distinctive relation to "the present," *l'actuel.*

Whereas his critics mistakenly read him as a universal thinker, whether that meant being a nihilist or an irrationalist, Foucault situates *himself* as a "specific" intellectual who does not speak in the voice of Reason, Justice, Progress, Objectivity, or any other discourse rooted in the prophetic traditions of the Good Society.[27] Thus the singularity and ambiguity he associates with the Iranian Revolution represents an important feature of his critical genealogy. In a 1977 interview, more than a year prior to his Iranian Revolution writings, he remarks:

> I dream of the intellectual who destroys evidence and generalities, the one who, in the inertias and constraints of the present time, locates and marks the weak points, the openings, the lines of force, who is incessantly on the move, who doesn't know exactly where he is heading nor what he will think tomorrow for he is too attentive to the present; who, whenever he moves, contributes to posing the question of knowing whether the revolution is worth the trouble, and what kind (I mean, what revolution and what trouble), it being understood that the question can be answered only by those who are willing to risk their lives to bring it about.[28]

Foucault did not know that soon after he would be writing the same lines not as an abstract concept but with reference to a particular historical actuality, some of whose constitutive events he was able to observe first-hand. "The collective will is a political myth. . . . It's a theoretical tool. . . . I thought that the collective will was like God, like the soul, something one would never encounter. I don't know whether you agree with me, but we met in Tehran and throughout Iran, the collective will of a people."[29] And later, in May 1979, after witnessing the radical transformative acts of ordinary Iranians, he writes wonderingly, "The man in revolt is ultimately inexplicable. There must be an uprooting that interrupts the unfolding of history, and its long series of reasons why, for a man 'really' to prefer the risk of death over the certainty of having to obey."[30]

Foucault's genealogical analysis has led his critics to read his work as a "subject-less" history—thus inconsistent with his passionate defense of the revolutionary movement in Iran. However, in his genealogy, he was skeptical of the notion of the subject per se, the reference to which "is either transcendental in relation to the field of events or runs in its empty sameness throughout history."[31] His historiography is inimical to the conception of a subject that is situated in a progressive historical teleology. Rather, he links his genealogical studies to a modality of social critique that he describes as a "critical ontology of the present" that at the same time considers "the historical analysis of the limits that are imposed on us and an experiment with the possibility of going beyond them."[32]

For Foucault, a critical ontology of the present introduces a new manner of posing the question of modernity, a manner that he saw as consistent with the philosophical attitude but not the doctrinal reification of Enlightenment. This question is raised no longer in a "longitudinal relationship to the Ancients but in what could be called *sagittal* relationship with its own present."[33] Here Foucault uses the medical term "sagittal," literally meaning arrowhead, as a spatial image to emphasize the self-referential character of post-Enlightenment history and the Kantian impulse to recognize the problems of our time with reference to the time and place of its first appearance. As Deleuze and Guattari point out:

> It is not that the actual is the utopian prefiguration of a future that is still part of our history. Rather, it is the now of our becoming. When Foucault admires Kant for posing the problem of philosophy in relation not to the eternal but to the Now, he means that the object of philosophy is not to contemplate the eternal or reflect history but to diagnose our actual becomings: a becoming-revolutionary that, according to Kant himself, is not the same as the past, present, or future revolutions.[34]

But in order for one to think about the question of becoming, one needs to pose another critical question about our own actuality: that is, the way we engage and experience our life circumstances. This is not an issue of analyzing the truth, rather one of what we could call "an ontology of ourselves."[35] By no means do the relationship to and the primacy of the present indicate Foucault's inclination toward what his critics often construe as a radical relativism of *anything goes*. Through this ontology, he tries to recognize and promote a spiritual and ethical self who is willing to pay the price of a transformative engagement with his or her actuality. "For Foucault," Paul Rabinow observes, "in order to establish the right relationship to the present—to things, to others, to oneself—one must stay close to events, experience them, be willing to be effected and affected by them."[36.]

Foucault's engagement with the Iranian Revolution offered an important historical link between his earlier critical genealogy and his later philosophy of the present, ethical self, and the hermeneutics of the subject. The following is the way he captures this constellation of ideas:

> One sees that for the philosopher to ask the question of how he belongs to this present is to no longer ask the question of how he belongs to a doctrine or a tradition. It will also no longer simply be a question of his belonging to a larger human community in general, but rather it will be a question of his belonging to a certain *us*, to an *us* that relates to a characteristic cultural ensemble of his own actuality.[37]

Belated Liberal or the Unrepentant Philosopher of the Present?

Was Foucault's essay "What Is Enlightenment?," published before his death in 1984, a masked conversion to liberalism? Did the atrocities committed by the Islamic Republic during its reign of terror (1981–83) force him to curb his eagerness to experiment with transcending the "historical limits imposed upon us"? Should we read "What Is Enlightenment?" as his long awaited admission that he erred in his search for spirituality in politics?

According to Afary and Anderson, the answer to these questions is an unqualified yes. They interpret the essay to be an indirect apology for his mistaken enthusiasm. They base their reading on the following passage, in which he suggests that

> the historical ontology of ourselves must turn away from all projects that claim to be global or radical. In fact *we know from experience* that the claim to escape from the system of contemporary reality so as to produce the overall programs of another society, or another way of thinking, *another culture*, another vision of the world, has led only to the *return of the most dangerous traditionalism.*[38]

By italicizing "experience," "another culture," and "dangerous traditionalism," Afary and Anderson conclude that "it is likely" that Foucault was referring to his own earlier writings on the Iranian Revolution. Not only do they misread him, but more importantly, in order to prove their point, they also alter the original English translation and change the word "tradition" at the end of the citation to "traditional*ism*." A term often associated with religious movements. Not a single translation of his essay uses the term "traditionalism" here. Even the translation they have cited from Paul Rabinow's collection uses the word "tradition" and not "traditionalism." It is evident in the text that the totalitarian traditions of which he speaks are references to fascism and Stalinism, and not, as Afary and Anderson would have it, the Iranian Revolution.

In contrast to Afary and Anderson, I argue that not only did Foucault refrain from reversing his position on the Iranian Revolution, he expanded his *reportage* into a more coherent philosophy of enlightenment, ethics, and spirituality.

Foucault's commentary on Kant's *Was ist Aufklärung?* was not the first and only time that he *directly* addressed the question of enlightenment. Collected in a single volume under the title *The Politics of Truth*, the first published instance of this series of essays appeared in early 1978 and the last is a modified version of the same text published in 1984.[39] If there is a single common theme in all of his writings on the enlightenment, it must be the distinction he makes between "enlightenment as a critical attitude in the present and the Enlightenment (or even *Les Lumières*) as a philosophical-period concept characteristic of modernity as a fixed mature sociological state."[40] He saw the Iranian Revolution in light of the first form of enlightenment, *a critical attitude in the present*, and as a possible exit from the congealed and doctrinal rationality it came to represent in the nineteenth and twentieth centuries.

In Foucault's reading of Kant, a critical attitude, which is made possible by "man's release from his self-incurred tutelage," gives rise to an autonomous subject. But this autonomy affords the subject neither independence from the conditions of its constitution nor a possibility for moral and historical transcendence. For Foucault, the subject is autonomous, as Anita Seppä argues, "in the sense that it is capable of critique, but this critique has no purely transcendental or ahistorical value because it is always historically situated and contextual."[41]

Commenting on Jean Daniel's *L'Ere des rupture*, Foucault observes that the skepticism toward grand historical schemes is no longer a philosophical speculation. "One sought," he writes, "less and less to position oneself according to the great geodesics of history: capitalism, the bourgeois class, imperialism, socialism, the proletariat. Bit by bit, people began to give up pushing the 'logical' and 'historical' consequences of choices to inadmissible and intolerable limits."⁴² This assertion offers a clue that the *dangerous tradition* to which he refers in his "What Is Enlightenment?" essay has nothing to do with the Iranian Revolution. Rather, given the tenor of his entire corpus on enlightenment, he remains skeptical toward global and radical emancipatory politics he associates with Enlightenment rationality. He makes his point more explicitly in the paragraph immediately following the passage I cited earlier as an alleged proof of his recantation. Foucault declares:

> I prefer the very specific transformations that have proved to be possible in the last twenty years in a number of areas that concern our way of being and thinking, relations to authority, relations between sexes, the way in which we perceive insanity or illness; I prefer even these partial transformations that have been made in the correlation of historical analysis and the practical attitude to the programs for a new man that the worst political systems have repeated throughout the twentieth century.⁴³

It is important to note that Foucault wrote his first installments ("What Is Critique?" and "What Is Revolution?") on enlightenment *before* his involvement in the Iranian Revolution. More significantly, he was writing during a post-1968 period when the idea of "the end of revolutions" dominated the European intellectual milieu.⁴⁴ Foucault's meditations on enlightenment in 1978 were motivated by a series of questions about the possibility of critical thought and reinvention of the political, after the hopes of a revolution had, as he put it, "gone astray in a despotic rationality."⁴⁵ Moreover, in all his writings on enlightenment, including the ones he wrote after the Iranian Revolution, Foucault wonders about how the despotic *lumière* of the pitiless twentieth century supplanted the hopeful revolutionary impulse that motivated Kant's *Aufklärung*.

Rather than a "search for formal structures with universal value," critical philosophy must correspond to a historical investigation into the processes and events that have shaped every minute detail and particularities of our life experiences. Neither is this kind of critical philosophy transcendental nor is its purpose the realization of a metaphysics of freedom that operates like science. This critical philosophy "is seeking to give new impetus, as far and wide as possible, to the undefined work of freedom."[46]

In his two Dartmouth lectures about the beginning of the hermeneutics of the self in 1980, one can recognize a subtle but evident sign of the mark the revolutionary movement in Iran left on Foucault's thought. He argues that philosophy loses its critical character if it seeks to "determine the conditions and limits of our possible knowledge of an object." Instead, we must advance "a critical philosophy that seeks the conditions and indefinite possibilities of transforming the subject, of transforming ourselves."[47] The latter point becomes significant in Foucault's reassessment of Kant's view on enlightenment and the emphasis he places on *Ausgang*, a way out, as a constitutive feature of the modern subject. Rather than a nod to Kantian formalism, Foucault's emphasis on *Ausgang* inverts Kant from appealing to universal norms and values to particular indeterminate possibilities. Rather than a simple call upon Reason, Foucault considers *sapere aude* ("dare to know," "have the courage, the audacity, to know") to signify "a process in which men participate collectively and an act of courage to be accomplished personally."[48] In a rare attempt to define modernity, Foucault read the Iranian Revolution *back into* Kant's *Was ist Aufklärung?* Here he deviates from speaking of modernity as an epoch or "set of features characteristic of an epoch."

> Thinking back on Kant's text, I wonder whether we may not envisage modernity rather as an attitude than as a period of history. And by "attitude" I mean a mode of relating to contemporary reality; a voluntary choice made by certain people; in the end, a way of thinking and feeling; a way, too, of acting and behaving that at one and the same time marks a relation of belonging, and presents itself as a task.[49]

In describing what he means by an attitude, Foucault shows a closer affinity with Baudelaire's conception of modernity than that of Kant. For Baudelaire, Foucault writes in the same essay, "modernity is the attitude that makes it possible to grasp the 'heroic' aspect of the present moment . . . it is the will to 'heroize' the present." Foucault understood the "heroic" aspect of the present as a counter-Kantian end to the transcendental illusions that had shaped an elective self-image of the enlightenment subject. Here, along with Baudelaire, Foucault throws doubts on the image that modern "Man" is in search of himself, to discover his hidden truth.

To "heroize" the present means to strive for incessant invention and creation of the self *without connecting that self to a transcendental subject*. In this context, Foucault distanced himself from the kind of humanism to which his critics claim he subscribed toward the end of his life.

Also, here Foucault looks at modernity as rupture and unremitting discontinuity of time, distancing himself yet again from the Kantian progressive vision of modernity as growth from immaturity *(Unmündigkeit)* to enlightenment *(Aufklärung)*.[50] This rupture situates the present not as a link between the past and a historically inevitable future but rather as a "heroic" moment of *possibilities*. Possessing an enlightened attitude, Foucault says in echoing Baudelaire, "consists in recapturing something eternal that is not beyond the present instant, nor behind it, but within it."[51] Similar to his antidoctrinal defense of the Shi'ite character of the revolutionary movement in Iran, Foucault regards enlightenment as an attitude without normative proclivities. The thread that connects us with the Enlightenment, he reiterates, "is not faithfulness to doctrinal elements, but rather a permanent reactivation of an attitude . . . a philosophical ethos that could be described as a permanent critique of our historical era."[52]

Foucault emphasizes that we must recognize ourselves as beings who are, to a certain extent, historically determined by the Enlightenment. But that determination also renders the question of being for or against the Enlightenment irrelevant.

> You either accept the Enlightenment and remain with the tradition of its rationalism (this is considered a positive term by some and used by others, on the contrary, as a reproach); or else you criticize the Enlightenment and then try to escape from its principles of rationality (which may be seen once again as good or bad). And we do not break free of this blackmail by introducing "dialectical" nuances while seeking to determine what good and bad elements there may have been in the Enlightenment.[53]

Did Foucault see a moment of a different kind of modernity brought into being in the Iranian Revolution? Did the revolution elicit a reevaluation of his thoughts about the Enlightenment? In my opinion, the answer on both accounts is yes. Consider this: rather than projecting the doctrinal premises of the Enlightenment onto Islam, or depicting Islam as the ideology of the vanguard clergy, Foucault identified religion itself for Iranians to be a phenomenon through which they have constructed new modes of subjectivity, authority, and political identity. For Foucault, Islam was neither a burden of the past nor a blueprint for the future. Shiʻi Islam was the context for a creative reinvention of the self, without reference to an a priori, transcendental subject (the very foundation of Foucault's theory of ethics). In a later work, without a direct reference to it, Foucault re-affirmed his earlier antiteleological position on the Iranian Revolution. "Never mind whether [a revolution] succeed[s] or fail[s], that has nothing to do with progress, or at least the sign of progress we are looking for."[54]

Whether revolutions are destined to realize the totalitarian potential of their utopian discourse, whether revolutions can really carve out a space that escapes the instrumental rationality of a spiritless world, is a matter of history. In response to critics who chastised him for failing to anticipate the postrevolutionary reign of terror in Iran, Foucault empha-sized the beautiful indeterminacy of human action. "I cannot write the history of the future, and I am also rather clumsy at foreseeing the past. However, I would like to grasp *what is happening right now*, because these days nothing is finished, and the dice are still being rolled."[55] The kind of ambiguity that he ascribes to human action, particularly in his later writings, remains a core element of his philosophy. "The main interest in life," he would later propose in an attempt to define the meaning of truth and spirituality, "is to become someone else that you were not at the beginning. . . . The game is worthwhile insofar as we don't know what will be the end."[56]

Spirituality and the Ethical Subject

Foucault's later concerns with how the subject *constitutes* itself through the "spiritual" practices of care of the self might appear as a retreat from the margins of irrationality to the center of rational liberalism. This view, put forward by James Miller in his popular biography *The Passion of Michel Foucault*, links "Foucault's belated interest in liberalism"[57] with the events of postrevolutionary Iran—a view largely replicated by Afary and Ander-son.[58] Miller wonders why, despite his newly found sympathies toward liberalism, Foucault remained uncritical of his earlier obsession with the revolution. "The furies that now gripped Iran," Miller writes, "went far beyond anything that Foucault, or almost any other observer, had dreamed possible." Exaggerating the atrocities committed by the postrevolutionary regime during the first few months of its reign, he further remarks that

> homosexuals were dispatched to firing squads. Adulterers were stoned to death. The chimera of a "political spirituality" was dispelled by the reality of a ruthless theocracy. . . . In this context, Foucault could, in principle, have expressed his newfound sympathy to a certain style of liberal reasoning, perhaps even applying the maxim that "one always governs too much" to a critique of Khomeini's new Islamic regime. In practice, he did nothing of the sort. Unrepentant, he stood by his enthusiasm for the revolution in Iran—and justified it in no uncertain terms.[59]

Although Miller points out that by the time he wrote his last essay Foucault's so-called liberal awakening had already occurred, he does not question why he remained unrepentant about his support of the revolution. "By default," he concludes, "much of the French left—including Foucault, despite his momentary enthusiasm for the Iranian revolution—found itself embracing a kind of liberal (and chastened) vision of what politics might achieve, a vision given its most dramatic expression in the 'human rights' movement that was then still gathering momentum in the Soviet Union and Eastern Europe."[60]

Rave reviews of Miller's biography and the ardent reception it enjoyed illustrate how a commonplace view epitomizes Foucault's project as the triumph of liberalism over the critique of universal Reason.[61] Not only did Miller depoliticize Foucault by aestheticizing him as a Nietzschean samurai obsessed with death, he further misconstrued his oeuvre as a failed attempt to think and act outside of universal enlightenment rationality. Reading Foucault's later interest in ethics and the *constitutive*, rather than the *fabricated*, subject as a liberal/humanist conversion relies on a misconception of both his earlier and later works.[62]

Foucault's later engagement with Kant and the Enlightenment was neither celebratory nor derogatory. He tries to carry critical enlightenment in a new direction away from "the tribunal of Reason, in which Kant had enclosed it."[63] In this new direction, he traverses Kant's peculiar notion of public and private reason by collapsing it into a single act of critique as *praxis*—the courage to *know* and the courage to *act*. Kant offers a counterintuitive description of public and private reason in the distinction he makes between the freedom to reason and the duty to fulfill social obligations. He writes:

The Public use of one's reason must always be free, and it alone can bring about enlightenment among men. The private use of reason, on the other hand, may often be very narrowly restricted without particularly hindering the progress of enlightenment. By the public use of one's reason I understand the use which a person makes of it as a scholar before the reading public. Private use I call that which one may make of it in a particular civil post or office which is entrusted to him. Many affairs which are conducted in the interest of the community require a certain mechanism through which some members of the community must passively conduct themselves with an artificial unanimity, so the government may direct them to public ends, or at least prevent them from destroying those ends.[64]

In his famous example of tax collection, Kant argues that in his "private" affair the citizen "cannot refuse to pay the taxes imposed on him." But the same citizen, as his "public" duty, may express his "thoughts on the inappropriateness or even the injustice of these levies." Similarly, the clergyman, Kant points out, delivers his sermon, as a teacher, to ensure that his congregation "conform[s] to the symbol of the church which he serves, for he has been accepted on this condition." But in "public," as a scholar, he has the freedom to critique the same symbols and "to make suggestions for the better organization of the religious body and church."[65]

The use which an appointed teacher makes of his reason before his congregation is merely private, because this congregation is only a domestic one (even if it be a large gathering); with respect to it, as a priest, he is not free, nor can he be free, because he carries out orders of another. But as a scholar, whose writings speak to his public, the world, the clergyman in the public use of his reason enjoys unlimited freedom.[66]

Kant, as Foucault notes, regards the unrestricted exercise of reason as public when it circulates among peers, scholars, and critics in newspapers and other publications. But at the same time, Kant calls the private use of reason the responsibility of conforming to the duties of an office by a government functionary, teacher, or religious leader. Curiously, as Foucault remarks, "what Kant defines as private use is each individual's obedience, inasmuch as he is a part of the State, to his superior, to the Sovereign or his representative." In this context, Kant makes the public display of discontent in the form of "I will not obey you and your order is absurd" inconceivable.[67]

Foucault argues that in Kant's *Aufklärung* "there are limits to the manifestation of *courage*."[68] But courage stands at the center of Foucault's conceptions of critique and the way he defines spirituality and ethics. For Foucault, by having *the courage to know*, the subject offers himself "the right to question truth on its effects of power and question power on its discourses of truth." Thereby, he considers critique to be "the art of voluntary insubordination, that of reflected intractability. Critique would essentially insure the desubjugation of the subject in the context of what we could call . . . the politics of truth."[69]

The experience of the Iranian Revolution generated a major shift in Foucault's thinking regarding the politics and "games" of truth. Whereas in his earlier writings he highlighted regimes of truth in relation to constitutive discourses and coercive practices, in his later works, he explores "ascetic practices," not in the sense of "a morality of renunciation but as an exercise of the self on the self by which one attempts to develop and transform oneself, and to attain to a certain mode of being."[70] We need to be mindful here that Foucault inverts the notion of asceticism from its early Christian practices of disengagement from the world and adopts an idiosyncratic interpretation in which he understands ascetic practices as the condition of the exercise of freedom.

He also distinguishes between the exercise of freedom and liberation. The concept of liberation, he argues, presupposes a human nature that "has been concealed, alienated, or imprisoned in and by mechanisms of repression."[71] But he views freedom as a ceaseless act of becoming, which is realizable only through the care of the self.

But here also Foucault advances a radical pragmatist view in which neither the self nor one's obligations to others are conceived with any reference to a transcendental notion of humanity. Foucault sees no contradiction in the way he promotes the exercise of freedom through the care of the *self* and the necessary intersubjectivity that political action requires. Like many others who speak of the significance of ethics in social life, Foucault regards the self in a perpetual interactive, generative state. He considers ethics to be the act of self-creation, one's desire *and* ability to transform oneself. In that regard, his theory of care of the self has a closer affinity to Levinas's conception of "the ethical subject" than any form of utilitarian individualism. Levinas, like many others who speak of the significance of ethics in social life, regards the self in a perpetual interactive state. In his view, the self's exercise of freedom is only realizable through the acts of justice toward others.[72] Foucault's critics emphasize that self-creation, which according to Richard Rorty constitutes private reason, posits an irreconcilable act with the care of others and social justice, which compose public reason. "There is no way," Rorty observes, "to bring self-creation together with justice at the level of theory. The vocabulary of self-creation is necessarily private, unshared, unsuited to argument. The vocabulary of justice is necessarily public and shared, a medium for argumentative exchange."[73] It is this irreconcilability that Foucault tries to overcome.

It is not farfetched to interpret Foucault's care of the self as a form of utilitarian individualism. Particularly when he attempts to illustrate how a perpetual care of the self would generate communal and social transformation. For example, in response to the question whether "care of the self, separated from care for others, runs the risk of becoming an absolute," he suggests that in care of the self, one thinks of others.[74] "He who takes care of himself," Foucault maintains, "to the point of knowing exactly what duties he has as a master of a household and as a husband and father will find that he enjoys a proper relationship with his wife and children."[75] Divorced from the historical context of its production, his assertion could be easily understood as a form of "self-centered ethics" and "cult of self."[76]

Foucault distinguishes the Stoic notion he advances in his care of the self as something inherently *relational*. He argues that the separation between care of the self and "social activities"—that is, all the responsibilities one ought to fulfill as subject, "those activities that Greek thought grouped together as 'economic'"—developed after the advent of Christianity. "In the Stoics," Foucault insists, "there is an intricate connection between care of the self and the economic, which they try to make as strong as possible."[77] Care of the self and access to the truth not only impose demands on the self, they also rearrange and reshape one's relation with others and with one's environment. That is why Foucault poses this question as a founding question, particularly in the Platonic tradition, of all philosophy: "What is the price I have to pay for access to the truth? This price is situated in the subject himself in the form of: What then is the work I must carry out on myself . . . to be able to have access to truth?"[78]

Foucault's incessant reminder of the price one has to pay in order to become an ethical subject offers the best clue that for him care of the self does not simply imply a blithe private life. Given the fact that he had already spoken of the spirituality of the revolutionary movement in Iran and had witnessed the transformative effect of the revolutionary act on the streets of Tehran, one can easily situate his concern with the price one has to assume in order to be an ethical subject in the Iranian Revolution. Foucault describes care of the self as a spiritual act, the purpose of which is access to truth. But one must not understand this access, as he explicates in his very first lecture on the hermeneutics of the subject at the Collège de France on January 6, 1982, as a problem of knowledge. Foucault expounds:

> We could call "spirituality" the search, practice, and experience through which the subject carries out the necessary transformations on himself in order to have access to truth. . . . We will call "spirituality" then the set of the these researches, practices, and experiences, which may be purifications, ascetic exercises, renunciations, conversions of looking, modifications of existence, etc., which are, not for knowledge but for the subject, for the subject's very being, the *price to be paid for access to the truth*. (15)

In this lecture, Foucault identifies three characteristics for spirituality, in all of which again one may detect the residues of his observations of Iranians marching on the streets of Tehran. The first is that, rather than a simple act of knowledge, spirituality postulates that having access to the truth requires the subject to "change," "transform," and "shift and become, to some extent and up to a certain point, other than himself . . . there can be no truth without a conversion or a transformation of the subject" (ibid.). The second characteristic also has to do with this conversion, which may take place "in the form of a movement that removes the subject from his current status and condition." Foucault calls this movement, quite conventionally, "the movement of *erōs* (love)." This movement is not complete unless it is sustained by "an elaboration [and transformation] of the self by the self" for which one takes responsibility in "a long labor of ascesis *(askēsis)*." These are the modalities, Foucault argues, "by which the subject must be transformed in order finally to become capable of truth." Last, and more importantly, spirituality assumes that truth will have a consequence on the subject. He calls the effects of the truth on the subject "rebound" *(de retour)* (15–16).

> The truth enlightens the subject; the truth gives beatitude to the subject; the truth gives the subject tranquility of the soul. In short, in the truth and in access to the truth, there is something that fulfills the subject himself, which fulfills or transfigures his very being. In short, I think we can say that in and of itself an act of knowledge could never give access to the truth unless it was prepared, accompanied, doubled, and completed by a certain transformation of the subject; not of the individual, but of the subject himself in his being as subject. (16)

Although this passage on the significance and consequence of truth bears resemblance to the Gnostic movements, Foucault insists that his conception is motivated by *acts of spirituality* and not concerns with access to knowledge *(connaissance)*, which is the characteristic of gnosis. Now, not only does Foucault describe the subject in its historical milieu, but he also emphasizes its ethical dimension. "We should remember," Frédéric Gros comments on *The Hermeneutics of the Subject*, "for a long time Foucault conceived of the subject as only the passive product of techniques of domination. It is only in 1980 that he conceives of the relative autonomy, the irreducibility, anyway, of the techniques of the self."[79]

But within realities of life, who can legitimately and practically engage in self-creation and transformation of the self? Are Foucault's ethical subjects the great men of history who shape the direction and condition of others' lives? Is a common man capable of taking care of his self? In his second Collège de France lecture, Foucault addresses the basic limitation of the Stoics and Cynics in their call for the care of the self. "To take care of the self," he cautions against the generalization of the Stoic principle, "one must have the ability, time, and culture, etcetera, to do so. It is an activity of the elite" (75). Also, one needs to bear in mind that for the Athenian Stoics the aim and meaning of taking care of oneself is "to distinguish the individual who takes care of himself from the crowd, from the majority, from the *hoi polloi* [the majority as opposed to the competent elite] who are, precisely, the people absorbed in everyday life" (75). The care of the self in its ancient context was also a deeply political action not in the way Foucault rearticulates it, but as an answer to the question: "How can one govern well?" Being concerned about the care of the self is "a privilege of governors, or it is also a duty of governors because they have to govern" (74).

I would like to argue that witnessing the revolutionary movement in Iran had a profound impact on his thought, helping Foucault to envision the care of the self and spirituality as the real possibility for and the responsibility of the common man. For him, at the time he was delivering his lectures on the hermeneutics of the subject, only months after his passionate writings on the Iranian Revolution, spirituality was no longer merely a property of the selected elite. As he repeated on numerous occasions in his reportage, he had seen how Iran became the spirit of a spiritless world and how ordinary people transformed themselves into irreducible, fearless, and spiritual subjects. More importantly, one can easily identify the reflection of this encounter in the way Foucault identifies two important features of the spiritual subject: first, the ability to create an "ethical distance" from one's functionary responsibilities (that is, the ability "not to feel deprived of what will be taken from him by circumstances") (540); and second, the audacity to speak truth to power.

Parrhesia: From Dare to Know to Dare to Act

In his last entry on the Iranian Revolution on May 11–12, 1979, Foucault reiterated the historical significance of the revolutionary movement. One must recognize the transformative character of a moment when an entire people say, "I will no longer obey," Foucault wrote, and are willing to "risk their lives in the face of power that they believe to be unjust. . . . There must be an uprooting that interrupts the unfolding of history, and its long series of reasons why, for a man 'really' to prefer *the risk of death over the certainty of having to obey*."[80] In his later writing, Foucault develops his observation into a theory of fearless acts of "truth-telling." After a massacre had happened a few days prior to his arrival in Tehran in September 1978, he thought that he would find a "terrorized city," but what he witnessed was "an absence of fear and an intensity of courage."[81] Much like his first observations in Tehran, in his last lectures in Berkeley in 1983, he chose the theme of the audacity to speak and of acting courageously. In a seminar entitled "Discourse and Truth," Foucault offered six lectures in which he delves into the Greek and Roman rhetorical tradition and revives and redefines the concept of *parrhesia*, loosely translated as "fearless speech."[82]

Despite the topic of the series, in his concluding lecture he remarks: "My intention was not to deal with the problem of truth, but with the problem of truth-teller or truth-telling as an activity." Foucault emphasizes that he did not intend to develop a sociological description of "truth-tellers" in different societies, but rather he wanted to show how Greek philosophy has reworked the problem of truth and viewed it from the standpoint of the act of truth-telling. The lectures were organized around four key questions:

> Who is able to tell the truth? What are the moral, the ethical, and the spiritual conditions which entitle someone to present himself as, and to be considered as, a truth-teller? About what topics is it important to tell the truth? (About the world? About nature? About the city? About behavior? About man?) What are the consequences of telling the truth? What are its anticipated positive effects for the city, for the city's rulers, for the individual, etc.? And finally: what is the relation between the activity of truth-telling and the exercise of power, or should these activities be completely independent and kept separate? Are they separable, or do they require one another?[83]

Here Foucault revives a well-known preoccupation of Socrates in an activity that involves politics, rhetoric, ethics, and questions such as who is able to tell the truth, about what, with what consequences, and with what relation to power. In order to engage these questions, Foucault introduces the term *parrhesia* and defines it as "a verbal activity in which a speaker expresses his personal relationship to truth, and risks his life because he recognizes truth-telling as a duty to improve or help other people (as well as himself)."[84] He recovers *parrhesia* from Euripides's plays, particularly from *Ion*, in which Foucault situates the most obvious example of *parrhesiastic* games and easily identifiable acts of the *parrhesiastes*.

Whereas in his lectures later the same year at the Collège de France, Foucault focuses on *parrhesia* as a moral virtue—"you admit the truth to yourself even if it threatens your self-image," and associates it with care of the self—in his Berkeley talks he highlights its political virtue: "You tell the Prince the truth even if it costs your head."[85] Although the accents are different in these two occasions, one can easily identify in Foucault's articulation that the moral virtue of speaking plainly and directly to the self is both the point of departure as well as the consequence of truth-telling of *parrhesiastes* and fearless speech addressing the "Prince." Thereby, Foucault links moral and political virtue in *parrhesiastic* acts of transformation.

Although Foucault collects examples from Greek and Roman rhetorical traditions, he turns *parrhesia* into an act far beyond a rhetorical gesture. In his etymological description, he locates the root of the word in "pan" (everything) and "rhema" (that which is said). With that reference, he defines the concept as a type of relationship between the speaker and the speech act without shrouding it in any rhetorical forms. Here Foucault makes an important distinction between rhetoric, which affords the speaker the means of capturing audience's minds, and *parrhesisates* acts, which allows the audience to learn directly what the speaker believes without fear of its consequences. By making *parrhesia* a human activity of dangerous and risky speaking, "Foucault strips the rhetorical tradition of its foremost trope of advocacy."[86] What is embedded in Foucault's use of *parrhesia* is its confrontational feature in situations of social inequality and asymmetry of power. "The commitment," Foucault elaborates, "involved in *parrhesia* is linked to a certain social situation, to a difference of status between the speaker and his audience, to the fact that the *parrhesiastes* says something which is dangerous to himself and thus involves risk."[87]

Situating Foucault's Last Lectures

"For Foucault," Paul Rabinow reminds us, "in order to establish the right relationship to the present—to things, to others, to oneself—one must stay close to events, experience them, be willing to be effected and affected by them."[88] One should always be conscious of the complexities of how one's life circumstances shape and condition one's ideas and thought. In this chapter, I tried to illustrate how Foucault's encounter with and reflections on the Iranian Revolution informed his later writings on ethics and spirituality. In this, neither do I want to draw a perfunctory and unmediated connection between events and his thoughts nor do I intend to follow Heidegger's view on the irrelevance of biographical information, illustrated most infamously by the way he opened his course on Aristotle with the words, "Aristotle was born, worked, and died."[89]

Although many commentators have argued that the Iranian Revolution left a mark on Foucault's writing, this mark is either dismissed as a fleeting moment of infatuation or as a transformative lesson in the perils of forsaking the Enlightenment's "normative yardstick." In this chapter, I demonstrated that despite the fact that he does not explicitly refer to the Iranian Revolution, it deeply affected his later writings in which he reaffirms his ideas of the revolutionary subject, and its inexplicability. Rather than a conversion to Enlightenment humanism as an unsaid admission to his error, Foucault's later writings represent a revisionist reading of the Enlightenment and Greco-Roman ethics in light of the Iranian Revolution.

The fact that he shifted the emphasis of his philosophy to the constituting acts of the subject (i.e., care of the self and *parrhesia*) is not disputed in Foucault scholarship. But the arena in which this shift occurs most often receives either a cursory treatment or no treatment at all. For example, in *The Cambridge Companion* (edited by Gary Gutting), only one reference exists in the entire book to the Iranian Revolution.[90] In describing the context of Foucault's 1981–82 lectures on *The Hermeneutics of the Subject*, the only revolution to which Frédéric Gros refers is the one in Foucault's mind. "What is philosophy today," Gros quotes Foucault, "if it is not the critical work that thought brings to bear on itself? In what does it consist, if not in the endeavor to know how and to what extent it might be possible to think differently." Gros continues:

> We should understand, then, precisely what it was that changed from 1976 to 1984. And for this the 1982 course turns out to be critical, located at the living heart of a change of problematic, of a conceptual revolution. But to speak of a "revolution" is no doubt too hasty, since what is involved, rather, is a slow maturation, of a development with neither break nor commotion, which brought Foucault to the shores of the care of the self. . . . This course constitutes a first reorientation in the general plan of his work, since we find in it, clearly expressed and conceptualized for the first time, the project of writing history of "truth activities" understood as regulated procedures which tie a subject to a truth, ritualized activities though which a certain subject establishes his relationship to a certain truth.[91]

Nothing could be more "un-Foucauldian" than a contextualization that has nothing to do with actual events—only the transformation of thought and the problematization of new concepts. How else can one comprehend Foucault's reflections on the Iranian Revolution except as precedents in writing history as "ritualized activities though which a certain subject establishes his relationship to a certain truth"?

Although John Rajchman does situate Foucault's ideas in actual historical events, he shows no interest in contemplating any connection between Foucault's writings on the Enlightenment, his reengagement with Kant, and his thoughts about the Iranian Revolution. "No doubt Foucault's trips to Poland during this period," he writes in the introduction to *The Politics of Truth*, "and, more generally, his philosophical sympathies with East European dissidence (with its own complicated relations with Enlightened Germany or France) together with his on-going discussions with the 'autonomous' movements in Italy (and the issue of 'red terrorism'), anticipate this event he did live to see and its role in the larger post-Marxist character of the debate over enlightenment."[92] Rajchman insists, rightly, that in returning to Kant, Foucault intended to show that the critical attitude of enlightenment belong to no "already-given civilization" or preconceived notions of politics. Further, Rajchman aptly points out that the crucial point in Foucault's writings on "the politics of truth" is that "while it thus belongs to no prior group and is contained in no prior form of knowledge, the critical attitude is essential for the very idea of the political."

Rajchman also stresses the significance of Foucault's interest in critical attitudes and social forces that emerge from "outside previously circumscribed situations" and those movements that introduce "new arrangements" of life outside the given possibilities.[93] Each of the important elements of Foucault's attempt "to invent a new style of critique, a new kind of critical philosophy"[94] bears close resemblance with the core ideas of his oeuvre on the Iranian Revolution. Yet here again Rajchman follows the lead of many others in failing to show this clear connection.

As one of the most important scholars who introduced Foucault to English readers, Paul Rabinow is more conscious of situating Foucault's last lectures on ethics and his writings on the care of the self in a historical context. He is one of the very few who speak of Iran and the Iranian Revolution as one of the arenas in which Foucault delivers his later work.

Although Rabinow highlights the significance of the Iranian Revolution for Foucault, he does not extend and link this importance *substantively* to his later writings. He argues that Foucault formulated an imperative that went "beyond overthrowing yet another corrupt, Western-supported authoritarian regime, an imperative he formulated thus: 'above all we have to change ourselves. Our way of being, our relationships with others, with things, with eternity, with God.'"[95] In Rabinow's contextualization the Iranian Revolution is there but without a meaningful connection to Foucault's concomitant preoccupation with ethics and the care of the self. The Iranian Revolution was not the only political event to which Foucault paid close attention. For many years, he considered himself a part of a movement against penal injustice and for prisoners' rights, he supported the dissident Solidarity union movement in Poland and participated in activities in their defense, and he marched with protesters defending the rights of Vietnamese refugees. But no singular event in Foucault's history generated such a distinct transformation in his thought as the Iranian Revolution. His writings on Iran remain controversial and largely ignored in relation to the development of his thought, except by those who want to baptize him posthumously as a born-again liberal who had learned the painful lesson of divesting himself from the universal referent of the Enlightenment in the reign of terror in Iran.

Conclusion

WRITING THE HISTORY
OF THE PRESENT

ONE OF THE IMPORTANT SOURCES that inspired the writing of this book was Susan Buck-Morss's controversial essay "Hegel and Haiti," published in the summer of 2000.[1] I had already read a Persian translation of Foucault's writings on the Iranian Revolution in a book published in Tehran in 1998, before I dis covered her essay.[2] Reading Foucault on the Iranian Revolution in Persian did not initially generate any serious intellectual curiosity in me. But reading Buck-Morss and the questions she raised on the origins of Hegel's idea of lordship and bondage led me back to Foucault and the Iranian Revolution with fresh interests. "Hegel and Haiti" raised significant conceptual questions that could similarly be raised in relation to *Foucault and Iran*—questions not only regarding the significance of Foucault's writings about the revolution but also on the profound mark that the event left on his thought. A response to those questions became more exigent as Foucault's essays found a second life in academic and political circles after the September 11 attacks and the inauguration of the "War on Terror."

Conventionally, intellectual historians draw the genealogy of Hegelian thought in connection with the writings of other philosophers, from ancient Greece (Plato or Aristotle) to other German philosophical traditions, most significantly that of Fichte. But Buck-Morss locates the famous metaphor of "struggle to death" between master and slave, "which for Hegel provided the key to the unfolding of freedom in world history," which has since its conception influenced political philosophers of the Left and the Right in a very concrete and empirical fashion. Hegel wrote *The Phenomenology of Mind* in 1805–6 during his residence in Jena, she writes, where he closely followed the events of the Haitian Revolution as it was reported and discussed in *Minerva*, a journal that covered the

French Revolution and later covered the revolutionary uprisings in Saint-Domingue from its inception in the early 1790s. "The Eyes of the World Are Now on St. Domingo," a *Minerva* headline read in 1804. And so were Hegel's, Buck-Morss argues.[3]

Although Hegel himself does not offer any clues as to how he conceived master–slave dialectics and their insertion into the historical struggle for freedom, Buck-Morss speculates that given the timing and his intellectual milieu in Jena in 1803, "Hegel knew about real slaves revolting successfully against real masters, and he elaborated his dialectic of lordship and bondage deliberately within this contemporary context."[4]

What is the significance of treating Hegel's lordship and bondage dialectics as an abstract device of historical interpretation or as a reference to a concrete historical experience? For Buck-Morss, *concretizing* Hegel's conceptual universe is a way out of the inherent "paradox between the discourse of freedom and the practice of slavery," so prevalent in Eurocentric views of history and justified by the prevalent Enlightenment rationality. Buck-Morss makes this crucial connection between Hegel and Haiti to bestow on the rebellious slaves of Saint-Domingue not only the mission of liberating the Haitians from the tyranny of the French but also, and perhaps more importantly, the responsibility of rescuing the universal History. "The Haitian Revolution was the crucible, the trial by fire for the ideals of the French Enlightenment."[5]

By situating Foucault in Iran, I have reached a different conclusion. In his writings on the Iranian Revolution, Foucault tried to be attentive to a constitutive paradox of the revolutionary movement. He thought that Iranians desired to make history and at the same time to be free from it, to be historical subjects without being subjected to its determinist logic, to be *included* in and *exit* from History. He found the display of this paradox in the singularity he observed in the revolutionary movement—in its religious expression, in the ambiguity of its assenting demands, in its distinct uncompromising rhythm, and in its inexplicable transformative power, which shrouded the whole rebellious nation. He coined the concept of "political spirituality" to capture that singularity. He thought that the revolutionary movement did not yield to the demands of a universal History and refused to make itself readily legible with references to foundational binaries of premodern/modern, secular/religious, reactionary/progressive, male/female, and subjugated/emancipated.

Understanding the Iranian Revolution requires a temporal map that recognizes the contingencies and indeterminacies within which the revolutionary movement unfolded. The revolution and its outcomes appear inevitable only to those who expunge those contingencies in and conceptualize the revolutionary movement in a historical narrative in which the colonized appears as the European past and Europe shows the colonized its own future. Foucault saw in the Iranian Revolution an instance of his antiteleological philosophy—a revolution that did not simply fit into the normative progressive discourses of history. What attracted him to the Iranian Revolution was precisely the same feature for which his critics ridiculed him: its ambiguity. For him, the revolutionary movement begot a new subject with an indeterminate relation to himself and to history. Rather than his fascination with death or his absorption in the aesthetics of violence, it was the inexplicability of the man in revolt that motivated much of his writing on the Iranian revolution.

Foucault conceptualized political spirituality not in defense of the establishment of an Islamic theocracy but rather in praise of the transformative power of the revolution. The spirituality he witnessed in the streets of Tehran had nothing to do with either doctrinal commitments to Islam or devotion to the undisputed leader of the revolution, Ayatollah Khomeini. As he elaborated in his later works, by spirituality he meant the acts and practices through which one could transform oneself into a new subject—*a subject that one could never imagine capable of becoming.*

In an elaborate and detailed series of lectures during the last few years of his life, Foucault linked the idea of spirituality to ethics and fearless speech. The revolutionary subjects in the streets of Tehran taught him the possibility of a transformative politics one can exercise outside normative conventions of the Enlightenment. The revolution showed him that in the care of self, rather than self-absorption, the ethical subject perpetrates self-creation and agrees to pay the price of it.

The postrevolutionary power struggles that gave rise to the consolidation of power by the clergy and the ensuing reign of terror should not cast doubt on the significance of Foucault's endorsement of the revolution. In response to his critics, he insisted that the manner in which the revolution was lived must remain distinct from its success or failure. We need to remind ourselves that it was the realpolitik of the postrevolutionary state that colonized the spiritual novelty of the revolt.

Ultimately, how one assesses Foucault's writings on the Iranian Revolution depends on the narrative through which one tells the story of the revolution and its outcome. In this book, I tried to debunk two commonplace assertions.

First, I disputed the view that the revolutionary movement unfolded with an internal friction between the secularist and Islamist forces, which eventually allowed the clergy to "steal" its leadership. There is no doubt that communists and liberal political organizations played an important role in the revolution. But they never understood themselves as the representatives of "secular" forces in the revolutionary movement. Indeed, a significant majority of communist organizations considered liberalism to be the main internal adversary of the revolutionary movement. Until a very late stage of the revolutionary movement, the liberals advocated: "Let the king reign but not govern!" To realize the full revolutionary potential of the masses, the communists believed, they had to prevail over liberal plots to save the monarch. For the entire period of the revolutionary movement of 1978–79, the Iranian Left remained firmly on the side of the anti-Shah and anti-imperialist radicalism, the undisputed leader of which was Ayatollah Khomeini.

Both conceptually and in practice, only in a Whiggish history did there exist a binary opposition between "seculars" and "Islamists" among the revolutionary forces. Political objectives were not expressed in those terms. Seculars as such were only those who *resisted* the revolution. So, in the Iranian context of 1978–79, to defend secularism politically meant to support the monarchy. During the same period, there were observers outside Iran who warned about the religious feature of the revolution. But Foucault tried to remain attentive to the revolutionary expressions inside Iran with all its ambiguities rather than projecting a normative European discourse of revolution back onto the Iranian uprising.

The tension between what a proper revolution should look like and the realities of the Iranian experience also shaped the representations of gender politics after the revolution. As I tried to illustrate in this book, the March 1979 rallies in Tehran against compulsory *hejāb* reflected a distinct rift between the way Iranian women who participated in these rallies understood their plight and the way Western feminists justified their intervention on behalf of their Iranian "sisters." The French and American feminists convened in Tehran and Paris to "save" Iranian women, with whom they had neither an organic nor a discursive connection. They stood in support of their Iranian sisters because they represented the universal demands of feminism and liberty. By contrast, in all cases in his reports, Foucault deliberately privileges the singularity of the Iranian voices over the tropes of universality and the indiscriminate language of Progress.

Second, I also tried to question the common assertion that the reign of terror was the *inevitable* result and the *natural* progression of Islamism. Without exception, those who criticized Foucault in 1978 to 1980 saw Islamism as a political movement for the realization of an essentialized Islam without significant distinction in its application in Iran or Saudi Arabia. They chastised him for his failure to distance himself from this "archaic fascism," and they linked this failure to Foucault's critical view of the Enlightenment rationality.

As a political ideology, Islamism has always been informed by the contingencies of time and place and has reflected particular historical trajectories of its emergence. As I showed in the preceding chapters, even Khomeini conceived distinct political theologies in different periods of his life. Once he advocated classical Shi'i political quietism and defended the monarchical order against chaos and unruliness; another time, toward the end of life, he adopted the principle of republicanism and electoral politics. Once he was against women's involvement in public life; later he insisted that without women's participation the revolution would fail. One cannot regard Islamism as a transhistorical ideology of oppression and identify its tenets with literal references to the Qur'an.

Foucault was indeed one of those subjects that the Iranian Revolution transformed—not to become a penitent liberal, as many have argued, but to recognize and commit to the possibility of a new form of subjectivity and political virtue in *parrhesiastic* acts of transformation. The revolutions of the "periphery," Haiti or Iran, have always burst asunder with a double consciousness: a demand to claim the universals and a desire to assert their singularity. It is in this underarticulated singularity of the revolutionary Iranians where I empirically situate Foucault's enthusiasm toward the end of his life about the care of the self and ethics.

Like Hegel before him, who never acknowledged the *real* slaves and the *real* masters in the struggle for freedom in world history, Foucault remained silent about the origins of his newfound interest in ethics and the hermeneutics of the self. His silence gave rise to a commonplace assertion that the critic par excellence of modern governmentality saw its prudence before the end of his life. By locating the origins of his conceptual shift in the revolutionary Iranian subjects, I have argued it was the thread of singularity that sewed Foucault's late work together, and not a latent appreciation of Enlightenment universality. We might call this, as has Žižek, "a defense of lost causes." But that precisely is the point of thinking about history without preaching its end.

Foucault's reports on the Iranian Revolution are not documents for understanding Islamism. He might have been fascinated by the aesthetics of the revolution or its death rituals, but what motivated his writing was his conviction that the Enlightenment rationality has not closed the gate of unknown possibilities for human societies. Such a conviction is unsettling and perilous, as the atrocities committed by the Islamic Republic attest. But nonetheless, how the present unfolds and what the future holds must not remain in the prison house of the past, be it in the instrumental rationality of the Enlightenment or in other kinds of fundamentalisms, religious or otherwise.

ACKNOWLEDGMENTS

I HAVE WRITTEN THIS BOOK with various sets of audiences in mind. As such, I am indebted to a diverse set of intellectual traditions and those who make these traditions possible, in their writings and in the networks that sustain these exchanges.

Much of this manuscript was written in Berlin during the magnificent year of 2010–11 as a fellow at the Wissenschaftskolleg zu Berlin. The staff at Wiko made the institute the fantastic place that it is with their generosity and cordiality. Julie Livingston, Kamran Ali, Syema Muzaffar, Tanja Petrovic, Karen Feldman, Niklaus Largier, Nancy Hunt, Iruka Okeke, Vikram Sampath, Fred Cooper, Jane Burbank, Steven Feierman, Vera Schulze-Seeger, Katarzyna Maria Speder, Georges Khalil, Toshio Hosokawa, Claire Messud, and Elias and Najla Khouri made life in Berlin even more pleasant and engaging.

My colleagues in the history department at the University of Illinois are just masters of creating the best working environment one can desire. Special thanks go to Diane Koenker, who oversaw this well-oiled machine during her chairwomanship and offered me invaluable solicited and unsolicited support. Antoinette Burton has always been a source of inspiration and encouragement; I have learned plenty from her and hope to continue to do so. For some unwarranted reasons, Maria Todorova has always championed my work. I thank her for that and, more importantly, for doing it so graciously. And Terri Barnes is the one colleague and friend everyone should wish for. The list of friends and colleagues is too long to be mentioned here. I also need to thank my dear friend Zsuzsa Gille for decades of friendship. Zohreh Sullivan makes life in the prairie simple and attractive. Faranak Miraftab, Ken Salo, Hadi Esfahani, Asef

Bayat, Linda Herrera, Niloufar Shambayati, Ken Cuno, Angelina Cotler, Jane Kuntz, Richard Powers, Usha and Rajmohan Gandhi, Jesse Ribot, Allyson Purpura, Michael Rothberg, Yasemin Yildiz, Emanuel Rota, Elenora Stoppino, and James Kilgore all know the value of a good community, into which they offered me a membership.

I am grateful to my colleagues at the Department of Sociology for their support, to Tim Liao for always being the voice of reason, and to Brian Dill, Anna Marshall, and Assata Zerai and all others for their tireless effort to bring life back to our small community. In addition, the Center for South Asian and Middle Eastern Studies has always been an amazing source of support, particularly under the directorship of Valerie Hoffman. The center could not exist without the dedication and expertise of Angela Williams.

I have been influenced by the incredible works of many great thinkers, some of whom I've had the privilege of knowing: Afsaneh Najmabadi, Minoo Moallem, Saba Mahmood, Asef Bayat, Raewyn Connell, Mohammed Bamyeh, Talal Asad, Niloofar Haeri, Ervand Abrahamian, Saïd Amir Arjomand, Edmund Burke (III), Donna Haraway, James Clifford, and Michael Burawoy are just a few among these.

I am especially indebted to all of those who read different versions of this manuscript and made invaluable suggestions, corrections, and comments. Sharon Ghamari-Tabrizi, Mohammed Bamyeh, and Jason Weidemann read earlier versions and helped me to advance a much clearer and more grounded argument. The anonymous readers' and Nasrin Rahimieh's comments were amazingly extensive and thought-provoking. I also extend my thanks to the series editors, Junaid Rana and Sohail Daulatzai, for their careful reading and recognition of the contribution of this book. Danielle M. Kasprzak followed through so carefully the whole process of the review and production of the book. She presented the manuscript to the editorial board and magically persuaded them that there indeed is something worthwhile in this book. Special thanks to Anne Carter for her logistical assistance.

I have taken a winding road to get to this privileged place of writing books and teaching at a university. This could not have been possible without the everlasting encouragement of my amazing family and friends, who never held back their support and love. My brothers, Bijan and Behdad, and my sister, Behjat, know how important they are in my life and how without them nothing in my life could have been possible. I thank my friends who have always been there for me whose names need to remain unmentioned here.

I cannot say enough about how patiently and judiciously Julie Livingston has read different versions of this manuscript and commented on them with unparalleled insight. How can one thank a pure labor of love and the generosity with which it has been delivered?

Finally, I dedicate this book to the memory of my mother, who passed away during its writing. I have never known a person who had such a faith in the power of hope. I dedicate this book to her memory because this is also a book about hope, about possibilities. I always wondered about the sources of her amazing resilience, the way she carried on marching, kept her feet on the ground, with her head high, her back straight, her mind focused, and her integrity intact. I hope she is looking down and can see a tiny portion of that integrity in the book I am dedicating to her.

NOTES

Introduction

1. Charles Krauthammer, "The Arab Spring of 2005," *Seattle Times*, March 21, 2005.

2. Alain Badiou, *The Rebirth of History: Times of Riots and Uprisings* (New York: Verso, 2012), 48.

3. For an insightful account, see Yasmin Moll, "The Wretched Revolution," *Middle East Report* 273 (2014): 34–39.

4. See Anthony Alessandrini, "Foucault, Fanon, Intellectuals, Revolutions," *Jadaliyya*, April 1, 2014, http://www.jadaliyya.com/pages/index/17154/foucault-fanon-intellectuals-revolutions.

5. See, for example, Georg Stauth, "Revolution in Spiritless Times: An Essay on Michel Foucault's Enquiries into the Iranian Revolution," *International Sociology* 6, no. 3 (1991): 259–80; Craig Keating, "Reflections on the Revolution in Iran: Foucault on Resistance," *Journal of European Studies* 27 (1997): 181–97; Michiel Leezenberg, "Power and Political Spirituality: Michel Foucault on the Islamic Revolution in Iran," *Arcadia* 33, no. 1 (1998): 72–89.

6. Janet Afary and Kevin Anderson, *Foucault and the Iranian Revolution: Gender and the Seductions of Islamism* (Chicago: University of Chicago Press, 2005).

7. For discussion on Foucault's Orientalism, see Ian Almond, *The New Orientalists: Postmodern Representations of Islam from Foucault to Baudrillard* (London: I.B.Tauris, 2007). Michael Walzer coined the term "infantile leftism" to describe Foucault's endorsement of the Iranian Revolution in his essay "The Politics of Michel Foucault," in *Foucault: A Critical Reader*, ed. David Hoy (Oxford: Basil Blackwell, 1986), 51–68.

8. See Afary and Anderson's epilogue, particularly the section "Western Leftists and Feminist Responses to September 11," in *Foucault*, 168–72.

9. Afary and Anderson, *Foucault*, 136.

10. Ibid., 137.

11. Slavoj Žižek, *In Defense of Lost Causes* (New York: Verso, 2009), 115.

12. Afary and Anderson, *Foucault*, 108.

13. I have borrowed this line from Žižek and his description of the clichés of intellectuals' revolutionary sentiments in *Lost Causes*, 107.

14. The controversy began after the Danish newspaper *Jyllands-Posten* published twelve cartoons on September 30, 2005, in most of which the Prophet Muhammad was depicted as a terrorist, with a ticking-bomb turban or promising virgin angels to suicide bombers. After the cartoons appeared in the newspaper, Muslims in Europe and elsewhere held large demonstrations against its publication. The demonstrations sparked a passionate debate about the limits of the freedom of expression and the place of the growing Muslim population of Europe in its liberal democratic landscape. See my commentary for further analysis: "When a Cartoon Is Not Just a Cartoon," *Iranian*, February 4, 2006, http://iranian.com/Ghamari/2006/February/Cartoon/index.html.

15. For a full text, see "Writers Statement on Cartoons," *BBC News*, March 1, 2006, http://news.bbc.co.uk/2/hi/europe/4764730.stm.

16. Bruce Cumings, "Black September, Infantile Nihilism, and National Security," in *Understanding September 11*, ed. Craig Calhoun, Paul Price, and Ashley Timmer (New York: New Press, 2002), 198.

17. Bruce Cumings, *The Korean War: A History* (New York: Random House, 2011), 151–53.

18. Bruce Cumings, "Some Thoughts Subsequent to September 11," November 2001, http://www.ssrc.org/sept11/essays/cumings.htm. The Social Science Research Council (SSRC) created a website for a wide range of views on the historical, sociological, and theoretical significance of 9/11. Cumings deleted this part from the published and more tempered version of his earlier contribution on the SSRC's website.

19. Many of these essays are collected in a two-volume book that came out of the SSRC website collection: Calhoun et al., *Understanding September 11*; Eric Hershberg and Kevin Moore, eds., *The Critical Views of September 11: Analyses from around the World* (New York: W. W. Norton, 2002).

20. The following passage from an op-ed Michael Ignatieff wrote for the *Guardian* on October 1, 2001, captures the core of this political philosophy: "What we are up against is apocalyptic nihilism. The nihilism of their means—the indifference to human costs—takes their actions not only out of the realm of politics, but even out of the realm of war itself. The apocalyptic nature of their goals makes it absurd to believe they are making political demands at all. They are seeking the violent transformation of an irremediably sinful and unjust world. Terror does not express a politics, but a metaphysics, a desire to give ultimate meaning to time and history through ever-escalating acts of violence which culminate

in a final battle between good and evil. People serving such exalted goals are not interested in mere politics." http://www.theguardian.com/world/2001/oct/01/afghanistan.terrorism9.

21. As it became clear a few weeks later, the anthrax attacks had nothing to do with any Jihadi groups. The FBI later disclosed that its agents had identified a disgruntled American microbiologist who worked at Fort Detrick as the suspect. He committed suicide before his official indictment. In the published version of her contribution to the SSRC series on 9/11, Benhabib revised this passage to "The attacks unleashed by these groups, especially the continuing threat to use biological and chemical weapons against civilian populations . . ." Seyla Benhabib, "Unholy Wars: Reclaiming Democratic Virtues after September 11," in Calhoun et al., *Understanding September 11*, 241.

22. Seyla Benhabib, "Unholy Politics," *SSRC*, November 2001, http://www.ssrc.org/sept11/essays/benhabib.htm.

23. Tariq Ali, *Clash of Fundamentalisms: Crusades, Jihad and Modernity* (New York: Verso, 2003), 3.

24. Marshall Berman, *All That Is Solid Melts into Air: The Experience of Modernity* (London: Verso, 1983), 347.

25. Jürgen Habermas, *The Philosophical Discourse of Modernity*, trans. Frederick G. Lawrence (Cambridge: MIT Press, 1995), 7.

26. For more on the conception of the West as the producer and non-West as the consumer of modernity, see Partha Chatterjee, *The Nation and Its Fragments* (Princeton: Princeton University Press, 1993).

27. David Held, "Violence, Law, and Justice in a Global Village," in Calhoun et al., *Understanding September 11*, 104.

28. Afary and Anderson, *Foucault*, 165.

29. See Edward Rothstein's furious attack on "cultural relativists" in his oft-cited editorial "Attacks on U.S. Challenge the Perspectives of Postmodern True Believers," *New York Times*, September 22, 2001, http://www.nytimes.com/2001/09/22/arts/connections-attacks-us-challenge-perspectives-postmodern-true-believers.html.

30. James Der Derian, "9/11: Before, After, and In Between," in Calhoun et al., *Understanding September 11*, 177. Also on the same topic, see Judith Butler, "Explanation and Exoneration; or, What We Can Hear," *Social Text* 20, no. 3 (2002): 177–88. She argues that by rehabilitating the term "excuseniks," the "just war" liberal Left "suggests that those who seek to understand how the global map arrived at this juncture through asking how, in part, the United States has contributed to the making of this map, are themselves, through the style of their inquiry, and the shape of their questions, complicitous with an assumed enemy" (182).

31. Salman Rushdie, "Let's Get Back to Life," *Guardian*, October 6, 2001, http://www.theguardian.com/books/2001/oct/06/fiction.afghanistan.

32. Raymond Aron, *Main Currents in Sociological Thought: Montesquieu, Comte, Marx, Tocqueville, the Sociologists, and the Revolution of 1848* (New York: Penguin Books, 1969), 19.

33. David Rieff, "There Is No Alternative to War," *Salon*, September 25, 2001, http://www.salon.com/2001/09/26/modernity/.

34. The title of Minc's editorial was an apparent inversion of Jean Baudrillard's editorial "L'esprit du terrorisme," which had appeared in the same paper five days earlier on November 3, 2001. Baudrillard ended his essay with this piercing passage: "In the terrorist attack the event eclipsed all of our interpretive models, whereas in this mindlessly military and technological war we see the opposite: the interpretive model eclipsing the event. Witness, thus, the artificial stakes, the non-place. *War as a continuation of the absence of politics by other means*" (my italics). Alain Minc, "Le terrorisme de l'esprit," *Le Monde*, November 7, 2001; translated by Donovan Hohn, *Harper's Magazine*, February 2002, 18.

35. Minc, "Le terrorisme."

36. They argued that "in France, the controversy over Foucault's writings on Iran is well known and continues to undercut his reputation. For example, during the debate over the September 11, 2001, terrorist attacks on New York and Washington, a prominent French commentator referred polemically and without apparent need for any further explanation to 'Michel Foucault, advocate of Khomeinism in Iran and therefore in theory of its exactions' in a front-page op-ed article in *Le Monde*." Afary and Anderson, *Foucault*, 6.

37. Fred Dallmayr, *Alternative Visions: Paths in the Global Village* (Lanham, Md.: Rowman and Littlefield, 1998). Dallmayr aptly observed that, "faced with the realities of global hegemony, non-Western cultures have to engage in a complex double gesture, to affirm or defend cultural traditions and identities while simultaneously opening the latter up to critical scrutiny and revision" (270).

38. Rothstein, "Attacks on U.S."

39. Ernest Gellner, *Postmodernism, Reason, and Religion* (London: Routledge, 1992), 75.

40. Gellner, *Postmodernism*, 95.

41. Der Derian, *9/11*, 184.

42. Afary and Anderson, *Foucault*, 163.

43. Ibid., 173.

44. Even the hostile Bush administration admitted that Iran played a "constructive role" in toppling the Taliban. A June 2002 brief for Congress, "Iran: Current Developments and U.S. Policy," highlighted that "Iran pledged search and rescue assistance to the United States and pledged to allow U.S. humanitarian

aid for the Afghan people to transit Iran en route to Afghanistan. U.S. officials initially called Iran's role in the anti-Taliban/al-Qaeda effort, including efforts to form a new government at the Bonn conference (ended in agreement December 5, 2001) "constructive." Kenneth Katzman, Congressional Research Service, The Library of Congress, June 2002, CRS 6.

45. For a detailed analysis of this transformation, see Behrooz Ghamari-Tabrizi, *Islam and Dissent in Postrevolutionary Iran: Abdolkarim Soroush, Religious Politics, and Democratic Reform* (London: I.B.Tauris, 2008).

1. Thinking the Unthinkable

1. James Miller's *The Passion of Michel Foucault* (New York: Doubleday, 1993) is a key text that reimagines Foucault's life and lifework around "limit-experiences." Miller depoliticizes Foucault's encounter with the Iranian revolution and relates it to his use of drugs and participation in sado-masochistic sexual rituals as an instance of his fascination with limit-experience.

2. For an insightful discussion of the notion of *Sittlichkeit* and its relation to the expressions of justice, see Weigang Chen, "Peripheral Justice: The Marxist Tradition of Public Hegemony and Its Implications in the Age of Globalization," *Positions* 13, no. 2 (2005): 329–78.

3. See the brilliant analysis of Charles Kurzman, *The Unthinkable Revolution in Iran* (Cambridge: Harvard University Press, 2004).

4. Amir Parviz Pouyan, one of the leaders of a communist urban guerrilla group called the Fadā'iān-e Khalq (The Devotees of People), advanced this theory in late 1960s, which came to be known as the thesis of "two absolutes." In his 1969 manifesto on the necessity of armed struggle, *On the Refutation of the Theory of Survival*, Pouyan identified the two chief causes that prevented the working class from rising against their oppression. "[Workers] presume," he wrote, "the power of their enemy to be absolute and their own inability to emancipate themselves [to be] absolute." And then he asked, "How can one think of emancipation while confronting absolute power with absolute weakness?" (4).

5. Although Jazani was one of the first theorists of armed struggle, he revised his position in prison. He criticized the leadership of the Fadā'iān for their blind devotion to armed struggle without a critical analysis of Iranian society. For further examination of the Fadā'iān movement, see Maziar Behrooz, *Rebels with a Cause: The Failure of the Left in Iran* (London: I.B.Tauris, 1999) and Peyman Vahabzadeh, *A Guerrilla Odyssey: Modernization, Secularism, Democracy, and the Fadai Period of National Liberation in Iran, 1971–1979* (Syracuse: Syracuse University Press, 2010).

6. Reza Baraheni, "Terror in Iran," *New York Review of Books*, October 28, 1976, 21–23.

7. For a chronology of the events in Qom Seminary, see "Āncheh dar 14–17 Khordād-e 54 dar Qom gozasht" [The events of June 4–7, 1975, in Qom], *Faslnāmeh Motāleʿāt-e Tārikhi* [Journal of historical studies] 6 (2005): 159–72; and Ali Shirkhani, "Harkat-e 17 Khordād 1354 Feizieh" [Qom seminary's movement of June 7, 1975], *15 Khordād Journal* 6, no. 25 (1997): 33–56.

8. "Āncheh dar," 162.

9. Shirkhani, "Harkat-e 17 Khordād," 45–46.

10. Ibid., 46–48.

11. "Āncheh dar," 171.

12. Cited in ibid.

13. Ibid.

14. Taheri Khoram-Abadi in *Savak va Ruhāniyat* [Savak and the clergy] (Tehran: The Office of the Islamic Revolution Literature, 1992), 128.

15. See Emadaddin Baqi, *Forudastān va farādastān* [The downtrodden and the dominant: An oral history of the revolution] (Tehran: Nedā-ye Emruz, 2001).

16. See the BBC's interview with Becker: http://www.bbc.co.uk/persian/arts/2012/10/121013_l41_book_goethe_becker_interview.shtml.

17. In describing the events of "ten nights" at the Goethe Institute, I have consulted the following sources: Writers' Association, *Dah shab* [Ten Nights] (Tehran: Amir Kabir, 1978); Mohammad Qobadi, "Kanun-e nevisnadegān-e Iran" [The Iranian Writers' Association], *Faslnāmeh Motāleʿāt-e Tārikhi* [Journal of historical studies], 2 (2004): 242–81; Baqer Parham, "Az kanun-e nevisandegān tā anjoman-e senfi-ye nevisandegān" [From a writers' center to a writers' professional association] *Rāh-e No* [New way], 1, no. 14 (1998): 18–24; The Research Office of *Kayhan*, "Kānun-e nevisandegān-e Iran, az zohur tā soqut" [The rise and fall of the Iranian Writers' Association], *Kayhan Fargangi* 144 (July–August 1998): 4–22.

18. SAVAK documents, 325/23824 and 312/3067. In Qobadi, "The Iranian Writers' Association," 251–52.

19. See Mahmoud Etemadzadeh (M. A. Behāzin), *Az har dari* [From here and there] (Tehran: Jam, 1991), 32–33.

20. Cited in Qobadi, " Kānun-e nevisandegān," 13.

21. Mahmoud Enayat, *Roshanfekrān va enghelāb* [Intellectuals and the revolution] (Los Angeles: Negin, 1991), 32. The Lawyers' Guild also launched a letter-writing campaign around the same time, focusing on the question of the judiciary's independence and respect for human rights. Their letters were more critical and assertive in tone but did not have the same kind of societal impact at the time. For a more detailed discussion, see Ervand Abrahamian, *Iran between Two Revolutions* (Princeton: Princeton University Press, 1982), 500–504.

22. Fereidun Tonkaboni, interview with BBC: http://www.bbc.co.uk/persian/arts/2012/10/121020_l41_book_tonekaboni_goethe_nights.shtml.

23. Transcribed from an audio recording and translated by the author.

24. Mohammad Ali Sepanlou, *Sargozasht-e kanun-e nevisandegān-e Iran* [A history of the Iranian Writers' Association] (Stockholm: Bārān, 2002).

25. Javad Tale'ei, "Shab-hā-ye she'r-e Goethe ertebāti bā voqu'e enqelāb nadāsht" [Goethe Institute's poetry nights had no connection to the Revolution], *Tārikh-e Irani* [Iranian history], October 12, 2012, http://www.tarikhirani.ir/Modules/News/Phtml/News.PrintVersion.Html.php?Lang=fa&TypeId=4& NewsId=2700.

26. Ruhollah Khomeini, *Sahifeh-ye nur* [The collected speeches and declarations of Imam Khomeini] (Tehran: Institute for the Publishing of Imam Khomeini's Works, 1999), 3:254.

27. Islamic Revolution Documentation Center Archive, *Ayatollah Mustafa Khomeini Files*, no. 393, 13.

28. Mehdi Bazargan, *Enqelāb-e Iran dar do harkat* [The Iranian Revolution in two movements], 5th ed. (Tehran: Nehzat-e Azādi Iran, 1984), 24.

29. Cited in Emad Baqi, *Tehrir-e shafāhi-ye enqelāb-e eslāmi* [Writing the oral history of the Islamic Revolution] (Tehran: Tafakor Press, 1994), 261.

30. For a discussion of the differences between these two historical moments, see Charles Kurzman, "The Qum Protests and the Coming of the Iranian Revolution, 1975 and 1978," *Social Science History* 27, no. 3 (Fall 2003): 287–325.

31. *Mustafa Khomeini Files*, no. 393, 91.

32. *Taqvim-e tārikh-e enqelāb-e eslāmi: Mordād 1356-Farvardin 1358* [The calendar of the Islamic Revolution: August 1976–March 1979] (Tehran: Soroush Publisher's Research Group, 1989), 40.

33. Sajjad Rā'i, "Payāmad-hā-ye margi asrār-āmiz" [Consequences of a mysterious death], *E'temād*, no. 2084, Supplement (October 21, 2009): 2.

34. *Taqvim*, 48–49.

35. *Ettelā'āt*, January 7, 1978, reprinted in *Taqvim*, 54–57.

36. *Taqvim*, 58.

37. Khomeini, *Sahifeh*, 3:330–49.

38. For a detailed report on (including the long-term effects of) the Tabriz uprising, see Rahim Nikbakht, "Qiām-e 29 Bahman Tabriz" [Tabriz February 18 uprising], *15 Khordād*, 1, no. 28 (1997): 162–207. The number of casualties, like all other events of revolutionary period, is greatly exaggerated.

39. The statement is reprinted in Ali Davani, *Nehzat-e ruhāniyun-e Iran* [The movement of Iran's clergy: A collection of documents and events, vol. 7] (Tehran: Imam Reza Foundation, 1981), 79–81.

40. Cited in Nikbakht, "Tabriz," 188–89.

204 | Notes to Chapter 1

41. Mohammad Reza Pahlavi, *Pāsokh beh tārikh* [An answer to history] (Tehran: Motarjem, 1992), 332.

42. Cited in Nikbakht, "Tabriz," 200.

43. The fourteen-point manifesto also called for the return of Ayatollah Khomeini from exile and a radical redistribution of wealth in the country. See the document in Davani, *Nehzat*, 7:121–23.

44. *Taqvim*, 86.

45. Khomeini, *Sahifeh*, 3:367–68.

46. Ibid., 367–75.

47. *Taqvim*, 96.

48. Claire Brière interview with Ayatollah Shari'atmadari, *Libération*, May 22, 1978, reprinted in Davani, *Nehzat*, 7: 164–67. Brière was critical of Foucault's conception of the revolutionary movement (see chapter 2), but she also was skeptical of the French feminists' "mission" to Iran (see chapter 4).

49. *Mardom* 6, no. 201 (March 20, 1978): 1. The op-ed pieces and news items in *Mardom*, from early 1976 to the end of the summer of 1978, when martial law was declared in Tehran, primarily reflected the interests of the Soviet Union in Iran. For example, in almost every issue of *Mardom*, Iran's exit from the Central Treaty Organization (CENTO) military pact was presented as one of the main demands of the revolutionary movement. CENTO was a cold war military alliance between Iran, Turkey, Pakistan, the UK, and the United States. People in Moscow were more concerned about Iran's membership in CENTO than people on the streets of Tehran.

50. *Ettelā'āt*, June 1, 1978, in *Taqvim*, 97.

51. *Taqvim*, 111.

52. Ibid., 112.

53. Fereydoun Hoveyda, *The Fall of the Shah* (New York: Simon and Schuster, 1980), 16–20.

54. Qoba was established in the early 1970s and operated under the imam-ate of Mohammad Mofatteh, one of the favorite disciples of Ayatollah Khomeini. For the significance of Qoba Mosque in the revolutionary movement, see Gholamreza Goli-Zavvareh, *Zendegi-Nāmeh shahid Mofatteh* [A biography of Mofatteh the Martyr] (Qom: Daftar-e 'Aql, 2010). The book also includes copies of SAVAK reports on Qoba Mosque.

55. Gholamreza Karbaschi, ed., *Haft-hezār ruz tārikh-e Iran va enqelāb-e eslami* [Seven thousand days of Iranian history and the Islamic Revolution] (Tehran: Center for the Documentation of the Islamic Revolution, 1992), 2:886.

56. *Bayānieh-ye moshtarek* [Joint statement], collection of documents in H. Movahhed, *Do sāl-e ākhar: Reform tā enqelāb* [The last two years: Reform to revolution] (Tehran: Amir Kabir, 1983), 152.

57. For the complete text of Bazargan's message, see Movahhed, *Do sāl-e ākhar*, 156–57.

58. Khomeini, *Sahifeh*, 4:167.

59. Davani, *Nehzat*, 7:265.

60. Ibid., 268.

61. Masoud Behnoud, *Dolathā-ye Iran az Sayyed Ziā tā Bakhtiyār* [The Iranian states from Sayyid Ziā to Bakhtiyār] (Tehran: Javidan, 1985), 776–78.

62. Khomeini, *Sahifeh*, 3:454.

63. Behnoud, *Dolathā-ye Iran*, 774.

64. Movahhed, *Do sāl-e ākhar*, 168.

65. *Taqvim*, 125.

66. For a fascinating collection of eyewitness accounts, see Davani, *Nehzat*, 8:54–85.

67. Khomeini, *Sahifeh*, 3:460–61.

2. How Did Foucault Make Sense of the Iranian Revolution?

1. Hamid Algar, *The Roots of the Islamic Revolution* (Oneonta, N.Y.: Islamic Publications International, 2011), 104. Algar points out that Massignon had his own personal reasons to believe, erroneously, that Hallaj represented the typical Sufi mystic in Islamic tradition. Shari'ati was very much influenced by Massignon and for political reasons he never questioned the validity of Massignon's claim.

2. Ali Shari'ati, *An Approach to the Understanding of Islam* (Lesson 1): http://www.shariati.com/english/lesson/lesson1.html.

3. Michel Foucault, "Iran: The Spirit of a World without Spirit," in Afary and Anderson, *Foucault*, 257. For the sake of consistency, I have used Afary and Anderson's translations of Foucault's essays on the Iranian Revolution. Four thousand dead was an inflated number that circulated after Black Friday. Wildly overstated numbers circulated effectively during the Shah's reign in order to exaggerate the extent of the brutality of the regime. An official and true estimate put the dead at 88 and wounded at 205. The Martyrs Foundation confirmed these numbers after the revolution. For a report on the actual numbers of casualties incurred by the political oppression of the Shah's regime, see Emad Baqi, *Barresi-ye Enqelab-e Iran* [An analysis of the Iranian Revolution] (Tehran: Sarabi, 2003).

4. Foucault, "Iran," 253.

5. Ibid., 251.

6. Michel Foucault, "Is It Useless to Revolt?," in Afary and Anderson, *Foucault*, 266.

7. Edward Said, *Beginnings: Invention and Method* (New York: Basic Books, 1975), 290.

8. Michel Foucault, "The Order of Discourse," in *Untying the Text*, ed. Robert Young (London: Routledge and Kegan Paul, 1981), 67.

9. Leezenberg, "Power and Political Spirituality."

10. Cited in ibid., 76.

11. Michel Foucault, "The Shah Is a Hundred Years behind the Times," in Afary and Anderson, *Foucault*, 194.

12. The term was coined by the French Marxist Orientalist Maxime Rodinson in his critique of Foucault. See Afary and Anderson, *Foucault*, 99–102.

13. Foucault, "The Shah," 198.

14. Michel Foucault, "A Revolt with Bare Hands," in Afary and Anderson, *Foucault*, 211. Foucault identified three paradoxes in the revolutionary movement: first, the ineffectiveness of one of the mightiest militaries in the world against peaceful demonstrators; second, the absence of internal conflicts; and third, the lack of future plans.

15. This is a reference is to the important strike of the oil workers in the Khuzestan that played a key role in the economic collapse of the Pahlavi regime.

16. For a discussion on Foucault's eschatological view, see Melinda Cooper, "The Law of the Household: Foucault, Neoliberalism, and the Iranian Revolution," in *The Government of Life: Foucault, Biopolitics, and Neoliberalism*, ed. Vanessa Lemm and Miguel Vatter (New York: Fordham University Press, 2014), 29–58.

17. Foucault, "A Revolt," 212.

18. Foucault, "Iran," 256.

19. Michel Foucault, "What Are the Iranians Dreaming *[Rêvent]* About?," in Afary and Anderson, *Foucault*, 209.

20. "Dialogue between Michel Foucault and Baqir Parham," conducted in September 1978, in Afary and Anderson, *Foucault*, 185.

21. Foucault, "Dialogue," 186.

22. See Michel Foucault, "Questions of Method," in *The Foucault Effect: Studies in Governmentality*, ed. G. Burchell, C. Gordon, and P. Miller (Chicago: University of Chicago Press, 1991), 73–86.

23. Jeremy R. Carrette, "Prologue to a Confession of the Flesh," in *Religion and Culture: Michel Foucault*, ed. Jeremy R. Carrette (New York: Routledge, 1999), 1–49.

24. Cited in Carrette, "Prologue," 1.

25. Michel Foucault, "On the Genealogy of Ethics," in *The Foucault Reader*, ed. Paul Rabinow (New York: Pantheon Books, 1984), 352 (my italics).

26. James Bernauer, *Michel Foucault's Force of Flight: Toward an Ethics for Thought* (Atlantic Highlands, N.J.: Humanities Press, 1991). For Foucault's view on religion and the paradoxical effects of the death of God and death of Man, see his selected writings in Jeremy Carrette, *Religion and Culture*.

27. James Miller, *The Passion of Michel Foucault* (New York: Doubleday, 1993).

28. Foucault explains: "The pastoral, the new diplomatic-military techniques and, lastly, police: these are the three elements that I believe made possible the production of this fundamental phenomenon in Western history, the governmentalization of the state." "Governmentality," in G. Burchell et al., *The Foucault Effect*, 104.

29. Michel Foucault, "The Hermeneutics of the Self," in Carrette, *Religion and Culture*, 162–63.

30. Carrette, *Religion and Culture*, 42.

31. Foucault, "Questions of Method," 82.

32. Foucault, "Iran," 252.

33. Most vociferous among those was the French Marxist Orientalist Maxime Rodinson, whose writings are translated by Afary and Anderson: "Islam Resurgent?," 223–39; "Khomeini and the 'Primacy of the Spiritual,'" 241–45; "Critique of Foucault on Iran," 267–77.

34. Michel Foucault, "Tehran: Faith against the Shah," in Afary and Anderson, *Foucault*, 200.

35. Foucault, "Tehran," 202.

36. Foucault, "Iran," 255.

37. See chapter 5 for a more detailed elaboration on the notion of care of the self.

38. Foucault, "Tehran," 201.

39. For an elaboration on this point, see Armando Salvatore, *Islam and the Political Discourse of Modernity* (Berkshire: Ithaca Press, 1997), 152–54.

40. Foucault, "Iranians Dreaming," 208.

41. Ghamari-Tabrizi, *Islam and Dissent.*

42. Foucault, "Iranians Dreaming," 205–7.

43. Salvatore, *Islam,*152.

44. Cited in Afary and Anderson, *Foucault*, 91.

45. François Furet, *Interpreting the French Revolution*, trans. Elborg Forster (Cambridge: Cambridge University Press, 1981).

46. Žižek, *Lost Causes*, 158.

47. Foucault, "A Revolt," 212.

48. Foucault, "Revolutionary Action: 'Until Now,'" in *Michel Foucault, Language, Counter-Memory, Practice*, ed. Donald F. Bouchard (Ithaca: Cornell University Press, 1980), 230.

49. Nancy Fraser, *Unruly Practices* (Minneapolis: University of Minnesota Press, 1989), 33.

50. Derrida famously remarked in an interview, "Indeed, I cannot conceive of a radical critique which would not be ultimately motivated by some sort of

affirmation, acknowledged or not." See Richard Kearny, "Dialogue with Jacque Derrida," in *Dialogues with Contemporary Continental Thinkers*, ed. Richard Kearny (Manchester: Manchester University Press, 1984), 118.

51. William Connolly, *Politics and Ambiguity* (Madison: University of Wisconsin Press, 1987), 107 (my italics).

52. Figuratively "perplexity," from *A-poria* in Greek, meaning literally "no passage."

53. In the preface to *Dialectic of Enlightenment*, Horkheimer and Adorno argue that Enlightenment is both necessary and impossible: necessary because humanity would otherwise continue hurtling towards self-destruction and unfreedom, and impossible because enlightenment can only be attained through rational human activity, and yet rationality is itself the origin of the problem. This was the aporia that led Horkheimer and Adorno to become ever more circumspect about the concrete political aims of critical theory. "Adorno's faith in the capacity of any theory to guide social, political, or moral emancipation soon waned to the point that he considered almost any collective political action to be premature, arbitrary, and futile." Gordon Finlayson, *Habermas: A Very Short Introduction* (Oxford: Oxford University Press, 2005), 8.

54. Jürgen Habermas, *The Philosophical Discourse of Modernity* (Cambridge: MIT Press, 1990), 283.

55. Michel Foucault, *Power/Knowledge* (New York: Pantheon, 1980), 142.

56. Richard Rorty, *Essays on Heidegger and Others* (Cambridge: Cambridge University Press, 1991), 173.

57. Foucault, *Power/Knowledge*, 142.

58. Ibid., 133.

59. Foucault, "On the Genealogy of Ethics," in *Michel Foucault: Beyond Structuralism and Hermeneutics* ed. Hubert L. Dreyfus and Paul Rabinow (Chicago: University of Chicago Press, 1983), 231–32 (my italics).

60. Foucault is borrowing the concept of "absolutely absolute" from Amir Parviz Pouyan, one of the leaders of a communist urban guerilla group called the Fadā'iān-e Khalq (The Devotees of People), which was established in 1970. See chapter 1, note 4.

61. Foucault, "Is It Useless to Revolt?," 63–64.

62. Žižek, *Lost Causes*, 109.

63. Gilles Deleuze, *Negotiations: 1972–1990*, trans. Martin Joughin (New York: Columbia University Press, 1995), 171.

64. Foucault, "Is It Useless to Revolt?," 266.

65. Frantz Fanon, *A Dying Colonialism*, trans. Haakon Chevalier (New York: Grove Press, 1965).

66. Fanon, *Dying Colonialism*, 60.

67. John McSweeney, "Religion in the Web of Immanence: Foucault and Thinking Otherwise after the Death of God," *Foucault Studies* 15 (2013): 90.

3. Misrepresenting the Revolution, Misreading Foucault

1. Afary and Anderson, *Foucault*, 105 (my italics). It is not clear at what point this "displacing" had happened in the revolutionary movement. Was there a period during the revolutionary movement that Marxists and the nationalist Left led the revolutionary movement?

2. Janet Afary, *The Iranian Constitutional Revolution, 1906–1911: Grassroots Democracy, Social Democracy, and the Origins of Feminism* (New York: Columbia University Press, 1996).

3. Transcribed and translated by the author from a YouTube posting of the trial.

4. See Akbar Ganji's essay "Ostureh-ye Khomeini cheguneh sākhteh shod" [How was Khomeini's legend constructed], posted on http://news.gooya.com/politics/archives/2014/06/181080.php. Ganji revisits the writings of key intellectual and literary figures, such as Reza Baraheni, Ehsan Naraqi, Daryush Shaygan, Bijan Jazani, Forough Farrokhzad, and many others, to show how they all romanticized a notion of revolutionary Islam and how Khomeini came to represent the embodiment of that romantic revolutionary ideology.

5. Majid Sharif-Vaqefi was gunned down in 1975, and his body was burned to prevent identification by SAVAK.

6. Cited in Ervand Abrahamian, *The Iranian Mojahedin* (New Haven: Yale University Press, 1992), 161–62.

7. Foucault, "Is It Useless to Revolt?," 263.

8. Foucault, "Iran," 257.

9. Bonnie Honig, "What Foucault Saw in the Revolution: On the Use and Abuse of Theology for Politics," *Political Theory* 36, no. 2 (2008): 301–12.

10. 'Ashura is the tenth day of the month of Muharram in the Islamic lunar calendar and the day that Shi'ites' third Imam was martyred in the battle of Karbala. The battle of Karbala, which took place in what is now Iraq, happened in AD 680 (year 61 of the Islamic calendar). Shi'ites believe that knowing that his victory was in his martyrdom, Imam Hussein fought against the mighty army of Yazid, the second caliph of the Umayyad dynasty, with only seventy-two of his companions.

11. For a historically informed and theoretically sophisticated study of Muharram rituals, see Babak Rahimi's *Theater State and the Formation of Early Modern Public Sphere in Iran: Studies on Safavid Muharram Rituals, 1590–1641* (Leiden: Brill, 2012). In the brief introduction to chapter 1, Rahimi shows how Foucault

consciously distinguished his reading of Muharram carnivalesque transgressions from "Christian rites of penitence in the display of shame and sorrow for the loss of a sacred ideal." Foucault highlights the feeling of the "intoxication of sacrifice" that leads "the Shi'ite people [to] become enamored with extremes." As Rahimi observes, "The reference to 'intoxication' plays a critical role in this interpretive thrust. By this, Foucault wants to draw attention to that which exceeds boundaries, especially everyday subjective ones" (31).

12. On Shari'ati's ideas, see Ali Rahnema, *An Islamic Utopian: A Political Biography of Ali Shariati* (London: I.B.Tauris, 2000); and Ghamari-Tabrizi, *Islam and Dissent*, chapter 5.

13. Afary and Anderson, *Foucault*, 54. The reference for the scene described in the alleyway is from Michel Mazzaoui, "Shi'ism and *Ashura* in South Lebanon," in *Ta'ziyeh, Ritual and Drama in Iran*, ed. Peter Chelkowski (New York University Press, 1979), 228–37.

14. Rahnema, *Islamic Utopian*, 272–75.

15. Ibid., 266–76.

16. In addition to Ali Rahnema's *Islamic Utopian*, see Kingshuk Chatterjee, *Ali Shari'ati and the Shaping of Political Islam in Iran* (New York: Palgrave Macmillan, 2011). For a very short review of Shari'ati's political significance, particularly in relation to the question of xenophobia, see Ervand Abrahamian, "Ali Shari'ati: Ideologue of the Iranian Revolution," *MERIP Reports* 102 (January 1982): 22–24. Abrahamian writes: "Westerners commonly perceive the Iranian Revolution as an atavistic and xenophobic movement that rejects all things modern and non-Muslim, a view reinforced by the present leaders of Iran. . . . This conventional wisdom, however, ignores the contributions of Dr. Ali Shari'ati, the main ideologue of the Iranian Revolution. Shari'ati drew his inspiration from outside as well as from within Islam: from Western sociology—particularly Marxist sociology—as well as from Muslim theology; from theorists of the Third World—especially Franz Fanon—as well as from the teachings of the early Shi'i martyrs" (22).

17. Ali Shari'ati, *Marxism and Other Western Fallacies: An Islamic Critique*, trans. R. Campbell (Berkeley: Mizan Press, 1980).

18. Abu Dharr was one of the warriors of Imam Ali. Shari'ati's first published work (1956) was a translation from Arabic of a book by Joudah Al-Sahhar called *Abu Dharr Ghaffari*, which had been originally published in Mashhad. *Abu Dharr, Collected Works*, vol. 3 (Tehran: Hosseiniyyeh Ershad, 1978).

19. For a detailed account of these campaigns, see Naser Minachi, *Tārikh-e Hosseinieh-ye Ershād* [A history of Hosseinieh-ye Ershād] (Tehran: Ershād Publications, 2005),120–23; Rahnema, *Islamic Utopian*, 271–76.

20. Ali Shari'ati, *Nāmeh beh Ayatollah al-Uzma Milani* [Letter to the Grand Ayatollah Milani], in *Collected Works* (Tehran: Qalam, 1996), 34:98–103.

21. Rahnema, *Islamic Utopian*, 123–24.

22. He died in 1977 in the UK of a heart attack at the age of forty-four. His followers attributed his sudden death to the Shah's intelligence officers. That is why they called him "our martyred teacher."

23. Mansur Hallaj (d. 922), who proclaimed *Ana al-Haqq* (I have merged with, I am, the Truth) was executed as a heretic. This verse is attributed to him: "Kill me, O my trustworthy friends—for in my being killed is my life" (translated by Annemarie Schimmel in her work *Islam: An Introduction* [Albany: State University of New York Press, 1992], 108). Shari'ati transformed Hallaj's mystic "death through love" into martyrdom for the cause.

24. For a full account of Shari'ati's agonistic moments, see chapter 11, "Mystical Murmurs," in Rahnema, *Islamic Utopian*, 144–60.

25. Umar succeeded Abu Bakr as the second caliph after the Prophet's death.

26. The direction toward which Muslims face during their daily prayer: Mecca, Saudi Arabia.

27. Shari'ati, *āri inchenin bud barādar* [Yes, brother! This is how it was], in *Collected Works* (Tehran: Entesharat-e Sabz, 1982), 24:309–13.

28. A term they borrow from the French Marxist Orientalist Maxime Rodinson.

29. See, for example, Vanessa Martin's comprehensive commentary, "Religion and State in Khumaini's *Kashf al-asrār*," *Bulletin of the School of Oriental and African Studies*, no. 1 (1993): 34–45; Michael Fischer, "Imam Khomeini: Four Levels of Understanding," in *Voices of Resurgent Islam*, ed. John Esposito (New York: Oxford University Press, 1983), 150–74; Gregory Rose, "*Velayat-e Faqih* and the Recovery of Islamic Identity in the Thought of Ayatollah Khomeini," in *Religion and Politics in Iran: Shi'ism from Quietism to Revolution*, ed. Nikki Keddie (New Haven: Yale University Press, 1983).

30. Ruhollah Khomeini, *Kashf al-Asrār* [Revealing the secrets] (n.p.: [1943]), 230–42. For a more detailed analysis of the evolution of Khomeini's ideas, see Behrooz Ghamari-Tabrizi, "The Divine, the People, the *Faqih*: On Khomeini's Theory of Sovereignty," in *A Critical Introduction to Khomeini*, ed. Arshin Adib-Moghaddam (Cambridge: Cambridge University Press, 2014), 211–39. Adib-Moghaddam's volume is an important contribution to a critical understanding of Khomeini's legacy. Also, for a detailed analysis of competing interpretations and appropriation of Khomeini's ideas and practices, see Babak Rahimi's "Contentious Legacies of the Ayatollah" in the same volume.

31. See Vanessa Martin's commentary, p. 40. For a comprehensive discussion on the transformation of Khomeini's views on governance, see Jamileh Kadivar, *Tahavvol-e goftemān-e siyāsi-e Shi'i dar Iran* [The transformation of Shi'i political discourse in Iran] (Tehran: Tarh-e No, 2000) and Mohsen Kadivar, *Hokumat-e velā'i* [Governance by guardianship] (Tehran: Nay Publishers, 1999).

32. Nuri was one of the most influential clergymen during the Constitutional Revolution of 1905–6. He insisted on the irreconcilability of the *shari'a* with constitutional laws. An early supporter of the Constitutional Revolution, Nuri became more suspicious of its premises and eventually declared it "fundamentally antagonistic to the spirit of Islam." See Mohammad Torkman, ed., *Rasā'el, e'lāmiyeh-hā, maktubāt, va ruznāmeh-hā* [Creeds, pronouncements, correspondences, and papers] (Tehran: Rasa Publishers 1983), 1:103. He berated the constitutionalists for writing a "document of perdition" (64) based on two principles of "liberty" and "equality," both of which "emanated from the West" and were "alien" to Muslims (106).

33. Ayatollah Khomeini, "Formation of the Council of the Islamic Revolution," in *Islam and Revolution, Writings and Declarations of Imam Khomeini*, trans. and annot. Hamid Algar (Berkeley: Mizan Press, 1981), 246–47.

34. Afary and Anderson compare Muharram rituals and passion plays with the fascist anti-Semitic appropriations of Christian passion plays, a claim that is hard to substantiate. They also make unsubstantiated references to Khomeini's hostility to an ambiguous group generically called "Iran's minorities": "[Khomeini] rekindled dormant religious biases that progressive intellectuals had tried to erase for decades. He said that the Shah was carrying the wishes of the Jewish state, a government that planned to uproot Islam and seize the economy with the help of Iran's minorities [!]" (58). Shari'ati, they claim, was influenced by "the most virulent forms of Christian anti-Semitism" (62). They quote Khomeini's interview on October 8, 1978, in which he rejects reformist attempts to save monarchy from the revolution. They interpret whenever Khomeini emphasizes the Islamic revolution and the will of God as "the depth of his hostility towards the National Front, the Left, . . . [and] Iran's religious minorities (including Zoroastrians)" (86). "Here, Khomeini was continuing his earlier attacks on Jews, Baha'is, and other non-Muslim Iranians (86).

35. For a detailed account, see Mahdi Ahouei, "Iranian Anti-Zionism and the Holocaust: A Long Discourse Dismissed," *Radical History Review* 105 (Fall 2009): 58–78.

36. Khomeini, *Sahifeh*, 4:45.

37. Ghamari-Tabrizi, *Islam and Dissent*, 50–53.

38. Khomeini's message, cited in Afary and Anderson, *Foucault*, 86 (italics added by Afary and Anderson).

39. Afary and Anderson, *Foucault*, 86.

40. Michel Foucault, "The Challenge to the Opposition," in Afary and Anderson, *Foucault*, 213–14.

41. According to Habibi, the five jurists who authored the first draft of the constitution were Ahmad Sadr Hajj Seyyed Javadi, Naser Katuzian, Mohammad

Ja'fari Langarudi, Abdolkarim Lahiji, and Abbas Minachi. For more, see Asghar Schirazi, *The Constitution of Iran: Politics and the State in the Islamic Republic*, trans. John O'Kane (London: I.B.Tauris, 1997), 38. In an interview, Ezzatollah Sahabi recalled that Fathollah Bani Sadr, another liberal jurist, was also a member of the committee. See Bahman Ahmadi Amu'i, *Eqtesād-e siyāsi-ye Jomhuri-ye Islami: Dar goftegu ba Ezzatollah Sahabi* [The political economy of the Islamic Republic: In conversation with Ezzatollah Sahabi] (Tehran: Jam-e No, 2003).

42. For a brief history of the period, see Schirazi, *The Constitution*, 22–38 and Mehdi Moslem, *Factional Politics in Post-Khomeini Iran* (Syracuse: Syracuse University Press, 2002), 11–46.

43. See Amu'i, *Eqtesād-e siyāsi*. Also, for a detailed report on the drafting of the new constitution, see Ghamari-Tabrizi, *Islam and Dissent*, chapter 3.

44. *Kayhan*, June 18, 1979, cited in Schirazi, *The Constitution*, 23.

45. Volumes 2 and 3 of Ayatollah Khomeini's *Sahifeh-y Nur* are largely devoted to his assertions about the meaning of an Islamic Republic and the role of the *ruhāniyat* in its affairs. For specific references to his position on the advisory role of the *ruhāniyat*, see Khomeini, *Sahifeh*, 2:250; 3:75–78, 110–11. Typical of these statements were: "I, and other *ruhāniyun*, will not hold a position in the future government, the duty of *ruhāniyun* is to guide, I shall only take upon myself the responsibility of guiding the future government" (3:135). On another occasion, he reiterated that he "never said that *ruhāniyun* are going to be in charge of the government, *ruhāniyun* have other responsibilities" (3:140).

46. Cited in M. Kadivar, *Hokumat-e velā'i*, 183.

47. Foucault, "Iranians Dreaming," 206.

48. Ibid.

49. Ervand Abrahamian, *Khomeinism: Essay on the Islamic Republic* (London: I.B.Tauris, 1993), 3.

50. Claudie Broyelle and Jacque Broyelle, "What Are the Philosophers Dreaming About? Was Michel Foucault Mistaken about the Iranian Revolution?," in Afary and Anderson, *Foucault*, 247–48.

51. Michel Foucault, "Foucault's Response to Claudie and Jacques Broyelle," in Afary and Anderson, *Foucault*, 249.

52. John Esposito, *Unholy War: Terror in the Name of Islam* (New York: Oxford, 2002).

53. Fred Halliday, *Islam and the Myth of Confrontation* (London: I.B.Tauris, 2002).

54. Paul Berman, *Terror and Liberalism* (New York: W. W. Norton, 2003).

55. See Berman's *New York Times* op-ed piece in which he defends the invasion of Iraq but questions the incompetence of the Bush Administration in executing it efficiently. For a thoughtful review of his book, see Anatol Lieven's

"Liberal Hawk Down," in the *Nation*, October 7, 2004, http://www.thenation.com/article/liberal-hawk-down. Lieven correctly argues that "Berman, this 'man of the Left,' offers a portrait of 'Islamic fascism' that is hardly distinguishable from that of such hard-line right-wing members of the Israeli lobby as Daniel Pipes. In terms of historical literacy, the argument is the equivalent of suggesting that because nineteenth-century European socialism and clerical conservatism shared a deep hostility to bourgeois liberalism, they somehow formed part of the same ideological and political tendency."

56. Rubin Barnett and Sara Batmanglich, "The U.S. and Iran in Afghanistan: Policy Gone Awry," MIT International Studies, October 2008, 3.

57. James Dobbins, *After the Taliban: Nation-Building in Afghanistan* (Washington, D.C.: Potomac Books, 2008).

58. Cited in Afary and Anderson, *Foucault*, 19.

59. Ibid.

60. Michel Foucault, "The Minimalist Self," in *Politics, Philosophy, Culture: Interviews and Other Writings, 1977–1984*, ed. Lawrence Kritzman (London: Routledge, 1988), 3.

61. For an insightful discussion of Foucault and silence, see Jeremy R. Carrette, "Silence and Confession," in *Foucault and Religion: Spiritual Corporeality and Political Spirituality*, 25–43 (London: Routledge, 2002).

62. Michel Foucault, *Discipline and Punish: The Birth of the Prison*, trans. Alan Sheridan (New York: Pantheon, 1977), 293.

63. In his 1982 Vermont lectures, Foucault also speaks positively of the Pythagorean pedagogical value of silence developed as an art of listening in opposition to the dialogic form found in Plato. "Technologies of the Self," in *Technologies of the Self: A Seminar with Michel Foucault*, ed. L. H. Martin, H. Gutman, and P. H. Hutton (London: Tavistock, 1988), 16–49.

64. Foucault specifically talks about this notion in two lectures: one at the Collège de France on March 3, 1982 (Michel Foucault, *The Hermeneutics of the Subject: Lectures at the Collège de France, 1981–1982* [New York: Picador, 2001], 331–55), and the other in October of the same year in Vermont (Foucault, "Technologies of the Self," 16–49).

65. Foucault, *Hermeneutics*, 341.

66. Michel Foucault, "Nietzsche, Genealogy, History," in *Michel Foucault: Language, Counter-Memory, Practice: Selected Essays and Interviews*, ed. D. F. Bouchard (Ithaca: Cornell University Press, [1971] 1977), 139.

67. Michel Foucault, *Security, Territory, Population: Lectures at the Collège de France, 1977–78*, trans. Graham Bruchell, ed. Michel Senellart (New York: Picador, 2009).

68. Norma Claire Moruzzi, review of *Foucault and the Iranian Revolution,* by Afary and Anderson, *International Journal of Middle East Studies* 38, no. 3 (2006): 492–94.

69. Michel Foucault, "The Mythical Leader of the Iranian Revolt," in Afary and Anderson, *Foucault,* 220.

4. The Reign of Terror, Women's Issues, and Feminist Politics

1. Letter by Atoussa H., in Afary and Anderson, *Foucault,* 209–10.

2. See Joan Wallach Scott, *The Politics of the Veil* (Princeton: Princeton University Press, 2010); Saba Mahmood, *Politics of Piety: The Islamic Revival and the Feminist Subject* (Princeton: Princeton University Press, 2011); and more recently, Lila Abu-Lughod, *Do Muslim Women Need Saving?* (Cambridge: Harvard University Press, 2013).

3. Another critic who took political Islam seriously and began to think about its revolutionary significance was Norman O. Brown. Between 1980 and 1981 Brown delivered seven lectures on Islam, which eventually were collected and published thirty years later as *The Challenge of Islam: The Prophetic Tradition,* ed. Jerome Neu (Santa Cruz: New Pacific Press, 2009). In his first lecture he admits: "An essential ingredient in the impetus that leads to my being here offering to lecture on the challenge of Islam comes from the Ayatollah Khomeini, and my discovery of my total inability to situate what was happening . . . and relate what was happening to our understanding of what was going on in the world. . . . There is a truth in saying that I owe it to Ayatollah Khomeini to have been, as it were, woken up from my dogmatic slumber, and required to consider the subject of these lectures" (1). In contrast to the dominant Orientalist perception of Islam, Brown considers Islam to be a part of Western tradition rather than "a barbarism from outside." "Islam," he argues, "is not another Oriental cultural tradition. It is an alternative, a rival interpretation of our tradition." That perhaps is the most controversial claim that Brown advances in these lectures: that Islam can also offer a political path for Westerners. One needs to keep in mind that these lectures were delivered right after the Iranian Revolution and in the wake of the American hostage crisis. This, in turn, adds to the significance of Brown's bold intervention. "Islam," Brown remarks, "is a wager that Christianity has gone wrong" (3). Under the influence of the Iranian Revolution, Brown also became more interested in Shi'i Islam and its interpretive approach to Prophetic tradition. He points out how through Shi'ism Islam became *realpolitik.* As Jay Cantor writes in his introduction to these lectures, "The existential nature of prophecy . . . is inevitably intertwined with the problem of succession, of interpretive (which is to say political) authority." It is in this context that Brown

concludes his first lecture with these piercing words: "I end with a vision of two kinds of social criticism alive in the world today: Marxism and Islam. Two still-revolutionary forces. Two tired old revolutionary horses. Neither of them doing very well, but it would be a mistake to take any comfort from their failure. The human race is at stake. And they both, Marxism and Islam, would agree on one proposition: There will be one world, or there will be none" (12).

4. Abdallah Laroui, *The Crisis of the Arab Intellectual: Traditionalism or Historicism?*, trans. Diarmid Cammell (Berkeley: University of California Press, 1976), 60.

5. "Foucault's Response to Atoussa H.," in Afary and Anderson, *Foucault*, 210.

6. Ibid.

7. There is a wealth of literature that demonstrates that gender relations and the situation of women in Iran must be understood in practice, not merely based on a formal reading of legal codes and rights. The seminal work of Parvin Paidar, *Women and the Political Process in Twentieth-Century Iran* (Cambridge: Cambridge University Press, 1997), is the best example of such an approach. For a nuanced study of the changes in religious discourses on women and gender relations, see Ziba Mir-Hosseini, *Islam and Gender: The Religious Debate in Contemporary Iran* (Princeton: Princeton University Press, 1999). For a detailed study of women's social and economic status under the Islamic Republic, see Roksana Bahramitash and Shahla Kazemipour, "Myths and Realities of the Impact of Islam on Women: Changing Marital Status in Iran," *Middle East Critique* 15, no. 2 (2006): 111–28; Roksana Bahramitash, "Market Fundamentalism versus Religious Fundamentalism: Women's Employment in Iran," *Middle East Critique* 13, no. 1 (2004): 33–46; Homa Hoodfar, "Iranian Women at the Intersection of Citizenship and the Family Code: The Perils of 'Islamic Criteria,'" in *Gender and Citizenship in the Middle East*, ed. Suad Josef (Syracuse: Syracuse University Press, 2000); Homa Hoodfar and Samad Assadpour, "The Politics of Population Policy in the Islamic Republic of Iran," *Studies in Family Planning* 31, no. 1 (2000): 19–34.

8. See Mir-Hosseini, *Islam and Gender*. For a more general discussion of historical changes in Islamic discourse on women, see Leila Ahmed, *Women and Gender in Islam: Historical Roots of a Modern Debate* (New Haven: Yale University Press, 1992), particularly part 3.

9. Paidar, *Women and the Political Process*, 359.

10. For two excellent examples of how patriarchal ideologies generate paradoxical objective realities in the American context, see Rebecca Klatch, *Women of the Right* (Philadelphia: Temple University Press, 1988); and Kathleen Blee, *Women of the Klan: Racism and Gender in the 1920s* (Berkeley: University of California Press, 1991).

11. Kurzman, *The Unthinkable Revolution*.

12. There existed four major tendencies in the Iranian Left. The first, represented by the Tudeh Party (People's Party, est. 1941), followed a pro-Soviet platform. The party supported the Islamic Republic so long as it followed an anti-American policy and allowed the Tudeh Party to continue its legal operation. The second, represented by the Organization of the Fadā'iān (Devotee) Guerrillas (est. 1970), advocated armed struggle and was critical of Tudeh Party's conciliatory and reformist agenda against the Shah. After the revolution the two tendencies followed the same strategy in defending the new regime. The third tendency, much smaller than the first two, represented by the Organization of Peikār (Struggle) for the Liberation of the Working Class (est. 1978), was the Marxist faction of the radical Islamist organization Peoples' Mojāhedin. It followed an independent line and promoted the same radicalism against both capitalism and its American supporters as well as the Soviet social-imperialist expansionism. The fourth tendency, represented by Ranjbarān (Toilers) Party, followed a Maoist line. Ranjbarān was the only party on the Left that defended the liberal policies of the provisional government.

13. Published in *Kār* [Labor], no. 3 (March 23, 1979): 8. The number of martyrs of the revolution is highly exaggerated. The total number of people killed during the Shah's regime ranged between three to four thousand.

14. In a lecture two years after his forced resignation, Bazargan lamented, "As much as our revolution was grand and succeeded with the speed of light, the postrevolutionary transformations—which was dubbed as 'permanent revolution'—also happened with firework and 'radicalism.' But in a sense, it also was a revolution against the revolution. All the elements—such as pride in nationhood, humanism, and freedom—that created a national unity during the revolution turned into excuses for unfounded accusations, animosity, and frenzy." See Mehdi Bazargan, "Enqelāb-e Iran dar do harkat" [The Iranian Revolution in two movements], *Collected Works* (Tehran: Bazargan Foundation, 2012), 23:304.

15. Shari'ati directly used the term on many occasions in his lectures without making a reference to its Marxist origins. "There is a thesis called 'permanent revolution' that demonstrates how it is possible to intervene in the seemingly inevitable process of stagnation of a society. It is conceivable to exert a vanguard leadership over a society to sustain a permanent revolution by constantly reinventing the means of its livelihood." See *Islamology* (Tehran: Entesharat-e Shari'ati, 1981), 2:65. Shari'ati might have also been inspired by Régis Debray's *Revolution in the Revolution*, which had significant currency in French Left intellectual circles during his residence in Paris from 1960 to 1965.

16. *Peikār*, no. 3 (May 14, 1979): 1.

17. Published in *Peikār*, no. 5 (May 27, 1979): 5.

18. *Kār* 1, no. 12 (May 23, 1979): 12.

19. Rodinson, "Critique of Foucault on Iran," 270–72.

20. There was never an "imposition of *chador*" (the black head-to-toe veiling) after the revolution, but this is often the way feminist critics of Foucault frame the issue. I will discuss this later in this chapter.

21. Cited in Rosemarie Scullion, "Michel Foucault the Orientalist: On Revolutionary Iran and the 'Spirit of Islam,'" *South Central Review* 12, no. 2 (1995): 16–40.

22. Nima Naghibi, *Rethinking Global Sisterhood: Western Feminism and Iran* (Minneapolis: University of Minnesota Press, 2007), 65.

23. Afsaneh Najmabadi, "Hazards of Modernity and Morality: Women, State and Ideology in Contemporary Iran," in *Women, Islam and the State*, ed. D. Kandiyoti (Philadelphia: Temple University Press, 1991), 48–76.

24. Najmabadi, "Hazards," 49.

25. Afsaneh Najmabadi, "Veiled Discourse-Unveiled Bodies," *Feminist Studies* 19, no. 3 (1993): 487–518.

26. Najmabadi, "Hazards," 65.

27. Jalal Al-e Ahmad, *Gharbzadegi* [Westoxication] (Tehran: Ravaq, 1962), 56. Al-e Ahmad does not advocate a return of women to domestic responsibilities. Rather, he believed that the changes in women's status were cosmetic and that in order to have meaningful gains women needed to enjoy equal opportunities with men and take part in fulfilling their social responsibilities. He continues: "Until the day that the contribution of men and women are recognized in society, they gain equal pay for their labor and women assume positions of responsibility in society, and equality in its true material and spiritual meaning is not established between men and women, women's emancipation remains an empty slogan. It only would add to the masses of consumers of facial powder and lipstick, products of western industries. This is another face of *gharbzadegi*. What is at stake is the leadership of the nation, the path on which women are not taking" (57).

28. Ayatollah Montazeri, *Kayhān*, January 16, 1979, 3.

29. Khomeini, *Sahifeh*, 5:189.

30. The law was enacted in 1967 and gave women more rights in divorce and custody matters. Since its conception, the clergy by and large opposed its basic premises, which many believed violated the Islamic views on women's role in the family. To appease traditionalist clerics who remained skeptical of the revolution and the promised Islamic Republic, Ayatollah Khomeini annulled the law in February 1979. But in October of the same year, the Revolutionary Council passed the Bill on Special Civil Courts, which restored the prerevolutionary ordinances. Shortly after the Revolutionary Council passed the new bill, emphasizing the central role women played in the revolution, Khomeini called upon women

to think of marriage as a contract in which they could stipulate even the right to initiate divorce. Accordingly, while the law instituted men's unilateral right to divorce their wives, it also recognized in practice the right of citizens to include provisions in the marriage contract that could undermine the same laws. In 1982 a ministerial order reinstated all the provisions of the 1967 law. See Ziba Mir-Hosseini, *Marriage on Trial: A Study of Islamic Family Law* (London: I.B.Tauris, 1993), 54–56; and Schirazi, *The Constitution of Iran*, 217.

31. Khomeini, *Sahifeh*, 6:328–29.

32. For a more detailed history of the Iranian Left's position, see Haideh Moghissi, *Populism and Feminism in Iran: Women's Struggle in a Male-Defined Revolutionary Movement* (New York: St. Martin's Press, 1994), 139–58. Although I disagree with Moghissi's conclusions, there is good documentary evidence in her narrative of women's protests during this period. Also see Mahnaz Matin and Naser Mohajer's invaluable two-volume collection of documents in *Khizesh-e zanān dar Esfand 1357* [Iranian women's uprising in March 1979] (Paris: Noqteh, 2013).

33. The statement of the National Union of Women, published in *Jahān-e Novin* 5 (March 29, 1979): 8 (my italics).

34. Ahmad Shamlou, the influential Iranian poet and cultural critic, founded the magazine in the summer of 1979. It was shut down in May 1980 after the publication of its thirty-sixth issue. The majority of the contributors to this literary and political magazine were Left-leaning intellectuals.

35. Diana, "Gerāyesh-e zanān beh sāzmān-dehi dar mobārezāt-e ejtemā'ei" [Women's propensity toward organizing in social struggles"), *Ketāb-e Jom'eh* 1, no. 30 (1979): 41.

36. Cited in Nima Namdari, "Dāstān-e ejbāri shodan-e hejāb dar Iran: Gām-e avval, chādor barā-ye 'arusak-e farangi" [The story of making *Hejāb* compulsory: First step, veil for the Western doll), http://www.meydaan.com/Showarticle.aspx ?arid=438.

37. Naser Takmil Homayun, "Mikhāstand zan-e Irani arusak farangi bāshad" [They wanted the Iranian woman to become a Western doll], *Kayhān*, February 5, 1979, cited in Namdari, *Hejāb*.

38. The "nakedness" of women was a common reference to fashionable women who dressed in Western style and wore heavy makeup. The "naked woman" was not only a concept limited to the political lexicon of the clerical Islamists. In the moving account of his pilgrimage to Mecca, *Khasi dar meiqāt* [Lost in the crowd], 10th ed. (Tehran: Ferdows, 2005), Al-e Ahmad reports that in Saudi Arabia he realized that *gharbzadegi* was not a plague only inflicting Iranians. He writes that glossy magazines from Egypt and Lebanon were filled with stories of "tanks, drinking-wine, and naked women" (48). Samad Behrangi (1939–67), a

Marxist social critic and influential writer of children's literature, also uses the same terminology to identify "Western-looking" women. He considered the newly fashionable women's magazines to be a place for gossip about Western movie stars and erotic secrets for women on how to attract men. See *Kand-o kāvi dar masā'el-e tarbiyati-ye Iran* [An inquiry into the educational upbringing problems in Iran] (Tabriz: Mohammadi, 1965), 126.

39. *Kayhān*, no. 10656 (March 8, 1979): 2, cited in Namdari, *Hejāb*.

40. *Kayhān*, no. 10658 (March 11, 1979): 3, cited in Namdari, *Hejāb*.

41. Ibid.

42. She is using here Khomeini's famous expression for the need for unity: "unison of the word."

43. *Kayhān*, no. 10657 (March 10, 1979): 6, cited in Namdari, *Hejāb*.

44. See a detailed report in Matin and Mohajer, *Khizesh*, 1:51–96.

45. *Kayhān*, no. 10658 (March 11, 1979), reprinted in Matin and Mohajer, *Khizesh*, 1:81–82.

46. *Kayhān*, no. 10660 (March 13, 1979), reprinted in Matin and Mohajer, *Khizesh*, 1:82.

47. *Kayhān*, no. 10658 (March 11, 1979): 6, cited in Namdari, *Hejāb*.

48. Eliz Sanasarian, *The Women's Rights Movement in Iran: Mutiny, Appeasement, and Repression from 1900 to Khomeini* (New York: Praeger, 1982), 117.

49. Ibid., 117–19.

50. Ibid., 120.

51. *Kayhān*, no. 10658 (March 11, 1979): 2, cited in Namdari, *Hejāb*.

52. *Kayhān*, no. 10660 (March 13, 1979), reprinted in Matin and Mohajer, *Khizesh*, 1:96.

53. Khomeini, *Sahifeh*, 13:190–94.

54. For an earlier discussion of white women's burden in the South Asian context, see Kumari Jayawardena's edited volume *The White Woman's Other Burden: Western Women and South Asia during British Rule* (New York: Routledge, 1995). For another thoughtful account of the colonial context of feminist solidarity with colonial subjects, see Antoinette Burton, *Burdens of History: British Feminists, Indian Women, and Imperial Culture, 1865–1915* (Chapel Hill: University of North Carolina Press, 1994), particularly chapters 5 and 6.

55. Kate Millett, *Going to Iran* (New York: Coward, McCann, and Geoghegan, 1982), 19.

56. "Kate Millett in Iran to Aid Feminists; Calls Khomeini 'Chauvinist,'" *Chicago Tribune*, March 12, 1979, 2.

57. Gayatri Spivak, "Can the Subaltern Speak?," in *Marxism and the Interpretation of Culture*, ed. Cary Nelson and Lawrence Grossberg (Urbana: University of Illinois Press, 1988).

58. Almost half a century before Millett, another American woman, a Christian missionary named Ruth Frances Woodsmall, wrote: "Undoubtedly the barometer of social change in the Moslem world is the veil. Where the veil persists without variation, the life of the Moslem woman is like the blank walled streets of Bhopal, India, which afford no outlook from within and no contact from without." Cited in Naghibi, *Rethinking Global Sisterhood*, 37. See chapter 3 of this work for an insightful analysis of Kate Millett's journey.

59. bell hooks, "Sisterhood: Political Solidarity between Women," *Feminist Review* 23 (Summer 1986): 125–38.

60. Donna Haraway, *Simians, Cyborgs, and Women: The Reinvention of Nature* (New York: Routledge, 1991), 155.

61. Millett, *Going to Iran*, 177. For a person who is so attentive to how others pronounce her name, it is quite disturbing to read how, like the old colonial habits, Millett reproduces the names of the characters in her narrative phonetically without any attempt to verify their correct spelling. Almost none of the names of the people she refers to is spelled correctly. Not only does she show in her narrative how Iranian actors exist only in relation to her, but in her conspicuous disregard for the correct spelling of their names she further marginalizes them. A few examples of her phonetic spelling: The famous Iranian poet Siyavosh Kasra'ei appears as "Sylvashroe Khasroe" (78); Ayatollah Taleqani as "Tolerani" (22); her contacts Taraneh as "Terranie" (189), Fereshteh as "Ferdosheh" (128), Hormoz as "Hermoz," Niloufar as "Nelufar" (134), etc.

62. Meyda Yeğenoğlu, *Colonial Fantasies: Towards a Feminist Reading of Orientalism* (Cambridge: Cambridge University Press, 1999), 95–120.

63. For an insightful discussion on the topic, see Antoinette Burton's "The White Women's Burden: British Feminists and the Indian Woman, 1865–1915," *Women's Studies International Forum* 13, no. 4 (1990): 295–308. Burton argues that British feminists "deliberately cultivated the civilizing responsibility as their own modern womanly burden because it affirmed an emancipated role for them in the imperial nation state" (295).

64. Naghibi, *Rethinking Global Sisterhood*, 60–61.

65. For a thorough discussion of Orientalist feminism, see Joseph Massad, "Women and/in 'Islam': The Rescue Mission of Western Liberal Feminism," chapter 2 in *Islam in Liberalism* (Chicago: University of Chicago Press, 2015).

66. Title of a news report by Michael Burns, *Baltimore Sun*, March 27, 1979.

67. John Kifner, "Iran's Women Fought, Won, and Dispersed," *New York Times*, March 16, 1979.

68. Ibid.

69. Jonathan Randal, "Sexual Politics in Iran: Kate Millett Finds That Tehran's Feminists Are Not United," *Washington Post*, March 12, 1979 (my italics).

Despite the fact that Millett's press conference resembled a scene from a theater of the absurd, it received considerable press coverage in the United States. All the major newspapers ran stories about the event. Many wondered, without a sense of irony, about Iranian women who showed no interest in associating themselves with Millett and her entourage. In a story entitled "Hassled, Heckled Kate Millett Not Leaving Iran, Yet," printed in the *Los Angeles Times* (March 16, 1979), we learn that Millett's press conference was interrupted by a "hostile Iranian woman," who said: "We don't need foreign women to come here to solve our problems. She does not have the right to decide what is happening in Iran."

70. Randal, "Sexual Politics in Iran."

71. "Women March against Khomeini," *Newsday*, March 9, 1979, 13Q. This report, as many others, repeated the same fiction that women were chanting "Down with Khomeini," something that was utterly inconceivable only a few weeks after the revolution. "Foes of Khomeini Focusing on Issue of Women's Rights" was another front-page headline in the *New York Times* by Youssef Ibrahim, published on March 12, 1979. "Khomeini's Ballot Attacked as Iranian Women Continue Protests" was the headline in the *Irish Times* on March 12, 1979.

72. Michael Burns, "Thanks, but No Thanks," *Baltimore Sun*, March 27, 1979.

73. Betsy Amin-Arsala, "In Iran, to Veil or Not to Veil?" *New York Times*, April 21, 1979. The author is introduced as a "Peace Corps volunteer in Afghanistan in the 1960s" who says that "while she is not technically a practicing Muslim, she married that world and has been a participant-observer for 15 years."

74. Mangol Bayat, "The Iranian Woman's Long March," *Newsday*, March 29, 1979, 94.

75. Judith Cummings, "Demonstrations in City Back Iranian Women's Rights," *New York Times*, March 16, 1979.

76. In May 1979 the *Village Voice* revealed that Steinem and the powerful sponsors of *Ms. Magazine* pressured Random House to delete the entire chapter in which it was documented that Steinem worked for the CIA beginning in 1958, spying on Marxist students in Europe and disrupting their meetings. Steinem has repeatedly defended her collaboration with the CIA, and argues: "I was happy to find some liberals in government in those days who were far-sighted and cared enough to get Americans of all political views to the festival," she told the *New York Times*. And to the *Washington Post*, she said: "In my experience the agency was completely different from its image: it was liberal, nonviolent and honorable." See Hugh Wilford, *The Mighty Wurlitzer: How the CIA Played America* (Cambridge: Harvard University Press, 2008), 146–48.

77. Claude Servan-Schreiber, *Nous sommes toutes des Iraniennes*, cited in Matin and Mohajer, *Khizesh*, 2:87.

78. Laila Said, *A Bridge through Time: A Memoir* (New York: Summit Books, 1985), 219.

79. Burns, "Thanks, but No Thanks."

80. Ibid.

81. For a detailed account of the itinerary of the delegation, see Servan-Schreiber, *Nous sommes toutes des Iraniennes*, 86–95. The four members who made the trip were Katia Kaupp, a *Le Nouvel Observateur* journalist; Maria Antonietta Macciocchi; Micheline Pelletier-Lattès, an independent photographer; and Claire Brière, a former *Libération* reporter.

82. Interview with Claire Brière, in Matin and Mohajer, *Khizesh*, 250.

83. Ibid., 251.

84. Observing the *hejāb* in public became compulsory three years later.

85. Gregory Jaynes, "Future Veiled for Iranian Women," *Chicago Tribune*, May 6, 1979 (my italics).

86. Ibid.

87. Ibid.

88. Michel Foucault, "Open Letter to Prime Minister Mehdi Bazargan," in Afary and Anderson, *Foucault*, 261.

89. Ibid., 263.

90. Afary and Anderson, *Foucault*, 115–16.

91. Gayatri Spivak, "Three Women's Texts and a Critique of Imperialism," *Critical Inquiry* 12, no. 1 (1986): 243–61.

92. Kifner, "Iran's Women."

93. Ibid.

94. For a discussion on changes in abortion rights and women's inheritance, see Behrooz Ghamari-Tabrizi, "Women's Rights, *Shari'a* Law, and the Secularization of Islam in Iran," *International Journal of Politics, Culture, and Society* 26, no. 3 (2013): 237–53.

95. I have outlined and discussed all these developments in religious knowledge in my book *Islam and Dissent*.

96. The topic is discussed in Lydia Sargent's edited volume *Women and Revolution: A Discussion of the Unhappy Marriage of Marxism and Feminism* (Cambridge, Mass.: South End Press, 1981). Although contributors to Sargent's volume primarily debate the issue from a neo-Marxist view and try to delink women's emancipation from production and labor processes, they share with liberal feminists the sentiment of the universality of women's bodies and feminism as the site for unmediated political expression. For a critique, see Judith Butler's seminal *Gender Trouble: Feminism and the Subversion of Identity* (London: Routledge, 1999), chapter 1.

97. Nancy Fraser and Linda Nicholson, "Social Criticism without Philosophy: An Encounter between Feminism and Postmodernism," *Theory, Culture, Society* 5, no. 2 (1988): 384.

98. Roksana Bahramitash, "Islamic Fundamentalism and Women's Economic Role: The Case of Iran," *International Journal of Politics, Culture, and Society* 16, no. 4 (2003): 552–68.

99. Bahramitash, "Market Fundamentalism versus Religious Fundamentalism," 33–46.

100. For a detailed analysis of the politics of reproduction in Iran, see Homa Hoodfar's various studies, including: "Volunteer Health Workers in Iran as Social Activists: Can 'Governmental Non-governmental Organizations' Be Agent of Democratization?," Women Living under Muslim Laws, Occasional Papers no. 10, 1998; (with Samad Assadpour) "Where Religion Is No Obstacle: The Politics of Making a Successful Population Policy in the Islamic Republic of Iran," *Studies in Family Planning* 31, no. 1 (2000): 1–17; "Devices and Desires: Population Policy and Gender Roles in the Islamic Republic," in *Political Islam*, ed. Joel Beinin and Joe Stork, 220–33 (Berkeley: University of California Press, 1996).

101. Foucault, "Iranians Dreaming," 206.

5. Was ist Aufklärung?

1. Foucault, "Open Letter," 261.

2. Broyelle and Broyelle, "Philosophers Dreaming," 248–49.

3. Claudie Broyelle, Jacques Broyelle, and Evelyne Tschirhart, *China: A Second Look*, trans. Sarah Matthews (Atlantic Highlands, N.J.: Humanities Press, 1980).

4. Richard Curt Kraus, Review of Broyelle, Broyelle, and Tschirhart, *China: A Second Look*, *Journal of Asian Studies* 40, no. 3 (1981), 573.

5. "Foucault's Response to Claudie and Jacques Broyelle," in Afary and Anderson, *Foucault*, 249–50.

6. Immanuel Kant, "*Was ist Aufklärung?*," in Michel Foucault, *The Politics of Truth*, trans. Lysa Hochroth and Catherine Porter (Los Angeles: Semiotext(e), 2007), 29.

7. Michel Foucault, "What Is Critique?," in *The Politics of Truth*, 47.

8. John Rajchman, "Enlightenment Today," introduction to *The Politics of Truth*, 25.

9. For a background context, see Paul Rabinow's introduction to his edited volume of Foucault's *Ethics, Subjectivity and Truth* (New York: New Press, 1997), xx–xxi.

10. Michel Foucault, "The Masked Philosopher," in *The Politics of Truth*, 322.

11. Ibid., 323.

12. Michel Foucault, "For an Ethics of Discomfort," in *The Politics of Truth*, 122.

13. There is a large body of literature on Foucault's late transformation and his so-called "death-bed" confession of his earlier mistakes. Afary and Anderson interpret Foucault's short essay on the Enlightenment according to this view (I shall discuss this later). Among more explicit advocates of Foucault's recantation are Eric Paras, *Foucault 2.0: Beyond Power and Knowledge* (New York: Other Press, 2006); Geoff Danaher, Tony Schirato, and Jen Webb, *Understanding Foucault* (New York: Sage, 2000); Lois McNay, *Foucault and Feminism* (New York: Polity Press, 1992); Timothy O'Leary, *Foucault and the Art of Ethics* (New York: Continuum, 2002). For an insightful critique of the conventional periodization of Foucault's oeuvre, see Jeffrey Nealon, *Foucault beyond Foucault: Power and Its Intensification* (Stanford: Stanford University Press, 2007).

14. Michel Foucault, *The Order of Things* (New York: Vintage, [1966] 1973), 387. His earlier writings are also marked by a shift from his focus on the archeology of knowledge to the development of his genealogy of the modern individual as subject in *The Order of Discourse*, in *Untying the Text*, ed. Robert Young (London: Routledge and Kegan Paul, [1970] 1981); *Discipline and Punish: The Birth of the Prison* (New York: Vintage Books, [1975] 1995); and the first volume of *The History of Sexuality* (New York: Vintage Books, [1976] 1990).

15. Similar to his theory of power, Foucault did not have a hierarchical conception of resistance. He saw power as generative and not something that could be abolished, but at the same time, "power creates its own resistance." Foucault, *Discipline and Punish*, 73.

16. Alain Badiou, *Infinite Thought: Truth and the Return to Philosophy*, trans. Oliver Feltham and Justin Clemens (New York: Continuum, 2005), 6.

17. Gary Gutting, ed., *The Cambridge Companion to Foucault* (Cambridge: Cambridge University Press, 1994).

18. Roy Boyne, *Foucault and Derrida: The Other Side of Reason* (London: Unwin Hyman, 1990), 144.

19. Jana Sawicki, "Foucault, Feminism, and Questions of Identity," in Gutting, *Cambridge Companion*, 286–87.

20. Michel Foucault, "Structuralism and Post-Structuralism," in *The Essential Works of Foucault, 1954–1984*, ed. J. D. Faubion, vol. 2, *Aesthetics, Method, and Epistemology* (New York: Free Press, 2000), 452.

21. Michel Foucault, "The Subject and Power," in Faubion, ed., *Essential Works*, 3:327.

22. Charles Taylor, "Foucault on Freedom and Truth," *Political Theory* 12, no. 2 (1984): 152.

23. Jürgen Habermas, "Taking Aim at the Heart of the Present," in *Foucault: A Critical Reader*, ed. David Couzens Hoy (New York: Basil Blackwell, 1986), 93.

24. Nancy Fraser, *Unruly Practices: Power, Discourse and Gender in Contemporary Social Theory* (Cambridge: Polity Press, 1989), 29.

25. Nancy Hartsock, "Foucault on Power: A Theory for Women?," in *Feminism and Postmodernism*, ed. L. Nicholson (New York: Routledge, 1990), 159.

26. Michel Foucault, "A Powder Keg Called Islam," in Afary and Anderson, *Foucault*, 240 (my italics).

27. For Foucault's discussion of the "universal" and "specific" intellectuals, see "Truth and Power," in Rabinow, *The Foucault Reader*, 51–75.

28. Michel Foucault, "Power and Sex," in *Politics, Philosophy, Culture: Interviews and Other Writings*, ed. L. Kritzman (New York: Routledge, 1988), 124.

29. Foucault, "Iran," 253.

30. Foucault, "Is It Useless to Revolt?," 263.

31. Foucault, "Truth and Power," 59.

32. Michel Foucault, "What Is Enlightenment?," in Rabinow, *The Foucault Reader*, 50.

33. Michel Foucault, "What Is Revolution?," in Rabinow, *The Politics of Truth*, 86.

34. Gilles Deleuze and Félix Guattari, *What Is Philosophy?* (London: Verso, 1984), 112–13.

35. Foucault, "What Is Revolution?," 94.

36. Rabinow, introduction, xviii.

37. Foucault, "What Is Revolution?," 85.

38. Foucault, "What Is Enlightenment?," cited and italicized in Afary and Anderson, *Foucault*, 137.

39. See Rajchman, "Enlightenment Today," 18. There are five other essays on enlightenment in *The Politics of Truth*: "What Is Critique?," "What Is Revolution?," "What Is Enlightenment?," "For an Ethics of Discomfort," and "What Our Present Is."

40. Rajchman, "Enlightenment Today," 22.

41. Anita Seppä, "Foucault, Enlightenment, and the Aesthetics of the Self," *Contemporary Aesthetics* 2 (2004), http://www.contempaesthetics.org/newvolume/pages/article.php?articleID=244.

42. Foucault, "On the Ethics of Discomfort," 124. This essay later was published as the preface to Jean Daniel's *L'Ere des rupture* (Paris: Grasset, 1979).

43. Foucault, "What Is Enlightenment?," 114.

44. The most relevant discussion of the "end of revolutions" was put forward by François Furet in his widely debated book in 1978, called *Interpreting*

the French Revolution, trans. Elborg Forester (Cambridge: Cambridge University Press, 1981).

45. Michel Foucault, cited in Rajchman, "Enlightenment Today," 11.

46. Foucault, "What Is Enlightenment?," 46.

47. Michel Foucault, "Subjectivity and Truth," in Rabinow, *The Politics of Truth*, 152–53.

48. Foucault, "What Is Enlightenment?," 35.

49. Ibid., 39.

50. *Unmündigkeit* and *Aufklärung* have largely been appropriated in civilizational/colonial contexts. Garrett Green argues that the English translation of *Unmündigkeit* as "immaturity" subtly "shifts the underlying analogy from a legal to a psychological context." What Kant had in mind with the concept *Unmündigkeit*, Green posits, was not only being a "minor," but more generally, a state of being in need of representation or guardianship. For example, in his commentary on "the fair sex," Kant viewed women as *unmündig*, and therefore, "prime candidates for enlightenment." Garrett Green, "Modern Culture Comes of Age: Hamann versus Kant on the Root of Metaphor of Enlightenment," in *What Is Enlightenment? Eighteenth-Century Answers and Twentieth-Century Questions*, ed. James Schmidt (Berkeley: University of California Press, 1996), 291–305.

51. Foucault, "What Is Enlightenment?," 39.

52. Ibid., 42.

53. Ibid., 43.

54. Michel Foucault, "Kant on Enlightenment and Revolution," trans. Colin Gordon, *Economy and Society* 15, no. 1 (1983): 88–96, 94.

55. Michel Foucault, "The Mythical Leader of the Iranian Revolt," in Afary and Anderson, *Foucault*, 220.

56. Michel Foucault, "Truth, Power, Self," in *Technologies of the Self*, ed. Luther Martin et al. (Amherst: University of Massachusetts Press, 1988), 9.

57. Miller, *Passion*, 312.

58. They prefer Miller's intellectual genealogy of Foucault and the way he links Foucault's personal life to his philosophy. From Miller they also borrow the notion that Foucault's interest in the Iranian Revolution stemmed from his fascination with death. Afary and Anderson, *Foucault*, 7

59. Miller, *Passion*, 312. Miller situates Foucault's last essay, "Is It Useless to Revolt?," written in May 1979, within a language of hyperbole and sensationalism about the casualties of the postrevolutionary summary trials during its first three months. The point is not to discount the magnitude of these summary executions, but one needs to situate these atrocities in the context of postrevolutionary politics, not merely as Khomeini's plan. The majority of secular leftist groups demanded swift justice in Jacobin-style public trials, and hundreds of

thousands demonstrated in front of Khomeini's residence and called for the execution of military chiefs and SAVAK operatives. At the time Foucault wrote his essay, two hundred high-ranking officers and cabinet members of the old regime had been executed—homosexuals had *not* been dispatched to firing squads nor had adulterers been stoned to death. Stoning for adultery was added to the Islamic Penal Code much later, in 1983. It is true that during the reign of terror from 1981 to 1985, and later in 1989, thousands of members of opposition groups were executed in the Iranian prisons. But one should not read the dynamics of the postrevolutionary power struggle and the Islamic regime's bloody project of the consolidation of power back into the revolutionary *movement* that toppled monarchy in Iran. It was this movement that Foucault wrote about, not its post-revolutionary institutionalization.

60. Miller, *Passion*, 314.

61. While mostly rebuked by Foucault scholars, the book received glowing reviews in almost all major newspapers, news magazines like the *Nation* and *New Republic*, and other media. There were few notable exceptions to this overwhelming celebratory response. See Wendy Brown, "The Passion of Michel Foucault," *difference* 5, no. 2 (1993): 140–50. Also, on Miller's misconception of Foucault's ethics, see William Connolly, "Beyond Good and Evil: The Ethical Sensibility of Michel Foucault," *Political Theory* 21, no. 3 (1993): 365–89. Connolly wrote this article as a response to one of the prepublication presentations Miller delivered on his book.

62. For a good discussion of the continuity between Foucault's conception of the subject in his early and late work, see Sebastian Harrer, "The Theme of Subjectivity in Foucault's Lecture Series *L'Herméneutique du Sujet,*" *Foucault Studies* 2 (May 2005): 75–96. Harrer argues: "A popular view on [Foucault's] late period holds that at some point his oeuvre, Foucault turned away from analyzing the power/knowledge mechanisms that *fabricate* subjects, and turned to analyzing how subjects *constitute* themselves. This view sometimes implies the idea that these notions, 'constitution' and 'fabrication', refer to two *distinct* phenomena" (76).

63. Rajchman, "Enlightenment Today," 23.

64. Kant, *"Was ist Aufklärung?,"* 31.

65. Ibid., 32.

66. Ibid., 33.

67. Foucault, "What Is Critique?," 78.

68. Ibid., 79 (my italics).

69. Ibid., 47.

70. Michel Foucault, "The Ethics of the Concern for the Self as a Practice of Freedom," in Rabinow, *Ethics*, 282.

71. Ibid.

72. Emmanuel Levinas's conception of "the ethical subject" is primarily a critique of Heidegger's ontological philosophy. He believes that rather than being an ontological realization of its authenticity, the self must constitute itself through interaction with others as an ethical subject. Ethics, Levinas argues, must be liberated from an "ontological imperialism" that has transformed humankind into the position of slaves to an "anonymous Being." See Levinas, *Totality and Infinity* (Pittsburgh: Duquesne University Press, 1969), 44–46. "To affirm the priority of *Being*, over the *existent*," Levinas remarks, "is to subordinate the relation with *someone* who is an existent (the ethical relation) to a relation with the *Being* of the *existent*, which, impersonal, permits the apprehension, the domination of the existent and subordinates justice to freedom" (45). For a precise and illuminating critique of Levinas, see Steven Gans, "Ethics or Ontology: Levinas and Heidegger," *Philosophy Today* 16 (Summer 1972): 117–21. For a stimulating discussion of the topic, see Karl Simms, ed., *Ethics and the Subject*, special volume of *Critical Studies* 8 (1997).

73. Richard Rorty, *Contingency, Iron, and Solidarity* (Cambridge: Cambridge University Press, 1989), xiv.

74. Foucault, "Ethics," 288–89.

75. Ibid., 289.

76. David Hiley uses this phrase to identify the problem he associates with Foucault's critique of power/knowledge normativity. Hiley points out the contradictions in Foucault's rejection of the binary opposition of individual–society and offers an insightful reading of how Foucault situates himself vis-à-vis the Enlightenment. David Hiley, "Foucault and the Tradition of Enlightenment," *Philosophy and Social Criticism* 11 (1985): 63–83. Also, for an engaging assessment of the problem of politics in Foucault's radical pragmatism, see Jon Simons, *Foucault and the Political* (London: Routledge, 1995), particularly chapters 6–9.

77. Michel Foucault, *The Hermeneutics of the Subject: Lectures at the Collège de France, 1981–1982*, ed. Frédéric Gros (New York: Picador, 2005), 59.

78. Foucault, *Hermeneutics*, 189.

79. Férédric Gros, "Course Context," in Foucault, *Hermeneutics*, 525.

80. Foucault, "Is It Useless to Revolt?," 263.

81. Foucault, "Iran," 257.

82. Foucault's lectures were published in a volume called *Fearless Speech*, ed. Joseph Pearson (Los Angeles: Semiotext(e), 2001).

83. Foucault, *Fearless Speech*, 169–70.

84. Ibid., 19.

85. Thomas Flynn, review of *Fearless Speech*, in *Notre Dame Philosophical Reviews* 4 (2002), http://ndpr.nd.edu/review.cfm?id=1223.

86. Thomas Goodnight, *"Parrhesia*: The Aesthetics of Arguing Truth to Power," in *Dissensus and the Search for Common Ground*, ed. H. V. Hansen (Windsor: OSSA, 2007), 5.

87. Foucault, *Fearless Speech*, 13.

88. Rabinow, introduction, xviii.

89. Hannah Arendt quotes this passage from Heidegger's lectures in "Martin Heidegger at Eighty," in *Heidegger and Modern Philosophy*, ed. M. Murray (New Haven: Yale University Press, 1978), 297.

90. James Bernauer and Michael Mahon, "The Ethics of Michel Foucault," in Gutting, *Cambridge Companion*, 141–58. "When he was criticized," they argue, "for his initial sympathetic analysis of the revolution, Foucault refused to dismiss the moral achievement of those who made the revolution when it resulted in new political repression" (144). Bernauer and Mahon recognize the link between Foucault's conception of ethics and his political views on the revolutionary movement in Iran. But this chapter is a rare exception.

91. Férédric Gros, "Course Context," 509.

92. Rajchman, "Enlightenment Today," 11.

93. Ibid., 14–16.

94. Ibid., 19.

95. Rabinow, introduction, xxiii.

Conclusion

1. Susan Buck-Morss, "Hegel and Haiti," *Critical Inquiry* 26, no. 4 (Summer 2000): 821–65.

2. Michel Foucault, *Irani-hā cheh ro'yā'i dar sar dārand?* (What are the Iranians dreaming about?), translated into Persian by Hossein Masumi Hamedani (Tehran: Hermes, 1998).

3. Buck-Morss, "Hegel and Haiti," 837–38.

4. Ibid., 844.

5. Ibid., 837.

INDEX

Abrahamian, Ervand, 102, 202n.21, 209n.6, 210n.16, 213n.49

Abu Bakr, 211n.25

Abu Dharr Ghaffari, 88, 92, 210n.18

Abu-Lughod, Lila, 215n.2

activism, pessimistic, 70–72

Adib-Moghaddam, Arshin, 211n.30

Adorno, Theodor, 208n.53

adultery, stoning for, 228n.59

Afary, Janet, 5–6, 75, 197n.6, 197n.8, 209n.1–2; earlier work on Iranian constitutional revolution, 76–77; on Islamism, 5–6, 16, 76–82, 87, 104; misreading of Foucault and misrepresentation of revolutionary events, 5–6, 8, 13–15, 75, 168–69, 173, 209n.1, 225n.13 (*see also* *Foucault and the Iranian Revolution*); on roots of 9/11, 6, 13–16, 200n.36

Afghanistan: Islamic Republic's assistance in agreement on transitional government of, 105, 201n.44; Taliban regime in, 13, 16, 105, 200n.44

Ahmed, Leila, 216n.8

Ahouei, Mahdi, 212n.35

Alavid Shi'ism, 25, 62, 86, 87, 92

Al-e Ahmad, Jalal, 123–24; Daneshvar, widow of, 129–31; on westoxication, 123–24, 218n.27, 219n.38

Alessandrini, Anthony, 197n.4

Algar, Hamid, 205n.1

Algeria, revolution in: Fanon on revolution in, 72, 73; Shabestary on utility of the veil during, 129; Shari'ati on French atrocities in, 89

Ali, Ayaan Hirsi, 10

Ali, Imam, 79, 80, 88

Ali, Tariq, 12, 199n.23

Alleg, Henri, 89

Almond, Ian, 197n.7

al-Qaeda, 6; Afary and Anderson on rise of, 14; American strategic interests giving rise to, 13; post-9/11 Enlightenment moralists' characterization of, 12

Al-Sahhar, Joudah, 210n.18

Althusser, Louis, 29

Amal (Lebanese newspaper), 124

ambiguity: as core element of Foucault's philosophy, 173; in vision of future, revolutionary movement and, 58–59, 61, 165–66, 189

Amin-Arsala, Betsy, 222n.73

fascism, Islamism and, 104–5
fatwa against Rushdie, 105
Fearless Speech (Foucault), 229n.82.
    See also parrhesia (fearless speech)
feminist politics, 8, 111, 135–58,
    190–91; female body as universal
    referent for women's emancipatory
    politics, 154–55, 223n.96; feminist
    internationalism, 154; "feminist
    premonitions" and women's status
    under Islamic Republic, 155–58,
    190–91, 224n.100; Iranian women's
    groups' rejection of foreign inter-
    ventionism, 144–53, 222n.69;
    Millett's visit to Iran, 135–43;
    modern-yet-modest, Iranian
    feminist view as, 123; Second Wave
    feminism during 1970s, 154,
    156–57; Western white women's
    interventionism and, 135–43,
    190–91; women's protests against
    mandatory *hejāb* during Interna-
    tional Women's Day (1979), 8,
    121–22, 128, 148–50, 151, 190.
    See also Millett, Kate; women
Feminist Revolution (Redstockings),
    148
Fichte, Johann G., 187
Finlayson, Gordon, 208n.53
Fischer, Michael, 211n.29
Flynn, Thomas, 229n.85
F Magazine, 154
Foucault, Michel, ix, 205n.3, 205n.6,
    206n.8, 206n.11, 206n.14, 206n.19,
    206n.22, 206n.25, 207n.28–29,
    207n.34, 208n.55, 210n.11,
    212n.40, 213n.51, 214n.60,
    214n.62–67, 215n.69, 223n.88,
    224n.7, 225n.10–15, 225n.20–21,
    226n.26–33, 227n.54–56, 228n.70,

229n.77, 230n.2; Afary and Anderson on, 5–6, 8, 13–15, 75, 168–69,
173, 209n.1, 225n.13 (*see also Foucault and the Iranian Revolution*);
antiteleological genealogy of, 58,
108–9, 173, 189; Atoussa H.'s
critique of, Foucault's response to,
115, 161; Atoussa H.'s critique of,
in "An Iranian Woman Writes,"
113–14; as belated liberal or unrepentant philosopher of the present,
168–73, 185; on collective will, 19,
57–58, 61, 166; course of reading
on Islam and Iranian history,
55–57; essays on Iranian Revolution,
xi, 4–7, 8, 16–17, 59–72, 153;
essays on Iranian Revolution, as
journalism about ideas, 60; essays
on Iranian Revolution, main thrust
of critique of, 19, 58–59, 75, 76,
160–62, 200n.36; Fanonian predicament of, 72–74; gendered ambivalence toward question of rights
and civil liberties, 8, 153, 154–55;
grievance against French intellectuals, 161–62; indictment as main
poststructuralist culprit of cultural
relativism, 5–6, 105–11; on irreducibility of uprisings, 84, 159; on
Islamic government, 66–67, 101–2,
115, 159, 165; on Kant's notion of
public and private reason, 174–76;
last lectures, situating, 182–85,
191–92, 230n.90; later writings on
ethics and spirituality, common
misinterpretations of, 6–7, 160,
163–69, 173–74, 183–85; later
writings on ethics and spirituality,
effect of Iranian Revolution on,
163, 168, 172–73, 176, 178, 180,

explanations of Arab uprisings, 2–4; on international demonstrations of solidarity for women's rights in Iran, 148; naming of "Arab Spring," 2; on women's demonstrations in Iran, 144, 152, 154. *See also specific newspapers and other media*

Milani, Ayatollah, 89–90

Militant Muslim Students of Tabriz University, 38

Miller, James, 63, 68, 173–74, 201n.1, 207n.27, 227n.58–59, 228n.61

Millett, Kate, 135–43, 144, 148, 151, 153, 154, 220n.55–56; colonial roots of her mission to Iran, 137–39, 141, 220n.54; deportation order issued against, 143; *Going to Iran*, book on her ordeal in Iran, 137–43, 221n.61; invitation from CAIFI to speak at Women's Day rally in Tehran, 136, 139–40; press conference, 137, 141–43, 222n.69; Western media's depiction of visit of, 142, 144–47

Minachi, Abbas, 213n.41

Minachi, Naser, 210n.19

Minc, Alain, 14–15, 200n.34

Minerva (journal), 187–88

Mir-Hosseini, Ziba, 216n.7, 219n.30

Mirmajlessi, Mrs., 144, 155

Mirza Yusef Mosque (Tabriz), 38

modernity: critical ontology of the present introducing new manner of posing question of, 167–68; displacement of tradition of, in Iranian Revolution, 67; female body as site of negotiating, in Iran, 123; Foucault's attempt to define, as attitude and rupture, 171–72;

Foucault's reports as philosophical commentary on, 60–61; *hejāb* as one of key signifiers of, 122; revolution as regressive denunciation of, Afary and Anderson's reading of, 75, 106 (*see also Foucault and the Iranian Revolution*); structural position of the West as sole producer and non-West as everlasting consumer of, 13, 199n.26

modernization project, Shah's, 58, 60–61, 77

Mofatteh, Mohammad, 45, 204n.54

Moghaddam, General, 43

Moghissi, Haideh, 219n.32

Mohajer, Naser, 219n.32

Moharram, month of, 35

Mojāhedin, 42; adoption of Marxism by Islamist leadership (1975), 81–82; assassinations between 1981 and 1983 by, 103; Shari'ati and, 91–92

Moll, Yasmin, 197n.3

monarchy: legitimacy of, 24–25; liberal nationalists' belief in constitutional, 60, 98, 190; revolutionary movement and, 30, 51–52, 98. *See also* Shah of Iran

Monde, Le (newspaper), 14, 70, 100, 122, 161, 162; Khomeini interview, 40–42

Montazeri, Ayatollah, 124, 218n.28

Moqaddam-Salimi, Manuchehr, 79

Morsi, Mohamed, 3–4

Moruzzi, Norma Claire, 111, 215n.68

Mosaddeq, Mohammad, 131; CIA-designed coup toppling (1953), 25, 91, 132

Moshiri, Minou, 150

Moslem, Mehdi, 213n.42

BEHROOZ GHAMARI-TABRIZI is associate professor of history and sociology at the University of Illinois at Urbana-Champaign. He is the author of *Islam and Dissent in Postrevolutionary Iran: Abdolkarim Soroush, Religious Politics, and Democratic Reform.*